John Cantacuzene reigned as Byzantine Emperor in Constantinople from 1347 to 1354. He was a contemporary of Stephen Dušan of Serbia and of Osman, father of the Osmanli or Ottoman Turkish people.

A man of varied talents, as a scholar, soldier, statesman, theologian and monk, John Cantacuzene was unique in being the only Emperor to narrate the events of his own career. His memoirs form one of the most interesting and literate of all Byzantine histories. Following his abdication in 1354, he lived the last thirty years of his long life as a monk, a writer and a grey eminence behind the throne. This book is not a social or political history of the Byzantine empire in the fourteenth century. It is a biography of a much-maligned man who had a hope, however naive, of coming to terms with the emerging Muslim world of Asia and of winning the co-operation of western Christendom without compromising the Orthodox faith of the Byzantine tradition.

THE RELUCTANT EMPEROR

John VI Cantacuzene as monk

THE
RELUCTANT
EMPEROR

*A biography of John Cantacuzene,
Byzantine Emperor and monk, c. 1295–1383*

DONALD M. NICOL

Published by the Press Syndicate of the University of Cambridge
The Pitt Building, Trumpington Street, Cambridge CB2 1RP
30 West 20th Street, New York, NY 10011–4211, USA
10 Stamford Road, Oakleigh, Melbourne 3166, Australia

First published 1996

Printed in Great Britain at the University Press, Cambridge

A catalogue record for this book is available from the British Library

Library of Congress cataloguing in publication data
Nicol, Donald MacGillivray.
The reluctant Emperor: John Cantacuzene, Emperor and monk,
c. 1295–1383 / Donald M. Nicol.
p.   cm.
Includes bibliographical references and index.
ISBN 0 521 55256 7 (hc)
1. John VI Cantacuzenus, Emperor of the East, 1295–1383.
2. Emperors – Byzantine Empire – Biography. I. Title.
DF636.J6315N53 1996   949.5'04'092–dc20 95–30689 CIP

ISBN 0 521 55256 7

CONTENTS

PLATES

Frontispiece: John VI Cantacuzene as monk (Paris *BN* cod. gr. 1242 f. 123)

Between pages 114 and 115

1 John VI Cantacuzene as Emperor and monk (Paris *BN* cod. gr. 1242 f. 123)
2 John VI Cantacuzene presiding over a synod of bishops (Paris *BN* cod. gr. 1242 f. 5)
3 The Emperor Manuel II Palaiologos (detail from Paris, Musée du Louvre, cod. Ivoires 100, f. 2^r)
4 Alexios Apokaukos as Grand Duke (Paris *BN* cod. gr. 2144 f. 11)
5 The Emperors Andronikos III, John VI Cantacuzene and John V Palaiologos (fifteenth-century portraits from Cod. Mutinensis gr. 122 f. 294^v, Modena)
6 Stephen Dušan of Serbia and his wife Helena (fresco in Church of the Archangels, Lesnovo)
7 The Transfiguration (Paris *BN* cod. gr. 1242 f. 92^v)
8 Orhan and his father Osman, Emirs of Bithynia (sixteenth-century portraits from a MS in Istanbul University Library, Cod. Yildiz 2653/261)

ACKNOWLEDGMENTS AND
NOTE ON THE TEXT

I make no apology for latinising or modernising the family name of Kantakouzenos into the simpler and perhaps more familiar form of Cantacuzene. Otherwise, however, I prefer to render most names of persons and places in a form as near as possible to the original Greek. I have tried to limit my footnotes and references mainly to the primary sources. The bibliography includes many secondary authorities not cited in the notes. This may prove useful to those who would like to explore further the life of a unique figure of the Byzantine world of the fourteenth century.

Conceived thirty years ago in Dumbarton Oaks, the idea of this book has lived with me throughout my academic career in the Universities of Indiana, Edinburgh, and London, and in the Gennadius Library in Athens, before taking shape in Cambridge. I am indebted to the help and patience of numerous friends, colleagues and librarians in all these groves of academe. But once again my special thanks are due to the Cambridge University Press for finally bringing the book to the light of day after so long a gestation.

Page x blank

ABBREVIATIONS

B	*Byzantion*
BFG	R.-J. Loenertz, *Byzantina et Franco-Graeca*
BNJ	*Byzantinisch-neugriechische Jahrbücher*
BS	*Byzantinoslavica*
BZ	*Byzantinische Zeitschrift*
CFHB	*Corpus Fontium Historiae Byzantinae*
CSHB	*Corpus Scriptorum Historiae Byzantinae*
DOP	*Dumbarton Oaks Papers*
DR	F. Dölger, *Regesten der Kaiserurkunden des oströmischen Reiches*
EEBS	*'Επετηρὶς 'Εταιρείας Βυζαντινῶν Σπουδῶν*
JÖB	*Jahrbuch der österreichischen Byzantinistik*
JÖBG	*Jahrbuch der österreichischen Byzantinischen Gesellschaft*
MM	F. Miklosich and J. Müller, *Acta et Diplomata Graeca Medii Aevi*
MPG	J. P. Migne, *Patrologiae cursus completus. Series Graeco-Latina*
OCP	*Orientalia Christiana Periodica*
PLP	*Prosopographisches Lexikon der Palaiologenzeit*, ed. E. Trapp, H.-V. Beyer, R. Walther *et al.*
REB	*Revue des Etudes Byzantines*
RESEE	*Revue des Etudes Sud-Est Européennes*
Schreiner, *Chron brev.*	P. Schreiner, *Chronica byzantina breviora*
ZRVI	*Zbornik Radova Vizantološkog Instituta*

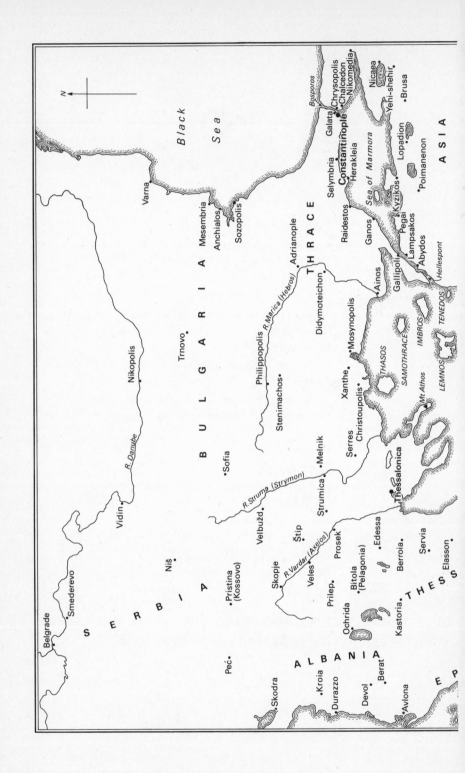

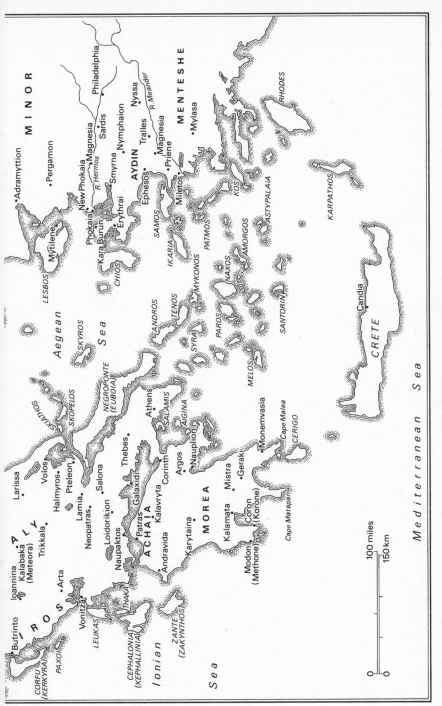

The Byzantine world, thirteenth to fifteenth centuries

INTRODUCTION

JOHN Cantacuzene, known in history as John VI, was Emperor
of the Romans in Constantinople for only seven years, from
1347 to 1354. He was, almost without knowing it, a contemporary
of Edward III of England, of Philip VI of France and of Andrea
Dandolo, Doge of Venice. As a Byzantine he was more closely
aware of being a contemporary and a neighbour of Stephen
Dušan of Serbia and of Osman, the father of the Osmanli or
Ottoman Turkish people. A man of varied talents as a soldier,
scholar, statesman, theologian, Emperor and monk, he was
unique in being the only Byzantine Emperor to record the
events of his own career. His memoirs or autobiography constitute one of the most interesting and literate of all the many
works of Byzantine history. In 1354 he abdicated and lived the
last thirty years of his long life as a monk, a writer and a grey
eminence behind the throne which he had occupied for so short
a time. It is arguable that his influence was more lasting and
beneficial as a monk and a theologian than it had been as an
emperor and a man of the world. There has been no monograph
on his life in English. An intriguing account in French,
published in 1845, is mainly a critique and a historical evalu-
ation of the man's own memoirs; and there is a studious analysis in German of the structure of the society in which he lived.
A German translation of his memoirs with notes and commentary is currently in progress.[1]

---

[1] Val. Parisot, *Cantacuzène homme d'état et historien, ou examen critique des Mémoires de
l'Empereur Jean Cantacuzène et des sources contemporaines* (Paris, 1845); G. Weiss, *Joannes
Kantakuzenos – Aristokrat, Staatsmann, Kaiser und Mönch – in der Gesellschaftsentwicklung
von Byzanz im 14. Jahrhundert* (Wiesbaden, 1969); *Johannes Kantakuzenos Geschichte*,
translated with notes and commentary by G. Fatouros and T. Krischer (Stuttgart,
1982, 1986–).

This book does not aim to present a social and political history of the Byzantine Empire in the fourteenth century. It is no more than a biography of a great and much-maligned and misunderstood man who lived through and tried as Emperor to direct the course of events during that century. The ghost of John Cantacuzene has been haunting me for about thirty years, for the idea of writing his life first came to me in 1964 during a year as a Visiting Fellow at Dumbarton Oaks, Washington D.C. I found to my surprise that almost nothing was known about his father and very little about his family background. My researches into these problems led me far beyond my intentions and resulted in my compiling a genealogical and prosopographical study of all the known members of the Byzantine family of Kantakouzenos up to about 1460.[2] By far the largest entry in this work is inevitably that relating to John Cantacuzene. But it does not venture beyond the bounds of recording the bare facts of his life. This book attempts to put some flesh on the bones of those facts and to offer some speculation about the nature of the man and about his achievements and failures.

The major source for his life is naturally his own memoirs. These he completed about 1369 when he was living in retirement as a monk. Of almost equal importance and value, however, is the historical work of his older contemporary Nikephoros Gregoras, whose narrative spans the years from 1320 to 1359. Gregoras was a statesman and a scholar, qualities which he shared with his friend John Cantacuzene. Their disagreement, as was so often the case in Byzantine society, arose over a matter of theology. From being a sober and reliable historian of his age and a useful control over the statements of Cantacuzene, Gregoras degenerated into a ranting and obsessive polemicist. There are no other Greek historians of the fourteenth century to whom one might turn for a second opinion on the career of John Cantacuzene. It is an indication of the Byzantine failure of nerve in that age that after he and Gregoras laid down their pens about 1360 the long and

---

[2] D. M. Nicol, *The Byzantine Family of Kantakouzenos (Cantacuzenus) ca. 1100–1460. A Genealogical and Prosopographical Study* (Dumbarton Oaks Studies XI: Washington, D.C., 1968).

continuous tradition of the writing of contemporary history in Greek dried up. The historians who revived the art all lived in the fifteenth century, after their Byzantine world had been rudely brought to its end by the Ottoman Turkish conquest of Constantinople in 1453. Of these only the historian Doukas has much to say about the former Emperor and monk John Cantacuzene; and his facts are of necessity derived from hearsay or reminiscences of a past which he never knew, however much he may have mourned its loss.

The last of the long line of Byzantine historians, Laonikos Chalkokondyles, who died in 1490, has little to say and nothing to add about the life and career of Cantacuzene. The theme of his history is not so much the decline and fall of the Byzantine Empire as the origins and rise to power of the Ottoman Turks who had precipitated the fall. This is of some interest, for Cantacuzene was the first Emperor who came face to face with the leaders of the Osmanlis or Ottoman people and had to deal with them on personal terms. There are unfortunately no Ottoman histories or records of his time, even though his daughter became the wife of Osman's son. There is, however, one other unique Turkish source which throws some curious light on the man. It is a long verse epic relating to the Deeds (*Destān*) of another Turkish leader, Umur Pasha, who succeeded his father as Emir of Aydin (Smyrna) in 1334. The poet was called Enveri and he finished his poem in 1465. His hero Umur became a devoted personal friend of John Cantacuzene and remained so until he was killed in battle in 1348.

These are the only contemporary literary sources for his life and career. None of his own private correspondence exists. Those of his letters that have survived are all of an official or diplomatic nature. His name was known in western Europe, not least to the Popes at Avignon with whom he corresponded on ecclesiastical affairs. He was known more closely to the Italians of Venice and Genoa who caused him much trouble by their squabbles over the markets of Constantinople and trade in Byzantine waters. He claims that he could read and speak both Latin and Turkish. These were rare accomplishments for a Byzantine, or rather a 'Roman'. For as a citizen, an Emperor and a monk of what he proudly called the Empire of the Romans, Cantacuzene would hardly have understood the word

'Byzantine'. Nor did he call himself a Hellene or a Greek, although Greek was his language and he wrote it with a directness and simplicity of style uncommon among the Byzantine literati of his age. The four books of his memoirs on which much of this biography is based present a lucid, sometimes graphic, sometimes prolix and tedious, and frequently apologetic and enigmatic picture of their author. He had a vision of an empire smaller but more manageable than that ruled by his imperial predecessors, though none the less Roman. He had a hope, however naive or misguided, of coming to terms with the new Muslim world of Asia Minor. He fancied that he might win the trust and co-operation of western Christendom without compromising the Orthodoxy of his Christian faith and the special qualities of the culture into which he was born. He tried to save the ship of the Byzantine church and state before it plunged headlong into the final hundred years of its millennial existence.

I

THE POLITICAL AND
SOCIAL BACKGROUND

'THERE is not, and there never was on this earth, a work
of human policy so well deserving of examination as
the Roman Catholic Church.'[1] Macaulay was impressed by the
longevity of the Papacy as an institution. He rated the Republic
of Venice as next in length of years. He may not have been
familiar with the term Byzantine Empire, for the word
Byzantine was devised mainly to obviate the clumsy concoction
of 'East Roman Christian' recommended by purists such as
Arnold Toynbee.[2] But Edward Gibbon's *Decline and Fall of the
Roman Empire* might have suggested to Macaulay that the most
enduring political institution that Europe had ever known
was the continuation of the Roman Empire centred upon
Byzantium or Constantinople. The Byzantine Empire lasted
for eleven hundred years and more, from the foundation of
Constantinople as the New Rome in AD 330 until its conquest
by the Turks and its transformation into the capital of the
Ottoman Empire in 1453. When John Cantacuzene, the subject
of this biography, came to prominence in about 1320, the
Empire was approaching its millennium. As a political edifice it
was feeling its age. Its foundations were no longer secure. Large
cracks were visible in its structure. It had lost many of the
outlying provinces which had once been part of its estate.

The Republic of Venice had a similarly long span of life. But
in its early years it had been one of the outlying provinces of
the Byzantine Empire; and as it became independent it
developed its own, fundamentally different political system.

---

[1] Thomas Babington Macaulay, review of the English translation of Leopold Ranke's
History of the Popes, in *The Edinburgh Review* (October 1840).
[2] A. J. Toynbee, *Constantine Porphyrogenitus and his World* (Oxford, 1973), *passim*.

The Byzantines inherited from the Hellenistic kingdoms and from the imperial Rome of antiquity the principle of monarchy. No other form of government was acceptable. Democracy, Greek though it was, seemed to them to be particularly offensive. The spiritual essence of the Byzantine state was the Orthodox Christian religion. The Christian Emperors of the Romans in Constantinople, beginning with Constantine the Great, were held to be the agents on earth of Christ. There was but one God in heaven. There could be only one Emperor in the world. The Emperor was the elect of God. He was also in theory the elect of his people. The Byzantines played at maintaining the ancient tradition of Rome that their Emperors were appointed by the senate, the army and the people, whose choice and acclamation revealed and implemented the will of God. This may have become no more than a pious fiction. The first Roman Emperors of the Julio-Claudian families had striven to perpetuate their line by heredity. Byzantine imperial families in the Middle Ages likewise strove to keep their power to themselves by founding or perpetuating a dynasty. There was no written constitution in Byzantium. But in theory the post of Emperor was a *carrière ouverte aux talents*. The point was proved in the ninth century by Basil I, the groom in the palace stables at Constantinople, who murdered his way to the throne in 867 and went on to establish the longest of all Byzantine imperial dynasties.

It is significant that the family line founded by Basil I had no name. It is known as the Macedonian dynasty, for all that its founder was of Armenian stock. The fact that neither he nor his imperial heirs boasted a surname or family names reveals the truth that in the golden days of the Byzantine Empire the concept of a hereditary aristocracy had not taken root. Nobility had no legal or constitutional definition, except in so far as it might be bestowed by the Emperor. Nor was it hereditary in the sense that its title and privileges passed to the heirs of its holder as in the feudal world of the west. Byzantine noblemen were *de facto* nobility in contrast to the *de iure* noblemen of western society. This was a notable break from the Roman roots of Byzantium; and it was no doubt partly due to the radical reform of society brought about by the militarisation of the Empire in the seventh and eighth centuries necessary for its survival after the losses and upheavals of the Arab and Slav invasions. Byzantium lived, survived and perpetuated itself under a form of universal martial law for many years. The commanders of its military provinces or themes were appointed for set periods by their Emperors. They had no right to convey their titles or their estates to their heirs. Their family or clan names were irrelevant. Many families were indeed forgotten or obscured in the fog of a dark age. The emergence of a new Byzantine aristocracy was one of the symptoms of the ending of that dark age. Towards the end of the eighth century family names began once again to become significant advertisements of wealth, of influence, of the possession of landed property or military distinction. A new aristocracy, or meritocracy, was emerging as the strait-jacket of martial law was relaxed. It was a sign that the battle for survival was being won. It was also a portent of trouble to come. For the acquisition of land and the peasants who went with it by family landlords eroded the highly centralised military, economic and social structure of the Byzantine government. The Emperors who tried to control and monopolise that structure from the hub of the wheel in Constantinople passed increasingly draconian laws to halt this development towards separatism and decentralisation. Yet the first Emperor to give warning of its effects and to legislate to arrest it was Romanos I (920–44), who had pulled himself up by his own bootstraps from an obscure Armenian background. A century later the great wealthy families of Phokas, Komnenos and Doukas were making their presence felt as landed magnates with growing family fortunes which were invested not in the state but in their own properties, their heirs and their dependants.

Such was the family of Cantacuzene, or Kantakouzenos, into which John was born at the very end of the thirteenth century. They originated probably in Asia Minor, where their first recorded member served his Emperor Alexios I Komnenos as a victorious military commander about 1100.[3] From the twelfth century onwards, however, their interests and their properties seem to have lain more in the European provinces of the Empire, in Macedonia, Thrace and Greece. Like many of their

[3] Nicol, *Byzantine Family*, no. 1.

peers, the family rose to prominence as leading lights in the military aristocracy, owners of vast landed estates, and of the social class known in their time as 'the powerful' (*dynatoi*). By the thirteenth century some of them were accepted into the élite of Byzantine society, the true hereditary aristocracy, known as the 'well-born' (*eugeneis*). Their sons and daughters married into the imperial families of Angelos, Komnenos and Palaiologos. John Cantacuzene did not have to pull himself up by his own bootstraps. He was born with a silver spoon in his mouth as one of those whom the Byzantines called 'the golden line' of nobility.[4]

The event that irreparably rocked the ancient foundations of the Byzantine Empire was the Fourth Crusade. The 'soldiers of Christ' had been inspired by the Papacy to drive the Muslims out of Jerusalem and the Holy Land. Most of them never got there. Manipulated by more materialistic instincts, not least those of the merchants of Venice, they attacked, plundered and appropriated the city of Constantinople in 1204, before addressing themselves to the conquest of its provinces in Europe and Asia. The so-called Latin Empire of Constantinople which the crusaders and Venetians set up as a consequence of their brigandage was never a success. But the violence and greed which had gone into its making had a lasting effect on the structure and the economy of the Byzantine Empire and, more significantly, on the minds of its people. The shock to their *amour propre* was irremediable. They had seen their hallowed institutions of church and state overthrown, their capital city burnt, devastated and despoiled. A Latin monarch had usurped the throne of their Emperors; a Latin and dissident bishop had usurped the place of their Patriarch in Constantinople. They found it hard to believe that the crusaders and their accomplices were worthy of the name of Christians. Even in the twelfth century there were signs that the centralised and unified Byzantine Empire was breaking up. After the Fourth Crusade its fragmentation was beyond repair. The Venetians

---

[4] See Angeliki E. Laiou, 'The Byzantine aristocracy in the Palaeologan period: a study of arrested development', *Viator*, 4 (1973), 131–51; Eva de Vries-Van der Velden, *L'élite byzantine devant l'avance turque à l'époque de la guerre civile de 1341 à 1354* (Amsterdam, 1989).

took over most of the sea ports and islands. The French conquered and settled in much of the Greek mainland. The only Byzantine provinces which remained free of the western colonialists were those that kept them out by force. Centres of resistance were formed, based on Nicaea in north-west Asia Minor and on Arta in Epiros in northern Greece. Nicaea became the capital of a Byzantine Empire in exile; and it was from there, after fifty-seven years of Latin occupation, that Constantinople, the true capital of the Empire, was recovered and restored to its rightful owners.

The Emperor in exile at Nicaea at the time was Michael Palaiologos. It was his army which had achieved the miracle; and it was he who, in August 1261, gratefully acknowledged that he was the elect of God and moved his seat of government to Constantinople. He is designated in history as Michael VIII. He himself liked to be known as the New Constantine, the second founder of the city that he had rescued. Many of his people, however, were aware that he had reached his throne in Nicaea by devious means and many were shocked when he legitimised his position by imprisoning and blinding the young heir apparent. The crime was overshadowed by the euphoria of the liberation of Constantinople from the Latins. The church, however, was slow to forgive the criminal; and for many years the New Constantine, Emperor of the restored Empire, failed to command the universal loyalty of his subjects. None the less, he succeeded in founding a dynasty of Emperors which lasted almost as long as that of the Macedonian line established by Basil I. The direct descendants of Michael VIII were destined to rule Constantinople and the remaining fragments of the Byzantine Empire to its bitter end in 1453. The dynasty of Palaiologos was the last Byzantine dynasty. The family line was interrupted by only one outsider. His name was John Cantacuzene.[5]

The house of Palaiologos into which Michael VIII was born was well-to-do and well connected. Michael could boast ancestral links with all three of the Byzantine imperial

---

[5] On Michael VIII: D. J. Geanakoplos, *Emperor Michael Palaeologus and the West, 1258–1282: A Study in Late Byzantine–Latin Relations* (Cambridge, Mass., 1959); D. M. Nicol, *The Last Centuries of Byzantium, 1261–1453*, 2nd edn (Cambridge, 1993), pp. 41–89.

dynasties before him. He was proud to advertise his noble
lineage by styling himself Michael Doukas Angelos Komnenos
Palaiologos. As the New Constantine he worked hard to put the
New Rome of Constantinople back on the map as a world
power, and to some extent he succeeded. Trade revived,
although it was mainly in foreign hands. The merchants of
Genoa had their reward for helping to oust their rivals the
Venetians from Constantinople. But the Venetians too were
soon forgiven and making still more profits from their lucrative
business ventures in Byzantine waters. As a diplomat Michael
had few equals. He made his name known if not feared in most
of the courts of western Europe. He married off his daughters,
natural and unnatural, to the rulers of Bulgaria, of the Mongols
of Persia and the Mongols of the Golden Horde in south Russia
and of the self-styled Empire of Trebizond. His son and heir-
presumptive was found a first wife from Hungary and a second
from Lombardy. He exchanged embassies with the Mamluk
Sultans of Egypt. This was imperial diplomacy on the grand
Byzantine scale. It was a scale which the revived Empire could
scarcely afford.

What he and his people had not expected was the sense of
grievance felt by many of the powers of western Europe since
the Greeks had deprived them of the glittering prize of
Constantinople. A movement, promoted by the Papacy and by
Venice, was soon afoot to win it back by means of another
crusade to recreate the Latin Empire and right the wrong done
to western pride and honour. It could be justified as a holy war
since the Byzantine church and people had wilfully rejected the
chance of professing obedience to the Church of Rome. The
Pope's champion as leader of this shabby cause was the King of
Sicily, Charles of Anjou, brother of the saintly Louis IX of
France. Michael VIII convinced himself, if not his subjects or his
church, that the way to avert this disaster was to convince the
Pope that the Orthodox Christians of Byzantium had now
seen the error of their ways and were ready to unite with the
Roman church. Many years of Michael's reign were wasted in
negotiations to achieve this diplomatic purpose. His limited
financial resources were spent on bolstering the defences of his
western frontiers against the chance that diplomacy might fail
and that the threatened crusade might after all be launched

across the water from Italy or Sicily. The threat was finally removed in 1282 when the proposed crusader, Charles of Anjou, was overthrown by revolution in his own Kingdom of Sicily. The revolt, known as the Sicilian Vespers, was at least partly sponsored by the astute diplomat Michael VIII Palaiologos.

He had outwitted his western enemies, but at a great price. He had formally united the Byzantine church with Rome. The union had been proclaimed at the second Council of Lyons in 1274. Michael was unpopular with his subjects on many other counts. His submission to the Papacy brought all his opponents together. It was widely construed as a betrayal of their spiritual identity as Byzantines. Those who opposed his policy were subjected to a reign of terror and persecution. It was an era which they and future generations never forgot. Michael died in December 1282, condemned by most of his people as a traitor and a heretic. The dreadful experience of the Fourth Crusade was still fresh in men's memories. The evidence of its effects was still visible and palpable in the western colonies that it had spawned throughout the Empire, the French principality on the mainland of Greece and in the Venetian and Genoese entrepots in Constantinople and throughout the Greek islands. Michael had been naive and unrealistic to expect people to pretend that it had never happened. Above all, he was insensitive to their deeply held religious feelings and convictions. The Fourth Crusade had caused them to wonder what sort of Christianity could have allowed it to happen. To suggest that the Orthodox Christians of Byzantium, whose church had for centuries questioned the claims and the theology of Rome, should make religious concessions for material advantage was not attractive. Orthodoxy had become synonymous with a form of nationalism. The Byzantines had acquired a lasting fear of being Latinised. They might have applauded their Emperor as their saviour from Latin aggression. But the cost was too high when it meant sacrificing their conscience.

There was another side to the account which Michael VIII bequeathed to his successors. His fear of invasion from Italy had led him to concentrate most of his military resources on defending the western approaches to his Empire. He had left his eastern frontiers too poorly defended. It was there at Nicaea that he had come to power. It was there that the seeds of disaster were being sown in the thirteenth century. During the years of exile at Nicaea there had been a balance of power and a recognisable frontier between Byzantium and the Seljuq Turks of Anatolia. The balance was broken with the arrival of the Mongols who, in 1258, had captured Baghdad and forced the Seljuq Sultans to become their vassals. The Mongol conquests further east stimulated a westward migration of countless tribes of Turkoman nomads. The Sultans encouraged them to press on towards the Byzantine frontier. Their livelihood depended on plunder; and, as fanatical Muslims, they were fired with the zeal of holy warriors or ghazis against the Christians. They were impervious to diplomacy. It was hard to know who their leaders were. They had no sense of ethnic or national unity. A well-equipped and disciplined army sent from Constantinople might have contained them. They found the going too easy; and as early as the 1270s their raiders were penetrating from the uplands of Anatolia down into the fertile valleys of western Asia Minor. The ancient walled cities such as Nicaea were for a time able to defend themselves. But soon they were isolated from one another as the raiders overran and occupied the surrounding countryside. By the time of Michael VIII's death in 1282 the rot had gone too far. The Byzantines had not the means or the strength to man the defences of their Empire on two sides at once. The new Turks began to settle and organise themselves into small principalities or emirates. Michael VIII Palaiologos no doubt saved his fragmented Empire from a second attack of Latinisation, a triumph for which his church and people gave him little thanks. But by neglecting his eastern provinces he left a legacy that was in the end to prove a far more deadly blow to all that remained of the Byzantine world.

His son and heir, who came to the throne in 1282 as Andronikos II Palaiologos, rightly saw that he must at once repair the wrongs that his father had done to the conscience of his people. He declared that the union with the Roman church was at an end and proclaimed himself as the champion and defender of true Orthodoxy. Not all the wounds were healed, for there were still those in the church and society who had hoped that the dynasty of Palaiologos would die with the death of its founder. An Emperor there must be, however. No alternative form of government was conceivable. Andronikos remained as such in name if not always in substance for more than forty years until 1328.[6] He was not gifted with his father's character and ingenuity in shaping the course of events and setting his stamp upon an age. He was an amiable if ineffective ruler, a man of letters and culture, piously Orthodox to a fault, but a victim rather than a manager of circumstances. Under his guidance the Byzantine Empire quickly sank to the status of a second-rate power, a monarchy beset by other monarchies, though still trailing clouds of imperial glory and imperial pretensions. The neighbouring Orthodox Kingdoms of Serbia and Bulgaria, having shaken off their political dependence on Constantinople, had pretensions of their own. The monarchies of western Europe were not much concerned with the fate of Byzantium. The Popes too, having lost patience with Michael VIII, were not interested in his successor who in any case kept well clear of them for fear of alienating his church. The mercantile Republics of Genoa and Venice continued to be the beneficiaries of Byzantium's economic weakness, to which their own activities had so greatly contributed. From time to time they went to war with one another over control of the markets of the Mediterranean and the Black Sea. They fought their sea battles in Byzantine waters while the Emperor watched or was forced to take sides and to pay them compensation for their losses. Andronikos played into their hands by his panic measures to stimulate the economy and reduce the Empire's commitments. He saved expenditure on the army by cutting down its numbers. He disbanded the navy altogether in the forlorn hope that his Italian allies would defend the Empire by sea. He introduced new taxes, some in money, some in kind. The revenue rose but it was the ordinary people who suffered and not the landed aristocracy or the still wealthy burghers of Constantinople. He devalued the coinage to about half of its former worth, thus encouraging men of affairs to put more trust in the new gold coinage being minted by Venice. The Venetians were not slow to see and to reap the advantage.

---

[6] On Andronikos II: Angeliki E. Laiou, *Constantinople and the Latins. The Foreign Policy of Andronicus II, 1282–1328* (Cambridge, Mass., 1972); Nicol, *Last Centuries of Byzantium*, pp. 93–147.

The most ominous portents of doom, however, were to be seen in the east, in Asia Minor, the former heartland of Byzantine power and resilience. By 1300 only a few isolated cities held out against the growing confidence and aggression of the new Turkish invaders. Byzantine resistance to them was weakened by the Emperor's reluctance to employ more soldiers and hampered by local rebellions or mutinies. The house of Palaiologos still had its political enemies in Asia Minor; a rival Emperor was indeed proclaimed there in 1295. The rebellion was suppressed; but it was symptomatic of a growing sense of despair among people who felt abandoned and neglected by their government. Streams of refugees began to pour into Constantinople to add to that government's problems. The Turks grew still more confident. In 1302 one band of them in Bithynia in the north-west of the country and dangerously close to the capital, defeated a Byzantine army in battle. Their leader was called Osman. As Emir of Bithynia he was to become the father figure of the Osmanli or Ottoman people. More floods of refugees swarmed across the Hellespont to Constantinople. Osman was only one of a number of such ghazi warriors then staking out their territorial claims in western and southern Asia Minor. The Emirs of Aydin and Menteshe to the north and south of the Meander river were the first to take to the sea and to raid the coastline and islands of the Aegean. The sailors who manned their ships were often Greeks who had been rendered unemployed when Andronikos disbanded the Byzantine navy. The Emir of Aydin captured Ephesos in 1304 and then Smyrna, and his pirate ships spread terror among the islands and as far away as the mainland of Greece. The Venetians saw their eastern trade routes being threatened and spread the word in western Europe.

The Emperor Andronikos clutched at every straw. After the defeat of his army by Osman in 1302 he gladly accepted the offer of help from a band of professional mercenary soldiers called the Catalan Company, who had just been paid off for their services in Sicily. They demanded a prodigious price, which put Byzantium in debt for many years to come; their activities in Asia Minor and elsewhere did more damage to the Christians than the Turks; and finally, after much bloodshed, they had to be driven out of the land that they had come to save. They drifted westward into Greece where they expelled the French colonial lords of Athens and transformed it into a Catalan Duchy. The Emperor's initiative, never very inventive, was then exhausted. It was not only his Christian subjects in Asia Minor who were desperate for action. The crowds of refugees reaching Constantinople had dreadful tales to tell and their numbers added to the existing poverty and hunger in the capital. The rich landowners who were losing their estates to the Turks also had their grievances against the government. By 1320 Andronikos had been on his throne for thirty-eight years. Things had gone from bad to worse. The circumstances might have been made for revolution or for reform. The Byzantines distrusted the idea of reformation. The Patriarch of Constantinople, Athanasios I, never tired of telling them that their misfortunes were being brought upon them by their sins. This they were prepared to believe. God was punishing them. Athanasios was a voluble and cantankerous saint. He mesmerised his Emperor Andronikos and he was idolised by the poor, not least by the destitute refugees in the city for whose relief and welfare he laboured. But he, like the Evangelist, knew that 'the poor always ye have with you' (John 12: 8). The order of society was ordained by God. The best that could be done was to inspire or to change its leadership. It was time to look for a younger and more enterprising Emperor.

The chance to bring about a dynastic if not a social revolution came in 1320. In October of that year the son and heir-apparent of Andronikos died. Michael Palaiologos, known in history as Michael IX, had been crowned as co-Emperor with his father in 1294. The ruling dynasty of Palaiologos seemed to be assured for another generation, for Michael's wife, an Armenian princess, produced two sons and two daughters. The elder of the boys, called Andronikos after his grandfather, developed into an unruly and extravagant young man. One of his amorous adventures which ended in family tragedy is said to have hastened the premature death of his father Michael IX in 1320. His grandfather disowned and disinherited him. His cause was championed by a clique of his friends and supporters, who easily persuaded him to take up arms and fight for his right to the succession. Most of them were of his own generation, young members of the hereditary landed aristocracy. Some were high-minded enough to hope that a successful palace revolution would unseat the now elderly Andronikos II and give the management of affairs to younger and more imaginative men loyally serving his disprized grandson. Others had less lofty motives seeing only a chance to make their names and perhaps their fortunes. Prominent among the more high-minded leaders of the revolt was John Cantacuzene.

2

THE OLD ORDER CHANGES
(1321–1328)

THE first recorded members of the family of Cantacuzene or Kantakouzenos served their Emperors as military commanders early in the twelfth century. By the time that John Cantacuzene came to prominence two hundred years later they were a rich, aristocratic and influential family, well endowed with landed property and connected through marriage to the ruling house of Palaiologos. Little is known about John's father except that he served Andronikos II as governor of the Byzantine province of Peloponnese or the Morea from about 1286 to 1294. He died in office there when he was no more than twenty-nine and it seems that his son John never knew him. John was a mother's boy and an only child, born probably in 1295, the year after his father's death. In his memoirs he speaks very rarely about his father. He claims to have been instructed in the martial arts by an uncle called Angelos who was a distinguished soldier.[1] It was his mother who brought him up, taught him, advised him and fed his ambition. She outlived her husband by almost fifty years and never married again. She was a woman of remarkable character and ability. Her son once accorded her the greatest accolade that a man of his time could bestow on a woman he admired, that she 'was gifted with a more than feminine strength of mind'. Others among her contemporaries praised her for her prudence, good judgment, resourcefulness and administrative

---

[1] The bare facts of the careers of John Cantacuzene and his parents are assembled and documented in Nicol, *Byzantine Family*, nos. 20, 21, 21a, 22; *Prosopographisches Lexikon der Palaiologenzeit*, ed. E. Trapp, H.-V. Beyer, R. Walther *et al.*, v, nos. 10942, 10973 (cited hereafter as *PLP*). John's uncle may have been John Angelos Synadenos, father of his later friend Theodore Synadenos.

ability.[2] She also had an ample fortune which she was happy to invest in the career of her only son. Her name was Theodora and, in the fashion of her age, she liked to be known as Theodora Palaiologina Angelina Cantacuzene. Her last surname she acquired from her husband. The two other names advertised her family connections with the older imperial line of Angelos and the ruling house of Palaiologos. Her son was proud to bear all three of his mother's surnames. He was devoted to her and in later years devoted to her memory. He owed her a great deal.

She was a watchful though not obsessive mother and she wisely arranged a suitable marriage for him while he was still young. In the person of Eirene Asenina, Theodora found a young woman of spirit with a character similar to her own. Eirene was a granddaughter of the Tsar of Bulgaria, John III Asen; and she became the wife of John Cantacuzene about 1318.[3] He was then twenty-three years of age. He was well known at court in Constantinople and held a minor and titular office in the administration. He got on well with the young Andronikos before and more especially after he had been disgraced. They were of much the same age. The old Emperor may have suspected that John's friendship with his grandson might lead to trouble. In April 1321 when trouble seemed to be brewing he ordered John to leave at once to take over the governorship of the Peloponnese. John declined to accept the post on compassionate grounds. It was the office which his father had held for eight years before his untimely death. The Peloponnese had sad associations for him and for his mother who had often told him that it would cause her grief if he were to be stationed there. The Emperor, however, seemed determined to move John away from Constantinople and from the company of the young Andronikos. He ordered him to take command in Thessaly. This, as John confesses, was a more attractive proposition since it gave him the chance to

[2] *Ioannis Cantacuzeni eximperatoris Historiarum Libri IV*, ed. L. Schopen and B. Niehbuhr, 3 vols. (*CSHB*, Bonn, 1828, 1831, 1832), I, p. 125 (cited hereafter as Cantac.); *Nicephori Gregorae Byzantina Historia*, ed. L. Schopen, 3 vols. (*CSHB*, Bonn, 1829, 1830, 1855), I, p. 530; II, p. 169 (cited hereafter as Greg.).
[3] On Eirene: Nicol, *Byzantine Family*, no. 23; D. M. Nicol, *The Byzantine Lady. Ten Portraits, 1250–1500* (Cambridge, 1994), pp. 71–81.

commandeer troops and supplies, for Thessaly in northern Greece was subject to attack from the Catalans who had taken over Athens.[4]

Thessaly was not what he wanted, however. He was already plotting with those of like mind who were eager to mount a *coup d'état* to right the wrongs that the old Emperor had done to his grandson. The conspirators made their headquarters in the city of Adrianople, two or three days' journey north of the capital. Adrianople, the modern Edirne in Turkish Thrace, was a prosperous and well-fortified city in the fourteenth century. The late Michael IX, father of the young Andronikos, had spent much time there and made many friends. The city had a large population and its own garrison of troops. Its citadel, commanding a fertile plain surrounded by hills, stood above the banks of the river Tunca which runs to join the Marica or Hebros just to the south of the city. Some 50 kilometres further south stood the smaller city and fortress of Didymoteichon which had access to the sea down the river Marica. It was a part of the Byzantine world which had, in 1320, been spared the attentions of the Turks. Landowners could still farm their estates; and it is likely that several who had lost their lands in Asia Minor had found new properties in Thrace. The cities of Adrianople and Didymoteichon both played a prominent role in the early career of John Cantacuzene.[5]

The conspiracy to promote the cause of the young Andronikos began to form in the early months of 1321. Apart from his friend John Cantacuzene, its leading lights were Syrgiannes Palaiologos and Theodore Synadenos. Syrgiannes was an ambitious and unreliable adventurer. His curious name betrayed his Mongol descent on his father's side, though his mother was a cousin of Andronikos II and related to the Cantacuzene family. He had been involved in rebellion in 1315 when acting as governor of Macedonia. Recalled to

[4] Cantac. I, pp. 77–86.

[5] Cantac. I, pp. 23–4. On Adrianople and Didymoteichon, see Catherine Asdracha, *La région des Rhodopes aux XIIIe et XIVe siècles. Etude de géographie historique* (Athens, 1976), pp. 130–48; R. Ousterhout, 'Constantinople, Bithynia, and regional developments in later Palaeologan architecture', in S. Ćurčić and Doula Mouriki, eds., *The Twilight of Byzantium* (Princeton, N.J., 1991), pp. 80–2. On Andronikos III: Ursula V. Bosch, *Kaiser Andronikos III. Palaiologos. Versuch einer Darstellung der byzantinischen Geschichte in den Jahren 1321–1341* (Amsterdam, 1965).

Constantinople he was put in prison. But when the Emperor conducted his re-shuffle of provincial governors in 1320 Syrgiannes was released and appointed to command the province of Thrace. It was an unwise appointment. It was no less unwise of John Cantacuzene to trust Syrgiannes as a loyal member of the conspiracy. Its third member was Theodore Synadenos, an older and more experienced man, who held the high military rank of *protostrator* and had been a close friend of Michael IX. He had been stationed in Thrace and knew the province well. He too was posted to another command, in Macedonia, in 1320. He too disobeyed his orders.

This triumvirate met in secret to discuss their plan of action. Adrianople, the centre of their operations, was under the control of Syrgiannes as the new governor of Thrace. Cantacuzene left his young wife at Gallipoli and returned to Constantinople to report to his friend Andronikos. While there he made the mistake of enlisting a fourth conspirator in the person of Alexios Apokaukos. Cantacuzene was never an acute judge of character. Apokaukos was something of a social upstart. He was not nobly born nor was he rich. He was a parvenu with an eye to the main chance. The best that even his friend Cantacuzene could say about him was that he had a keen and resourceful mind. In 1321 he was acting as chamberlain at the palace. Cantacuzene thought he might be useful in stirring up dissent in Constantinople. On 15 April 1321, the fourth day of Holy Week, John Cantacuzene left Constantinople and waited outside the city with some soldiers. Synadenos soon joined him on the road to Adrianople. On the night of 19–20 April the young Andronikos escaped on the pretext of taking a hunting party beyond the walls. Two days later he had joined his friends in Adrianople. The old Emperor was furious. At once he extracted an oath of loyalty from all his senators and officials, declared his grandson to be an outlaw, and bullied the hierarchy of Constantinople into excommunicating all present and future supporters of the rebel. But the rebel already had many supporters beyond the reach of his blustering grandfather.[6]

⁶ Cantac. I, pp. 25–40, 87–93; Greg. I, pp. 296–319. On the social standing and composition of the 'triumvirate', see G. Weiss, *Joannes Kantakuzenos – Aristokrat, Staatsmann, Kaiser und Mönch – in der Gesellschaftsentwicklung von Byzanz im 14. Jahrhundert*

The people of Thrace had quite recently been subjected to further ruinous taxation. By playing on their grievances the young Andronikos gained followers everywhere. He promised immediate remission of taxes for all. The publicans who were on their rounds were hunted down and the money that they had collected was taken to swell the coffers of the rebels so that they could recruit and pay for soldiers. By no means all of them were regulars but many of them, with the prospect of loot and plunder, were spoiling for a fight, not least a force of German mercenaries who may have formed part of the garrison of Adrianople and found it hard to know what was happening since they spoke no Greek. The Tsar of Bulgaria to the north of Thrace, who was married to a sister of Andronikos, offered to help the cause with 300 cavalrymen. His motives were far from selfless. The most hotheaded of the conspirators were for taking direct action by marching on Constantinople. Cantacuzene, however, advised a more cautious and less bellicose approach. After much argument his counsel prevailed, though it was thought wise to send a message to those in the capital warning them that an attack might be made. The old Emperor took the hint and sent a delegation to negotiate. It was headed by Theoleptos, Bishop of Philadelphia, and the mother of Syrgiannes, who was related to the families of Cantacuzene and Palaiologos. Early in June 1321, at Rhegion on the banks of the river Melas, between the port of Selymbria and Constantinople, a treaty was arranged. The Empire was to be partitioned between grandfather and grandson. They would rule as colleagues. Andronikos II as senior Emperor would control Constantinople; the young Andronikos would hold Thrace as his portion of Empire.[7]

It was an unsatisfactory arrangement and it lasted for only a few months. The crafty Syrgiannes changed sides. Some said that he was embittered after his wife had suffered from the lasciviousness of Andronikos. There is no doubt that he was jealous of the favouritism shown to Andronikos by John

---

(Wiesbaden, 1969), pp. 23–31. *PLP*, I, no. 1180 (Apokaukos); XI, no. 27121 (Synadenos); XI, no. 27167 (Syrgiannes).

[7] Cantac. I, pp. 97–119; Greg. I, pp. 319–21. Bosch, *Andronikos III*, pp. 19–25; Nicol, *Byzantine Family*, pp. 24–5, 38.

Cantacuzene. In November he deserted his supposed friends in Thrace and disappeared to Constantinople. This event was the signal for open war to break out between the rival claimants and their followers. It began in December 1321. The battle-ground was the province of Thrace. No decisive engagements were fought and in July 1322 both sides admitted their folly. A second settlement was agreed at a meeting at Epibatai on the coast near Selymbria. To ensure neutrality and fair play the negotiations were chaired by the Protos or superior of the monasteries of Mount Athos. All were agreed that the experiment of partitioning the Empire between grandfather and grandson had not worked. The monk of Athos no doubt reminded those present that in the theocracy of the Byzantine Empire, although there might be co-Emperors, there could be only one true Emperor of the Romans at a time. A treaty was again signed. The young Andronikos was mollified by a generous allowance from the imperial treasury. The future seemed more promising. After the formalities at Epibatai Andronikos rode to the palace at Constantinople. There he dismounted and kissed his grandfather's foot. It was a gesture contrary to the customary protocol, but it was greeted with cheers by those who witnessed it. After fifteen days in the palace he went back to his camp at Didymoteichon, where his wife, together with John Cantacuzene's mother, Theodora, had taken up residence.[8]

The part played by Cantacuzene in the sporadic warfare in Thrace in 1321–2 is not made as clear as it might be by one who was prone to paint his own achievements with a generous brush. After the treaty of July 1322 one assumes that he served the co-Emperors impartially. He is known to have helped ward off an attack on Thrace by the Bulgars in 1323. The old Emperor Andronikos is said to have announced that he had been so impressed by John's ability on this occasion that: 'If I were to die without heir I would advise the Romans to adopt this man as

---

[8] Cantac. I, pp. 119–25, 152–69; Greg. I, pp. 351–2, 358–9. *Chronica Byzantina Breviora*, ed. P. Schreiner, *Die byzantinischen Kleinchroniken (CFHB*, xii/1–3: Vienna, 1976–8), ii, pp. 229–30 (cited hereafter as Schreiner, *Chron. brev.*). This phase of the conflict is analysed at length by K. P. Kyrris, Τὸ Βυζάντιον κατὰ τὸν ΙΔ' αἰῶνα. Ἡ πρώτη φάσις τοῦ 'εμφυλίου πολέμου καὶ ἡ πρώτη συνδιαλλαγὴ τῶν δύο Ἀνδρονίκων (1321) (Leukosia, 1982).

their Emperor.'[9] The conflict with Bulgaria was brought to an end when its new ruler, Michael Šišman, took to wife the widow of his predecessor, for she was the sister of the young Andronikos. John further distinguished himself in driving away a large horde of Mongol horsemen who had come down through Bulgaria and pillaged the Marica river valley south of Adrianople. The only sour note in the apparent harmony between the co-Emperors in these years was sounded by the weasel Syrgiannes. The reconciliation in 1322 had upset his plans. He confided in other malcontents who were even more sinister than himself. They turned king's evidence against him and denounced him to the senior Emperor as a conspirator and potential assassin. Syrgiannes was put back in prison. His time was yet to come. The reconciliation which he had planned to disrupt was publicly advertised early in 1325. On 2 February, at a splendid ceremony in St Sophia, the young Andronikos was at last crowned as Emperor in his own right. The Patriarch Esaias officiated, as was proper. Everyone kept quiet about the fact that Andronikos had been crowned at least as co-Emperor nine years before. The senior Emperor, who had disowned him, was present at his second coronation. It was unfortunate that the old man suffered an accident during the procession to the cathedral: his horse slipped and threw him. Some saw this as an ill omen. They were not far wrong. The euphoria of the great occasion was not to last for long.[10]

It was probably now that John Cantacuzene, the proven friend and stalwart of the newly crowned Emperor Andronikos III, was promoted to the high rank and office of Grand Domestic or commander-in-chief of the armed forces of the Empire, which he was to hold for the next fifteen years. The army badly needed a generalissimo, a supreme commander who could shape its future and its strategy on a wider scale. The rivalries between the contenders for the throne, fought out in skirmishes in Thrace, had played into the hands of the Empire's enemies. The Turks in Asia Minor had made the most of their opportunities. Later in 1325 John Cantacuzene, in his capacity as Grand Domestic, led an army across the Straits to try to stop

[9] Cantac. I, pp. 182–6.
[10] Cantac. I, pp. 196–204; Greg. I, pp. 362–4, 373; Schreiner, *Chron. brev.*, II, p. 231.

the rot. He scored some limited success, though curiously his victory is not recorded in his memoirs. It is known only from two fulsome letters of congratulation written to him by one of the literati of Constantinople.[11] It was not a major victory. Those days were past. The Osmanlis in Bithynia had progressed from mere marauding in the countryside. They had grown confident enough to attack and besiege the walled cities. Brusa (Prousa) was the first to suffer. The young Emperor Andronikos III asked to be allowed to take a boatload of arms and supplies to the citizens to enable them to hold out. His grandfather forbade him; and on 6 April 1326 the hungry and neglected people of Brusa surrendered. It was the first great triumph for the Osmanlis and in due course Brusa was to become the first capital of the Ottoman people. In the next few years the other ancient Greco-Roman and Byzantine cities in Asia Minor were to succumb one by one to the Turks. Nor were Turkish soldiers unknown in Europe. Andronikos II had employed Turkish mercenaries to fight his battles in Thrace, in the hope that they could be relied upon to go home across the water when they had earned their pay. But some stayed as brigands and adventurers. In 1326 Cantacuzene was set upon by some of them, unhorsed and wounded in the foot while on his way to Didymoteichon.[12]

The final phase in the petty bickering over the possession of the throne was not long in coming. In May 1327 Andronikos III had a meeting with the new ruler of Bulgaria, Michael Šišman, who had recently become his brother-in-law. No doubt the meeting was a family occasion. It lasted for a week at Črnomen on the Marica river, some 20 kilometres west of Adrianople.[13] Cantacuzene was not present and so can take no blame for what ensued. Had he been there he might have advised his friend to be cautious; for rumours were coming from Constantinople that the old Emperor was restive. The peace between the two Emperors was clearly fragile; and there were other factors, some half understood, some only hinted at in the sources. It is

[11] Theodore Hyrtakenos, *Correspondence*, ed. F. J. G. La Porte-du Theil (Paris, 1798), nos. 54, 55.

[12] Cantac. I, pp. 206–7; Greg. I, p. 384; Michael Gabras, *Letters*, ed. G. Fatouros (Vienna, 1973), no. 411; Schreiner, *Chron. brev.*, II, pp. 231–2.

[13] Cantac. I, pp. 207–8; Greg. I, pp. 390–2; Schreiner, *Chron. brev.*, II, p. 233.

hard to know the truth, given that the two major authorities, John Cantacuzene himself and Nikephoros Gregoras his former friend, were so partisan and yet so full of detail. Both present the sordid squabble between the contestants entirely in terms of personalities. Neither looks for underlying causes, such as simple greed or ambition; neither has much to say about the distress and suffering brought upon the helpless victims of this struggle for power among the ruling aristocracy.

The third phase of the conflict was lent a more sinister colour by the active involvement in it of the Slav neighbours of the Empire. The Serbs as well as the Bulgars saw ways to advance their own interests. Michael Šišman of Bulgaria agreed to support his brother-in-law Andronikos III in return for help against his own neighbour, Stephen Dečanski of Serbia, who was known to be in alliance with the old Emperor in Constantinople. A dangerous precedent had been set when the foreign neighbours of the Empire were invited to take sides in the struggle for power between its rulers. Tension mounted in the summer and autumn of 1327. Portents of disaster were noted. There was an eclipse of the moon on 1 September; a pig ran amok in the cathedral of St Sophia.[14]

At the beginning of October Andronikos III moved his court from Didymoteichon to Selymbria on the coast, nearer to Constantinople, and then to Rhegion which was closer still. John Cantacuzene was with him and records the several exchanges of embassies that took place and the tedious speeches delivered on both sides. The old Emperor seems to have reached a state of panic. When his Patriarch refused to excommunicate the young Andronikos and counselled peaceful negotiations, he was told to mind his own business and not mix politics with religion. As the winter drew on and the old man became increasingly neurotic, feeling grew in favour of his grandson. He courted the loyalty of the people of Thrace by once again relieving them of taxation and promising them extravagant rewards for their support of his cause. His most loyal personal supporter remained the Grand Domestic John Cantacuzene, whose ample means, derived from his landed property, were readily available, as was the generosity of

---

[14] Greg. I, p. 385.

his mother Theodora, then resident at Didymoteichon, who gladly subsidised what she saw as the advancement of her only son.

For some weeks Andronikos III waited in vain for a response from his grandfather in Constantinople. On the advice of Cantacuzene and Synadenos he decided to twist the old man's arm. They took a force of 1,300 soldiers and marched to Constantinople. They got no further than one of the city gates, where a messenger informed them that it was his Emperor's order that they must withdraw at once. Clearly he was not going to give in. They went back to Selymbria and then reassembled at Didymoteichon. Their next ploy, no doubt inspired by Cantacuzene, was to strike a blow from another quarter. In December 1327 word had reached them that the city of Thessalonica in Macedonia was prepared to go over to them. Thessalonica, the second city of the Byzantine Empire, would be a great prize. Its people were none too happy about the alliance which Andronikos II had engineered with their northern neighbours in Serbia. They were tempted too by reports that the younger Emperor would relieve them of taxation. Their gamble was justified. In January 1328 Andronikos III and John Cantacuzene with his army stormed their way into the city to the acclamation of most of its inhabitants. The old guard held out for a while in the citadel until they were forced to surrender. Some of them fled to the court of the Serbian Kral, although he had prudently refrained from intervening. The other strongholds in the province of Macedonia soon followed the lead of Thessalonica and were persuaded without much difficulty to switch their allegiance.[15]

This unexpected shift in the balance of power in the Balkans prompted Michael Šišman of Bulgaria, the supposed ally of Andronikos III, to change sides and throw in his lot with the regime in Constantinople. The old Emperor, we are told, 'jumped at this offer like a storm-tossed ship in sight of haven'.[16] His grandson, who had treated Šišman as an honoured relative, was appalled. Again on the advice of Cantacuzene, he moved quickly to forestall any action by the Bulgarian troops

---

[15] Cantac. I, pp. 259–72; Greg. I, pp. 409–11.   [16] Greg. I, p. 411.

who were already on the scene. He persuaded their commander to withdraw and sent a reprimand to Šišman to remind him of the terms of their alliance.

The way was now set for the entry of the young Emperor into Constantinople. The people in the city were ready for almost any form of relief from their miseries. For two weeks or more a Venetian fleet had been blockading the Bosporos and the harbours of Constantinople to prevent Genoese food ships unloading their cargoes. It was a minor incident in the perennial trade war between Venice and Genoa; but the Byzantines were its victims. With no supply ships coming in to Constantinople or to the Genoese harbour of Galata across the Golden Horn there was near famine in the city. The old Andronikos had lost what little popularity he had left. The leaders of the opposition party were ready to receive their liberators.

On 23 May 1328 the triumvirate of Andronikos III, John Cantacuzene and Theodore Synadenos advanced to the walls of the city with about eight hundred soldiers. Two of the commanders of the garrison had offered to let them in on promise of a reward. The rest of the guards were encouraged to drink themselves to sleep. In the dead of night rope ladders were let down from the walls by the gate of St Romanos. The first over the walls opened the gate from within and the liberators silently made their way into the city. The old Emperor was in his bed. Twice he was told that something was amiss. Twice his friend and counsellor, Theodore Metochites, the Grand Logothete, assured him that it was no more than rumour. But when the noise and hubbub in the streets became audible the old man leapt from the bed on which he had been tossing and turning and took refuge by the icon of the Virgin Hodegetria. He was, not unreasonably, fearful for his own safety. The troops commanded by the Grand Domestic, however, had orders to offer no violence to any person or property. What they had achieved was God's purpose. At dawn on 24 May they hailed Andronikos III as their only Emperor. He went straight to the palace to receive the frightened and tearful submission of his grandfather and to assure him that no harm would come to him. The Patriarch Esaias, who had boldly refused to excommunicate the young Emperor, was brought out

of his monastic confinement and paraded on horseback through
the streets in a joyful procession of musicians and dancers.
There was a general feeling of relief.

Cantacuzene had seen to it that most of his soldiers were
encamped outside the city walls. There was little plundering
and looting, though some of the old Emperor's closest friends
and supporters were made to suffer, especially Theodore
Metochites. His palatial house was wrecked and ransacked
and his wealth was impounded by the imperial treasury. The
historian Nikephoros Gregoras was also a victim of popular
vengeance. As a philosopher he consoled himself by recalling
Solon who had sagely recommended that in such conditions of
political upheaval no citizen had the right to be neutral. The old
Emperor was Emperor no more. He was not disgraced. He was
not excommunicated. He was allowed to keep his imperial
insignia provided that he made no public appearances. His
Grand Logothete Metochites, however, was taken away to be
held under guard in Didymoteichon.[17]

---

[17] Cantac. I, pp. 285–306; Greg. I, pp. 415–28; Schreiner, *Chron. brev.*, II, p. 234. Bosch,
Andronikos III, pp. 39–52.

3

EMPEROR IN WAITING
(1328–1341)

T HE war between Andronikos II and Andronikos III lasted
for seven years and one month, from 19 April 1321 to 24 May
1328. So ends the first book of Cantacuzene's memoirs.[1] He tells
his own part in the ultimate triumph with a modesty which is
probably unfeigned, except in the eyes of critics looking for
sticks with which to beat him. All were agreed that the old
Emperor was treated with exemplary kindness and humanity.
But he was a broken and disappointed man. Senility and
blindness overtook him. In January 1330 he became a monk with
the name of Antonios and was known as 'the most pious and
Christ-loving Emperor Antonios the monk'.[2] It was a form of
address which John Cantacuzene was to understand and
appreciate twenty-five years later. Andronikos II died aged
seventy-four in February 1332 while dining with his widowed
daughter Simonis, whom he had once sacrificed on the altar of
diplomacy as a child-bride to the lecherous Kral of Serbia,
Stephen Milutin. His old friend and learned companion
Nikephoros Gregoras delivered a funeral oration. Thirty days
later his even more learned friend the Grand Logothete
Theodore Metochites also died; and in May of the same year
the Patriarch Esaias went to his reward in heaven. It was like
the passing of an age. It seemed that the older generation who,
under Andronikos II, had brought the Empire to despair if not
to ruin and precipitated a conflict for change, had bowed out
none too graciously and left the stage for younger men.[3]

---

[1] Cantac. II, p. 306 (*CSHB*), where the date '19 May' must be corrected to 24 May.
Greg. I, p. 427; Schreiner, *Chron brev.*, II, p. 234.
[2] Greg. I, p. 446.
[3] Cantac. I, pp. 431, 473; Greg. I, pp. 460–3, 474–81, 496; Schreiner, *Chron. brev.*, II,
pp. 239–42.

Andronikos III, now undisputed Emperor of the Romans, was about thirty-six when his grandfather died in 1332. His first wife, who came from Germany, had died childless. His second wife, whom he married soon after his coronation in 1325, was also a westerner. She was Joanna, or as the Greeks called her, Anna of Savoy. She spent the first years of her marriage at Didymoteichon and it was there that she gave birth to her first son, John, in June 1332. The happy event seemed to establish and assure the continuance of the dynasty of Palaiologos.[4] John Cantacuzene, who was also in his early thirties, had earned his position as the new Emperor's right-hand man. Theodore Synadenos, the third member of the triumvirate set up in 1321, was rewarded with the office of Prefect of the City of Constantinople. Cantacuzene, however, retained his rank of Grand Domestic and the military duties that it entailed. But once the fighting was at an end he asked to be relieved of some of the other imperial duties which had been wished upon him as an administrator. The important offices of secretary of state to the Emperor, of treasurer and collector of taxes were transferred to his protégé Alexios Apokaukos. It was a dangerous concentration of power in the hands of a man who was still hoping that his hour would come. Another adventurer looking for his opportunities in the changed political circumstances was Syrgiannes, who had been put in gaol by Andronikos II. Cantacuzene, who claimed to be related to him, pleaded for his release. Syrgiannes was set free. He was made to swear an oath of allegiance to the new government and sent off to take charge of Thessalonica, where it was hoped that the Emperor's mother, Maria, who lived there, would keep an eye on him. She was so taken with him that she adopted him as her son. After her death in 1333, his suspicious behaviour led to another warrant for his arrest. He was brought for trial in Constantinople but escaped and found his way to Serbia to continue his intrigues. He was finally rounded up by the Emperor's agents who exceeded their orders by murdering him. It was perhaps a fitting end to his ignoble career, as Gregoras concludes, since, in his opinion, Syrgiannes was 'the man most responsible for starting the war between the

---

[4] On Anna of Savoy: Nicol, *The Byzantine Lady*, pp. 87–95.

Emperors and the root cause of all the troubles that followed therefrom'.[5]

Cantacuzene was in many ways a simpler man than he appeared to be. He had befriended and liked Syrgiannes. He expected that those whose promotion and fortune he fostered would remain loyal as well as grateful. Another of his favourites who was to turn and bite the hand that fed him was Alexios Apokaukos. His power and influence also made enemies for him. The new Empress Anna of Savoy suspected that he had too much hold over her husband the Emperor. Her mother-in-law Maria felt much the same, though she preferred to live in Thessalonica and kept out of court circles in Constantinople. She was, however, madly jealous of Cantacuzene's mother, Theodora, whose wealth and ambition had played so great a part in her son's rise to power. The undercurrents of rivalry and intrigue were still strong, for all that the dust of civil war had died down. It did not pass unnoticed that as early as 1329 Andronikos had tried to persuade his friend Cantacuzene to accept the title of co-Emperor. Theodore Synadenos and even the young Anna of Savoy were invited to support the proposal, since Cantacuzene 'was already Emperor in all but name'. The man himself, however, resolutely declined the honour. He preferred to remain the power behind the scene.[6]

It remained to be seen whether the new regime in Constantinople had the strength or the policy to set the wreckage of Empire on a new and sounder course. The first to rush in to take his pickings was the Tsar of Bulgaria, who again marched into Thrace in June 1328. The immediate military response to his temerity surprised and chastened him. His army was driven away. He was forced to renew his treaty. Those who had supposed or hoped that Byzantium was ruined or exhausted by its own internal quarrels were startled to see that it had new vigour and power to fight back.[7]

The real test of the Empire's strength and resolve, however,

---

[5] Greg. I, p. 498; Cantac. I, pp. 329–39, 436, 456–7; Schreiner, *Chron. brev.*, II, p. 245. On the discrepancy in Cantacuzene's text here, see R.-J. Loenertz, 'Ordre et désordre dans les mémoires de Jean Cantacuzène', *REB*, 22 (1964), 222–37 (reprinted in Loenertz, *Byzantina et Franco-Graeca* [*BFG*], I, pp. 113–30).

[6] Cantac. I, pp. 363–70.

[7] Cantac. I, pp. 323–9; Greg. I, pp. 430–1.

lay in Asia Minor. The city of Brusa in Bithynia had fallen to Osman, leader of the Osmanli Turks, in 1326. Constantinople was still crowded with refugees who had fled across the water. Most of them would never go home and those who had not tried to escape were learning to make the best of life under their alien conquerors. Could the refugees ever be sent home? Could the tide of the Turkish invasion ever be turned back? These were some of the questions which the old regime in Constantinople had preferred to leave unanswered. Andronikos III and John Cantacuzene were determined to find answers. In May 1329 they crossed the sea with a hastily recruited army and on 1 June landed at Chrysopolis (Skutari) on the Asiatic side of the Bosporos. Their boats stayed on hand in case they were needed. They marched towards Nikomedia which the Turks were blockading and encamped at Pelekanon, from where they could see the enemy in the surrounding hills. An experienced soldier like Cantacuzene could tell that the Turks would have the advantage if it came to a fight. But the soldiers were fired by the thought of booty; and on 10 June battle was joined. Cantacuzene commanded the right wing of his army. The Osmanlis were led by Orhan, the son of Osman. After a number of indeterminate charges and counter charges and as night began to fall, Cantacuzene advised his Emperor that it would be best to retreat and prepare for another engagement in the morning. The Turks gave them no chance to retreat in an orderly fashion. Both their leaders were wounded. Rumour spread among the troops that the Emperor had been killed. The retreat became a rout, the men panicking to escape from the pursuing Turks. Cantacuzene did what he could to restore discipline. Andronikos, who could no longer mount his horse had to be carried to the coast at a place called Philokrene. There, after another skirmish, all the stragglers regrouped behind its walls. They had been badly mauled along their way and two of their officers, both relatives of Cantacuzene, had been killed. The dispirited army was led safely back to Chrysopolis and ferried home to Constantinople.[8]

The battle at Pelekanon was the first direct encounter on the

---

[8] Cantac. I, pp. 341–63; Greg. I, p. 458; Schreiner, *Chron. brev.*, II, pp. 235–6. Nicol, *Last Centuries of Byzantium*, pp. 169–70.

field between a Byzantine Emperor and an Osmanli Emir. It could be said that the action had surprised the Turks and relieved the blockade of the city of Nikomedia. But it was obvious that such relief could be no more than temporary. The Osmanlis were already masters of Bithynia. Given the overwhelming numbers and fanaticism of their warriors there could now be no military solution to the problem, at least in that part of Asia Minor which was closest to Constantinople. The point was underlined two years later. In March 1331 the city of Nicaea, once the capital of the Byzantine Empire in exile, surrendered to Orhan. Nikomedia held out until 1337. But by then Andronikos and Cantacuzene had initiated their new response to the Turkish peril. In August 1333 the Emperor went in person with a relief ship to Nikomedia to bring food to its starving inhabitants. He stayed for more than a week and arranged a meeting with Orhan at which a settlement was reached. It is not clear whether Cantacuzene was with him, although he records the event. Perhaps he was ashamed to report the exact terms of the settlement, which was in effect the first formal treaty between a Byzantine Emperor and an Osmanli Emir. For it is known from other sources that peace was bought by the Emperor's promise to pay to the Turks an annual tribute of 12,000 gold coins for possession of what little was left of Christian Bithynia. Gifts and pleasantries were exchanged and the Emperor went back to Constantinople.[9]

The payment of large sums of gold as a form of Danegeld was an old and well-established practice of Byzantine diplomacy. It was seldom regarded as degrading. It was often better and cheaper than warfare. It was certainly cheaper than trying to recruit, equip and maintain an army mighty enough to drive all the Turks back to what had once been the eastern frontiers of Byzantium. They were already too firmly established, not only in Bithynia but throughout western Asia Minor. The tentative treaty of 1333 may be seen as the first step in a new approach to the problem. The initiative of John Cantacuzene in this may be surmised more than stated. For his influence over his Emperor grew greater as time went on. In 1329, when Andronikos was convalescing from his wound at Didymoteichon, he had tried

---

[9] Cantac. I, pp. 446–8; Greg. I, p. 458; Schreiner, *Chron. brev.*, II, pp. 238, 243–4.

to invest his friend and companion in arms with the title of co-Emperor. Cantacuzene had modestly declined the honour. But it was increasingly evident that his was the guiding hand behind the foreign policy of the Empire. In 1330 Andronikos fell seriously ill at Didymoteichon and seemed near to death. He summoned Cantacuzene to his bedside and again offered him the title of Emperor. Again he declined to accept. To make his dying wishes still clearer, Andronikos then called his officials and his Empress, Anna, to witness that in the event of his death they would regard Cantacuzene the Grand Domestic as their leader and protector and as the guardian of his children, for Anna was again with child. At the Emperor's wish Cantacuzene then administered the oath of allegiance to the assembled company, 'as was the ancient custom on an Emperor's death'. In his extremity Andronikos asked if he might be ordained as a monk. This would have deprived him of his rights and privileges as Emperor. Cantacuzene refused to make the necessary arrangements and had a furious quarrel with one of the doctors, who felt that the Emperor's wish should be granted. A confessor was finally admitted to his presence, but only to administer the last rites. It was unnecessary; for, after sipping some holy water, Andronikos miraculously began to rally and revive. Before long he had made a full recovery.

It is a strange tale and it might be open to scepticism were it known only from the pen of Cantacuzene. But the essence of it is reported also by his friend Gregoras and, surprisingly, by the Turkish writer Enveri, who believed that the real Emperor at the time was, in any case, 'that artful man the Grand Domestic'.[10] Cantacuzene was not averse to blowing his own trumpet. Some of his achievements, however, are recorded only by others, as, for example, his 'singular heroism' during Andronikos's fatuous and unnecessary campaign against the Bulgars in 1331.[11] He had a greater talent for diplomacy than his Emperor and a greater gift for making and cultivating friends and allies, not all of them as desirable or as reliable as he hoped. That he was gullible in these matters is shown by the case of

---

[10] Cantac. I, pp. 391–411; Greg. I, pp. 439–50; Enveri, *Le Destān d'Umūr Pacha (Düstūrnāme-i Enverī)*, ed. Irène Mélikoff-Sayar (Paris, 1954), p. 93, lines 1313–70.
[11] Greg. I, p. 486. Bosch, *Andronikos III*, pp. 79–80.

the renegade Syrgiannes. It was as a result of that scandalous affair, when he was with the Emperor in Thessalonica, that Cantacuzene first met the Kral of Serbia, Stephen Dušan, who had succeeded Stephen Dečanski in 1331. Dušan was to become the architect of an extensive Serbian Empire in Macedonia. Cantacuzene met him when he came to Thessalonica for negotiations in 1333; and by his own account the two became firm friends.[12] How firm their friendship was and how much each man used the other for his own purposes came to be revealed in later years. Cantacuzene made, or claimed to have made, firm and useful friends in other quarters too. The most extraordinary of his friendships was with the Turkoman Emir of Aydin (Smyrna), Umur Beg. Umur's father had founded one of the new and enterprising Turkish Emirates on the west coast of Asia Minor. He completed the conquest of Smyrna in 1329.

Umur of Aydin was more than a simple ghazi warrior. He was a cultured and intelligent man. He answered a call for help from the Emperor and Cantacuzene when they were engaged in recovering the island of Lesbos from the Genoese adventurers who had appropriated it in 1335. He came in person to the Emperor's camp at Kara Burun between Chios and Smyrna; and it was there that Cantacuzene first met him.[13] His interview with the Emperor is recorded not only by Cantacuzene but also by the Turkish poet Enveri, who composed a heroic epic about Umur Pasha. The two accounts are like mirror images. Enveri quite naturally refers to the Emperor as the 'miscreant' Christian; Cantacuzene, with equal naivety, speaks of his new friend as 'the barbarian'. Umur was to honour the promises that he made at Kara Burun on several occasions and put himself out to honour his friendship with Cantacuzene. Even the generally prosaic Gregoras praised the humane character of Umur, noting that he was a man not devoid of a measure of 'Hellenic culture'; and he compared his friendship with Cantacuzene to that between Orestes and Pylades. Enveri tells a charming story of how Cantacuzene offered one of his three daughters, all of them as lovely as houris, in marriage to Umur.

---

[12] Cantac. I, p. 475.
[13] P. Lemerle, *L'Emirat d'Aydin. Byzance et l'Occident. Recherches sur 'La Geste d'Umur Pacha'* (Paris, 1957), pp. 108–15.

He was much moved by her beauty but sternly rebuked the offer. His religion could not permit such an incestuous union, for he and Cantacuzene were 'brothers'.[14]

The Byzantines of Constantinople, perhaps rather more than those in Asia Minor, must have been heartened to see at least some military and diplomatic action being taken against their enemies after the long years of inertia and internecine warfare before 1328. But in their eyes the greatest achievement of Andronikos III and his Grand Domestic was the restoration to their Empire of the provinces of northern Greece which had been wilfully alienated from their central government since 1204. The separatist rulers of Thessaly and Epiros, whose principalities had come into being after the Fourth Crusade, had never fully acknowledged their allegiance to the restored Empire in Constantinople. The habit of independence was inbred in them. Attempts had been made, especially by Michael VIII, to bring them to heel. But it was Andronikos III who succeeded. Events played into his hands. In 1333 the province of Thessaly was left in anarchy on the death of its ruling lord. The Emperor acted swiftly in ordering an army to march south from Thessalonica; and in a few weeks all the country as far south as the border of the Catalan Duchy of Athens and Thebes had been reclaimed. Michael Monomachos, the general who had accomplished his Emperor's purpose, was appointed as governor of the now imperial province of Thessaly.[15]

The reincorporation of the province of Epiros across the Pindos mountains from Thessaly came a few years later; and it was in this achievement that John Cantacuzene excelled himself by a remarkable display of his diplomatic and strategic talents. The pretext for mounting a large military offensive in that area came in 1337 when alarming reports reached Constantinople that the Albanians to the north of Epiros were causing trouble. It was not the first time they had done so. The Albanians were not partial to government of any kind. They

---

[14] Cantac. I, pp. 482–95; Greg. I, pp. 649–50; Enveri, *Le Destān*, pp. 83–5, lines 1035–84, p. 106, lines 1749–74. Lemerle, *L'Emirat*, pp. 175–6.

[15] Cantac. I, pp. 473–4. Bosch, *Andronikos III*, pp. 134–5; D. M. Nicol, *The Despotate of Epiros*, II, *1267–1479: A Contribution to the History of Greece in the Middle Ages* (Cambridge, 1984), pp. 101–4.

favoured free-lance banditry and plunder; and it was not easy to wage war on them in their mountain fastnesses where they knew all the escape routes and hiding places and where cavalry could not properly function. The detailed description which Cantacuzene gives in his memoirs of the fighting methods of the Albanians makes interesting reading. It was his idea to try new tactics against them. He called on his friend Umur of Aydin to lend him a force of about 2,000 Turkish foot-soldiers as mercenaries. Umur was glad to oblige his 'brother' and sent the troops from Smyrna. In the spring of 1338 a combined Turkish and Byzantine army set out from Thessalonica. The Albanian marauders were caught unawares, not so much by the attack as by the nature of the attackers. They had expected a cavalry force and had taken to their mountains where they could hide and pelt their enemies from above. But the Turkish infantry, being light-armed and agile, soon found their way around the hills and terrified the Albanians with their unfamiliar appearance and tactics. The Albanian bandits had met their match. The Turks slaughtered, plundered and took prisoners without mercy, as well as rounding up flocks of cattle, sheep and horses without number. Many of their prisoners were carried off to slavery in Asia Minor. The amount of booty was so great that the customary laws of war, by which one-fifth of any loot should go to the Emperor and one-fifth to his commander, could not be enforced. The Turks simply helped themselves to whatever they wanted 'as from an inexhaustible source of treasure'. Thus, as Cantacuzene smugly remarks, the Albanians paid the penalty for their crimes. The Greek-speaking inhabitants of the district were delighted. They had never seen an Emperor before. They heaped praises on him, regarding him as a god rather than a mortal.[16]

The Emperor wisely disbanded his Turkish mercenaries and sent them home to Umur with their loot and slaves before he went any further. It would not do to have his halo tarnished by news of their depredations. For it was now his intention to take his army south to negotiate or force the surrender of the province of Epiros. He had yet to discover how far the people of that long-defiant corner of the Empire were in a mood to

[16] Cantac. I, pp. 496–9; Greg. I, pp. 544–5.

abandon their independence; but the circumstances were promising. Affairs there had just passed into the hands of the widow of its former ruler, the *basilissa* Anna Palaiologina, and her son Nikephoros, who was still a boy. Anna was herself of the imperial line. She was not averse to making an honourable settlement with an Emperor of her own family and surrendering her province to him. Rumours of the conduct of his Turkish mercenaries in Albania was no doubt a strong incentive. But some of her people were in favour of continuing to defy the Emperor; and they had a willing ally in Italy across the water from Epiros in the person of Catherine of Valois, who claimed the unsubstantial title to the long defunct Latin Empire of Constantinople. Anna had her way, however, and accepted the Emperor's terms. She left her capital city of Arta and was escorted with the Emperor's retinue to Thessalonica where she was to be provided with a residence and an estate. The terms of her submission had stipulated that her son Nikephoros should be betrothed to one of the three daughters of John Cantacuzene and that he should leave Epiros with his mother. When the moment came for her to leave, however, her son had disappeared. He had been spirited away by those opposed to his mother's deal and abducted to Italy, to the court of Catherine of Valois. There he was to become the prince across the water for the diehards in Epiros. The Emperor could wait no longer. He appointed the ever-useful Theodore Synadenos as governor general of the restored province and, with Cantacuzene in command, left for Thessalonica.[17]

Eighteen months later they had to return to Greece to complete the operation. Nikephoros had been brought back to Epiros by his Italian friends as the young pretender to his heritage. The revolt was centred on Arta. Its leaders were Nikephoros Basilitzes and Alexios Kabasilas. They arrested Theodore Synadenos and held him captive in the castle of Arta. Some but not all of the other towns in the province joined the rebellion. Nikephoros was installed with a garrison of soldiers in the castle of Thomokastron on the coast, conveniently accessible to his allies in Italy. The Emperor was determined to prevent the revolt from spreading. He ordered Monomachos,

[17] Cantac. I, pp. 499–504; Greg. I, pp. 536–9, 544–6. Nicol, *Despotate of Epiros*, II, pp. 107–14.

the governor of Thessaly, together with John Angelos, a cousin of John Cantacuzene, to make for Arta; and in the spring of 1340 he and Cantacuzene arrived with reinforcements to find that the ground had been well prepared for them. They split their forces into three divisions to attack and lay siege to the three main centres of the revolt: Arta, the castle of Rogoi not far away, whose impressive remains still stand by the banks of the Louros river; and Thomokastron on the coast. The rebels had overestimated the strength of their following. Order was restored within a matter of months. It was done not so much by force as by the diplomacy and eloquence of John Cantacuzene, who bribed, bullied and talked the rebel leaders into surrender.

The long and circumstantial account of these events which he presents in his memoirs is worth quoting at length, for the speeches which he made illustrate his own powers of tact and persuasiveness and also something of his own political ideology. The castle of Rogoi had been taken over by the rebel Alexios Kabasilas. Cantacuzene recalled that he had met the man, befriended him and done him some favour when he was last in Epiros. In the hope that Kabasilas would remember and hand over his castle to a former friend, Cantacuzene went to Rogoi with a small bodyguard. Kabasilas saw him coming and sent a messenger to tell him not to come any nearer, for he was afraid that he might be compelled either to talk to him or to drive him away. He had sworn to have no truck with the enemy, while to turn away a man who had once befriended him would be bad manners. Cantacuzene replied that such words meant nothing. If Kabasilas drove him away he would only reveal himself as a devious and inconstant friend. Kabasilas protested that he could not deny that Cantacuzene was his friend; the thought caused him deep distress; but in the circumstances of war he could not speak for himself alone. He had his colleagues to consider. He feared that if he came down from the walls to hold private talks with Cantacuzene he might lose his self-control and be influenced by the bond of friendship to make a wrong decision. Finally Kabasilas was persuaded to come out as far as the bridge over the river and the two men talked from opposite ends of it. Their conversation was amicable until Cantacuzene abruptly came to the root of the matter by accusing his former friend of being the prime mover of the current rebellion against

imperial rule. He defended himself and his colleagues by
arguing that they were concerned only with the fact of their
long hereditary independence from Constantinople.

It was a battle of wits of a kind that Cantacuzene enjoyed.
Three days later he went back to Rogoi to continue the game.
Kabasilas saw him approaching and this time, after a calculated
delay, came out and crossed the bridge to talk man to man.
Cantacuzene talked at some length, pressing the point that it
was really not so terrible to live as a subject of the Emperor of
the Romans and certainly preferable to dying besieged by
that Emperor's army. They parted and went their ways. A
few days later they met again outside the walls of Rogoi and
Cantacuzene persuaded him to surrender himself and his
castle. His patience had been sorely tried; he was tired; and on
his way back to the camp at Arta Cantacuzene stopped to eat
and refresh himself by a stream. As he was resting, he saw
Kabasilas coming towards him at speed. He explained that he
had come on his own and with no guard as an earnest of his trust
in and friendship for Cantacuzene; for it was this that had
sapped his resolve to fight to the end. Kabasilas had his
reward. Having reported his success to his Emperor at Arta,
Cantacuzene went back to Rogoi the next day to bring the
rebels and their leader to pay homage. The Emperor received
them with kind words and no rancour. Kabasilas answered that
the kind words might apply to his comrades; but if he himself
had done anything to elicit the Emperor's kindness the credit
was due to John Cantacuzene alone, for it was his eloquence
that had captivated him and weakened his resolve to die rather
than surrender. This was a mystery which he could not fathom.
The Emperor was gratified by the mystery which his Grand
Domestic had achieved. He honoured Kabasilas with the gift of
an imperial title and rewarded his men proportionately to their
rank.[18]

Meanwhile the siege of the rebels in Arta continued. The
fortress of Arta stands on a hill above the city overlooking
the river Arachthos. It is an imposing building with massive
walls and only one entrance gate, which was well guarded. The
besieged were in no mood to surrender. They poured scorn on

[18] Cantac. I, pp. 509–17.

Alexios Kabasilas and his men, declaring that they would never give in even if they were to be offered 10,000 rewards. Once he was back in the Emperor's camp, Cantacuzene resolved to apply his psychological warfare which had proved so effective at Rogoi. He invited their leader Nikephoros Basilitzes to come down to the castle gate for talks. The talking was rather one-sided. Cantacuzene gave a historical résumé of how, in his view, the autonomy of the province of Epiros had come about as a consequence of the Fourth Crusade and the dismemberment of the Roman Empire to which it had belonged since the days of the first Caesar. The Emperors of Constantinople had, since 1261, repeatedly but vainly tried to win it back. The present Emperor's campaign was perfectly justified, for it was divinely inspired by his desire to recover a part of his patrimony. The young prince Nikephoros, for whose rights they claimed to be fighting, would never bring them true liberty. The Italians, on whose help he and they had called, were not their true friends. Cantacuzene dwelt on the foolishness of the rebels' stubborn resistance, on the damage that warfare and the presence of a besieging army was doing to the economy and agriculture of their land, and on the suffering being inflicted on the innocent victims of the rebellion.

Once again Cantacuzene's eloquence proved persuasive. Basilitzes called an assembly of his men inside the castle walls. Things had not gone as well as they had hoped. They had been under siege for about six months. They voted to surrender to the Emperor through his Grand Domestic, whom they trusted, knowing that he would arrange matters so that submission would seem sweeter than freedom. Cantacuzene accepted their surrender. Basilitzes and his men were brought to the Emperor's presence to seek and obtain his pardon. The gate of the castle of Arta was opened and the imperial army marched in. The surrender of Rogoi and then of Arta left the castle of Thomokastron as the last outpost of the rebellion. The Emperor could not leave Epiros until he had rounded up the last champion of its independence, the young Nikephoros, who was being besieged in Thomokastron. But an epidemic of dysentery had swept through the Emperor's camp during the long siege of Arta. Only one of his officers died of it but many of their horses and mules were afflicted, and he himself was far from well.

He could go no further. It was therefore left to Cantacuzene to go on alone to deal with the last pocket of resistance at Thomokastron and arrest Nikephoros.

Thomokastron was a long march from Arta. It had been under siege for some months but only from its landward side. This, as its defenders replied to the messages that Cantacuzene sent to them, was their strong point. They had access to the sea and they were daily expecting reinforcements to reach them in warships from their friends in Italy across the water. Three weeks after Cantacuzene reached Thomokastron thirteen ships from Taranto appeared offshore. They gave comfort to the besieged; but they rode at anchor well away from the coast and made no attempt to disembark their troops. They could see the enemy camp on the beach. Thomokastron was not going to be starved into surrender as Arta might have been. Its defenders would have to be persuaded. Cantacuzene saw another chance to exercise his rhetoric. After twenty-five days of besieging the castle he proposed that they send him a plenipotentiary for negotiations. They picked on the tutor of the young Nikephoros, an intelligent man of better breeding than most of them. The discussion that he held with Cantacuzene was, as before, mainly one-sided. Cantacuzene gave the young man a history lesson. The Italians, he said, had offered to help Nikephoros only from their own greed and ambition. Often in the past the Italians had invaded Epiros but they had never been able to occupy a single town by war or by siege, except for those that were ceded to them by treaty. Having failed in the past, how could they now expect to fare any better when the Emperor was on the spot with his army? The modest Italian force which was lying offshore would not dare to land its troops as long as the Grand Domestic and his men held the beach-head. Catherine of Valois, who was so eager to help them, for her own purposes, had taken a whole year to muster what few ships they could now see. Even these would soon melt away when they realised what they were facing, and the Italians would lose heart. Even if they sent a larger force and occupied the land, the outcome would be servitude for the inhabitants. The hope of Nikephoros and his supporters had been that their revolt would spread. That hope had proved to be baseless since the people of Arta and Rogoi had given in and benefited themselves by so doing. He and his men in Thomokastron should see the folly of their ways before the Emperor took over their land and property in other districts and drove their wives and children into exile.

To avoid this fate they should surrender and accept the rewards that would come to them. Nikephoros would be betrothed to a daughter of Cantacuzene who would bring him up as his own son. He would be honoured by the Emperor and made famous among the Romans. His friends and supporters would bask in his reflected glory and enjoy their share of his privileges.

The outcome was another triumph for Cantacuzene's powers of persuasion. The emissary went back to report to his colleagues in the castle and on the next day returned to say that they had decided to surrender. Nikephoros and their leaders were brought out to Cantacuzene, who led them to the Emperor at his camp. He left a garrison in Thomokastron to deter the Italians from attempting a landing. The Emperor welcomed the rebels at Arta and rewarded them for their good sense. He particularly welcomed the boy Nikephoros who had been lost and was now found, and invested him with an imperial title. Three weeks later, early in November 1340, after he had made arrangements for security in Epiros, the Emperor left for Thessalonica. Cantacuzene's cousin John Angelos was left as governor of Arta. Theodore Synadenos, who had suffered in prison there, was transferred to the governorship of Thessalonica. Nikephoros was taken to join his mother Anna and in the summer of 1342 he was married to Cantacuzene's daughter Maria. He was to prove to be a loyal and helpful son-in-law. After their return from Arta Cantacuzene's own eldest son Matthew, then aged about sixteen, married Eirene Palaiologina, a cousin of the Emperor. The wedding took place in Thessalonica. It signified a new and closer bond between the families of Cantacuzene and Palaiologos. It did not, however, imply that Matthew had become a prince of the blood or a potential successor to the throne. The right of succession still lay with John Palaiologos, the infant son of the reigning Emperor Andronikos III.[19]

---

[19] Cantac. I, pp. 518–25; Greg. I, pp. 553–4. Nicol, *Despotate of Epiros*, II, pp. 114–22. On Maria Cantacuzene the *basilissa* and on Matthew's marriage to Eirene Palaiologina: Nicol, *Byzantine Family*, nos. 27 and 24.

The question of the succession was, as it happened, to bedevil Byzantine society and politics for years to come. The crisis began when the Emperor got back to Constantinople from Thessalonica in the spring of 1341. He had been unwell and had no doubt over-exerted himself during the long campaign in Epiros. Shortly after his return he fell gravely ill. The doctors kept him alive for three days; but on the night of 14–15 June he died. Cantacuzene was at his bedside. When he saw that the end was near he advised the Empress Anna to look to the welfare of her children in case there might be trouble; and he set a special guard over the young John and his baby brother Michael. When it was clear that he was beyond medical help, the Emperor was moved to the city monastery of the Virgin Hodegetria. It was there that he died on 15 June and there that he was buried. He was in his forty-fifth year.[20]

It is at this point that Cantacuzene concludes the fortieth chapter of the second book of his memoirs and his older contemporary Gregoras the eleventh chapter of his *Roman History*. Both men recognised that it was a turning point in the history of their age. For Cantacuzene it was a sad event, for he had come to think of the young Emperor as his brother. Gregoras did what he thought was proper to the occasion by writing a formal lament and a eulogy of the deceased, tendentiously comparing his achievements with those of Themistocles, Pausanias, Alcibiades and even Alexander the Great. Such bombast was expected of Byzantine rhetoricians. What Gregoras most clearly reveals, however, is that he had much preferred the old Emperor Andronikos II to his grandson Andronikos III.[21]

[20] Cantac. I, pp. 557–60; Greg. I, pp. 559–60; Schreiner, *Chron. brev.*, II, pp. 250–1.
[21] R. Guilland, *Essai sur Nicéphore Grégoras: l'homme et l'oeuvre* (Paris, 1926), pp. 146–50.

4

WAR FOR THE THRONE

(1341–1347)

J OHN Cantacuzene begins the third book of his memoirs with
these words:

Upon the death of the young Andronikos [III] the worst civil war that
the Romans had ever known broke out. It was a war that led to almost
total destruction, reducing the great Empire of the Romans to a
feeble shadow of its former self. For this reason I have deemed it
necessary to relate the events of that conflict in detail, so that future
generations may learn what evils are generated by jealousy and also so
that my contemporaries may have a true account and not have to rely
on hearsay. For those who have written about this war either played
no part in it and served up the tales of the people or the reports of
others uncritically accepted; or, if they were participants on either
side, they knew nothing of their leaders' plans and counsels, nor were
they present at all the events in what was a long and continuous war
lasting for five years. No one can lay such charges against myself. For
I was party to all the plans, schemes and unrecorded stratagems of the
war and experienced all its vicissitudes. I therefore propose to relate
events as they were, adding nothing to the truth and taking care to
examine cases of blame or scandal attached to anyone, for it is not my
taste to speak ill of any. If my account seems sometimes to be at odds
with the popular version, this need cause no wonder, for truth rather
than popular opinion is my guide.[1]

Cantacuzene completed his memoirs in or before 1369. He
had had ample time to set his thoughts and his notes in order.
He had also had time to consult the account written by his former
friend Nikephoros Gregoras who died in 1361 and wrote the only
known history of his age to enlighten his contemporaries.[2] For,

---

[1] Cantac. II, pp. 12–14.
[2] Comparisons between the two men as historians are offered by Parisot, *Cantacuzène*,
pp. 5–29; and by R. Guilland, *Essai sur Nicéphore Grégoras* (Paris, 1926), pp. 251–7.

in spite of what Cantacuzene may say about the shortcomings of other historians or chroniclers of his time, none of their works has survived by which we might judge the truth or falsity of his statement. Gregoras is the only check that we have and he too, though less prolix, was not free from prejudice. Gibbon, who conscientiously ploughed through the 'enormous folios' of Cantacuzene, found in them more speciousness than veracity.

Instead of unfolding the true counsels and characters of men, he displays the smooth and specious surface of events, highly varnished with his own praises and those of his friends. Their motives are always pure; their ends always legitimate; they conspire and rebel without any views of interest; and the violence which they inflict or suffer is celebrated as the spontaneous effect of reason and virtue.[3]

The Emperor's death had been sudden and unexpected. It induced an atmosphere of crisis. His widow Anna stayed for three days in the monastery where he had died before going back to the palace to observe nine days of mourning. Cantacuzene as Grand Domestic felt responsible for the maintenance of law and order and also for the safety of her children. He stayed near them in the palace until he was sure that all was well. By his own account he wrote more than five hundred letters in thirty days to all the governors of the provinces and officials of the treasury ordering them to perform their duties as if their Emperor was still alive. Order and discipline were upheld. The Emperor's funeral service was a grand and solemn occasion conducted in the church of St Sophia, 'the largest of all churches under the sun', and yet not big enough to contain all the mourners. The celebrant was the Patriarch John Kalekas, or John of Apros, who had held his throne for seven years.[4] It was with the Patriarch that Cantacuzene first crossed swords. John Kalekas was no simple monk content to confine himself to his spiritual and theological duties. Like many a Patriarch of Constantinople before him he felt bound to have his say in the political affairs of the Empire. Like his meddlesome predecessor Athanasios he believed that

[3] E. Gibbon, *The History of the Decline and Fall of the Roman Empire*, ed. J. B. Bury (London, 1898), vi, p. 489.
[4] Cantac. ii, pp. 14–16. On the Patriarch John XIV Kalekas: *PLP*, v, no. 10288.

'priesthood was not granted to Christian people for the sake of Empire but Empire for the sake of priesthood'.[5]

It was unfortunate that the dying Emperor Andronikos III had not made his wishes clearer with regard to the succession. He had tried to do so when he was near death's door at Didymoteichon in 1330. He had nominated John Cantacuzene as guardian and regent of the Empire. He had more than once offered Cantacuzene the title of co-Emperor. At the moment of his death in 1341 circumstances were not the same. His son John Palaiologos had not been born in 1330. There was no evident successor to the throne. In 1341 John was nine years old. He was the heir-presumptive. There would have to be a regent until he came of age. Many people assumed that the regency would be in the hands of John Cantacuzene, who had been the late Emperor's closest friend and principal adviser in matters of politics and war. It was his own assumption. On the other hand there was much opposition to him as a person and as the spokesman and champion of the well-heeled aristocracy. Anna of Savoy, now the Dowager Empress, was glad to accept his protection and comfort in her hour of personal need. But she had always mistrusted his influence over her husband and may have feared that if he were appointed as regent he would exert the same influence over her infant son. She was a forceful woman and she was determined that no one should stand in the way of her son's imperial inheritance. Anna preferred to put her trust in the Patriarch as protector of the interests of her family until the young John Palaiologos was old enough to come into that inheritance. The Patriarch agreed. He saw himself as regent. He could point to the indisputable fact that the late Emperor had delegated him to take charge of affairs in Constantinople in 1334 and 1340 during his own absence in Thessalonica and Greece.[6]

The third and most devious actor on the political scene was Cantacuzene's supposed friend and protégé, Alexios Apokaukos. He had amassed a private fortune from the lucrative offices which the late Emperor had given him on

---

[5] *Letters of Athanasios*, ed. Alice-Mary Maffry Talbot, *The Correspondence of Athanasius I Patriarch of Constantinople* (*CFHB*, vii: Washington, D.C., 1975), no. 104, p. 264.

[6] Cantac. i, pp. 432–5, 451; Greg. i, p. 496; ii, pp. 579–84.

Cantacuzene's advice. Not long before the Emperor's death he had promoted Apokaukos to the position of Grand Duke or High Admiral of the fleet to guard the Hellespont against the Turks.[7] The uncertainty over the succession gave Apokaukos new opportunities to feather his own nest. He tried to induce Cantacuzene to press for the title of Emperor, no doubt calculating that he himself would reap still richer rewards. When this dodge failed, he changed tack and took to favouring the Patriarch and the Dowager Empress as regents. He had prepared for any eventuality by building himself a private castle at Epibatai on the Sea of Marmora, to which he could retreat if his plans went awry. The late Emperor had been wise to put little trust in Apokaukos. It was the fault of Cantacuzene not to see through the man.

The crisis was aggravated by a division of opinion over foreign policy. It was often the case when an Emperor died that the Empire's neighbours and enemies saw their chance to take advantage of an interregnum. In the summer of 1341 the Albanians stirred up trouble in Thessaly. Stephen Dušan of Serbia made a tentative incursion into Macedonia. In Bulgaria there had been another palace revolution. Michael Šišman had taken refuge in Constantinople. The new Tsar, John Alexander, demanded his extradition. The senate met to discuss what should be done. Cantacuzene was at the meeting, as were the Patriarch and the Empress Anna. The discussions were long and sometimes angry; nor did they have much to do with the Bulgarian problem. The burning question was the future of their own government. Cantacuzene reports the debate at tedious length. His version is a set-piece of self-justification. He claims that he offered to resign and retire from public life altogether rather than cause offence or discord by pressing his claim to a share in government. When the meeting adjourned he asked the Patriarch to intimate his intention of resigning to the Empress. She is said to have been grief-stricken at the idea. He went to talk to her himself. She was reduced to tears and implored him not to desert her and her children. He relented and gladly resumed his duties as Grand Domestic.[8]

The truth of Cantacuzene's offer of resignation lies, as has

----

[7] Cantac. I, pp. 535–41.   [8] Cantac. II, pp. 20–58.

been noted, hidden in the verbosity of the main actors in the drama, as reported by only one of them.[9] The offer may be as sincere or as false as the pretended resignation of Octavian Caesar in 27 BC. Perhaps the most interesting and revealing scene in the whole drama was the impatient outburst at the meeting of a junior senator, who brazenly demanded the right to speak first. Cantacuzene saw this rudeness as a clear sign of the prevailing disorder and anarchy in society. One of those present summed up the general indignation by posing the unthinkable question: 'What then?', he asked, 'Must we make a democracy of the Empire of the Romans, that anyone can say what he likes and compel his betters to give way?' Whatever form of government was to come out of the constitutional impasse in 1341, it would never be democracy. Cantacuzene took the outburst of the upstart revolutionary as a personal insult. He was deeply offended, partly on his own account, partly on account of the implied slur on the good order of society.[10]

It seemed that he had made his peace with the Empress and with the Patriarch. He had not had to resign; and he had work to do as commander-in-chief of the army. The morale and discipline of the soldiers was low. Their pay was in arrears. Money was short. Once again Cantacuzene found a useful friend. A certain Patrikiotes had made his fortune by his over-zealous activities as a tax-collector. He had thought of atoning for his sins by founding a monastery or giving his money to the poor. Cantacuzene proposed to him that, rather than being brought to court, Patrikiotes might absolve himself by redistributing his money among the army. In this fashion, the soldiers' arrears of pay were made good by the bounty of a remorseful millionaire, whose property in cash, as it turned out, amounted to 100,000 gold coins, with the worth of 40,000 more in moveable estate. The distribution of the cash took sixty days. The soldiers, officers and men, were delighted, expressed their readiness to go to war against Cantacuzene's enemies any-where and prepared their weapons and horses for battle.[11]

[9] Parisot, *Cantacuzène*, p. 167.
[10] Cantac. II, pp. 20–1.
[11] Cantac. II, pp. 58–64; Greg. II, p. 586. M. C. Bartusis, *The Late Byzantine Army. Arms and Society, 1204–1453* (Philadelphia, 1992), pp. 177–8. *PLP*, IX, no. 22077.

In July 1341 Cantacuzene felt confident enough to leave Constantinople at the head of his army to show the flag to the Bulgarians, who were still demanding the extradition of their former ruler. He left his mother Theodora to comfort and look after the Empress Anna, who made a pretty speech to him on his departure. The Patriarch assured him that all was well in the capital. He had suggested that the moment might have come for the young John Palaiologos to be crowned as Emperor. Anna was not in favour; and she was supported by Alexios Apokaukos. It was perhaps a mistake for him to leave Constantinople at such a moment. But his greatest mistake was to go leaving Apokaukos in so influential a position as commander of the fleet. It did not take him long to show the Bulgarians that he meant business, once he had collected the rest of his army at Didymoteichon. John Alexander was chastened into withdrawing his threats and his troops and renewed his treaty. At the same time Cantacuzene thwarted some Turks who were trying to land troops near Gallipoli and persuaded his Turkish friend Umur of Aydin, who had crossed over to Thrace to help him, to sail his ships up to the mouth of the Danube to terrorise the Bulgarians. He completed a good season's work by making a treaty with Stephen Dušan of Serbia.[12]

It was while he was in Didymoteichon in the summer of 1341 that messengers came to him from the Peloponnese bringing a proposition that might have changed the fate of the Byzantine Empire. They came not from the Greek inhabitants but from the French lords of the Morea. They were tired of paying allegiance to so feeble a sovereign as Catherine of Valois. They were ready to unite their principality with Byzantium, on condition that they could retain their lands and castles as fiefs though paying their dues and taxes to the Emperor or to an impartial governor. They had been impressed by the re-establishment of Byzantine rule in the north of Greece and concluded that John Cantacuzene, who had played a notable part in that operation, was effectively Emperor of Constantinople. It was an astonishing offer. The voluntary surrender of the Peloponnese after so many years of Latin rule

---

[12] Cantac. II, pp. 65–70; Greg. II, pp. 596–8. Lemerle, *L'Emirat d'Aydin*, pp. 141–3.

might have rescued the Byzantine Empire. For, as Cantacuzene put it:

If with God's help we were to win over the Latins in the Peloponnese, then the Catalans [in Athens and Thebes] will surely follow their example; and the Empire of the Romans would as before extend in an unbroken line from Greece to Constantinople, and we would easily find the strength to settle our accounts with the Serbians and our other foreign neighbours.

He could see that it was an opportunity not to be missed. He gave the messengers a gracious welcome and hoped that he could take up their offer in the following spring; and he sent back with them a messenger of his own to prepare the way for further consideration of their proposals. The opportunity did not come his way again.[13]

The restoration of the Peloponnese to the Empire was an exciting prospect, but it might involve another military expedition. Before he could properly contemplate it, Cantacuzene must make certain of his constitutional position. Word had reached him from Constantinople that Alexios Apokaukos had been caught planning a coup. As admiral of the fleet he had failed in his duty to prevent shiploads of Turks from crossing the Hellespont. It was now revealed that he had plotted to kidnap the boy John Palaiologos and hold him hostage until the Empress Anna agreed to appoint him master of affairs in Constantinople. She at once informed Cantacuzene of her suspicions. The culprit fled to his fortress at Epibatai. Cantacuzene sent a small force of troops to mount guard over him. These alarming events occurred towards the end of August 1341. In September Cantacuzene returned to the capital with his army. A day or two later, when he was conferring with the Empress in the palace, there was a hubbub in the courtyard outside. A crowd of his supporters, military men and some of the younger noblemen, were found to be haranguing the Patriarch. They were objecting to the fact that their hero had to enter the palace on foot like any commoner when he was of equal rank with the late Emperor. He claims to have found the

---

[13] Cantac. II, pp. 74–7, 80–1; Greg. II, p. 596. D. A. Zakythinos, *Le Despotat grec de Morée*, I (London, 1975), p. 76; Nicol, *Despotate of Epiros*, II, pp. 123–4.

disturbance embarrassing and to have complained to the Empress, who summoned the troublemakers and scolded them for behaving like barbarians.[14]

High on the agenda of his discussions with the Empress was the matter of Alexios Apokaukos, now under guard and deprived of all public office. She could agree with Cantacuzene's opinion that he should be pardoned and given yet another chance; and indeed, in view of the long catalogue of the iniquities and intrigues of the man which Cantacuzene here gives, it seems a curious opinion, dictated by a perverted sense of clemency or simply by poor judgment of character. Cantacuzene was perhaps too keen to put all his affairs in Constantinople in as good order as possible before he went back to Thrace. To this end, two proposals were made. One was that his own daughter Helena should be betrothed to the Empress's son John, the heir-presumptive. The other was that John should now be crowned as Emperor. The Empress was not in favour of either. Cantacuzene bade his farewells to her and to his mother Theodora on 23 September 1341. It was the last time that he saw his mother. It is hard to know why he was in such a hurry to go. It is possible that if he had stayed longer in Constantinople and kept a firmer grip on affairs, he might have saved himself and the Empire from a great deal of trouble and destruction. He was never one to make hard decisions quickly, except on the field of battle. Hesitancy was one of his failings. He left Constantinople for a second time with the problems of the succession and the regency still undecided.

He headed for Didymoteichon where his army was stationed. The fortress of Epibatai, where Apokaukos was under guard, was on his way. There he stopped, and there he made what he thought was his peace. Apokaukos was released and followed him as far as Selymbria, pretending to do him exaggerated honour as if he were Emperor. Either to get rid of him or to reward him for his allegiance, Cantacuzene pardoned him for his crimes and sent him off to Constantinople. Many in his entourage had advised him to arrest Apokaukos while he had the chance and to take him on to prison in Didymoteichon. He should have listened to them. For as soon as he was back

---

[14] Cantac. II, pp. 82–7.

in the capital Apokaukos set his intrigues in motion. The demonstration outside the palace had shown that the city was torn between the partisans of Cantacuzene and what might be termed the 'loyalists' who supported the Empress and her son. Apokaukos quickly made it his business to magnify the differences between them to his own profit. He might have chosen to patronise either faction. He felt that it would be easier to work his will on the Empress and the Patriarch, with whom he had already been in contact. He ate his humble pie before the Empress and begged her pardon for his past misdeeds. He approached Cantacuzene's mother and swore undying loyalty to her son. He then went to work on the Patriarch John Kalekas and whispered to him that it was Cantacuzene's plan to dismiss him and appoint in his place a monk called Gregory Palamas. The Patriarch, who knew Palamas, found this hard to believe. But little by little Apokaukos spun his web. The full story of his guile and cunning derives not only from the memoirs of Cantacuzene but from the less obviously prejudiced account of Gregoras, who goes so far as to say that the Patriarch's whole way of life changed. From being a man of the cloth he became entirely a man of the world. He took up his residence in the palace, spending whole days and nights with Apokaukos and the Empress, plotting the overthrow or the death of John Cantacuzene. In effect he appointed himself in the place of an Emperor with Apokaukos as his military commander and governor of Constantinople. The Empress, who rather admired him, was persuaded to give her approval to all these arrangements. She was taken in by the tales that Apokaukos told her; she began to believe that Cantacuzene, whom she had sometimes mistrusted, was plotting against her and her son John. She was still in many ways a foreigner, a stranger in a strange land; and she must have found it hard to tell truth from fiction in the devious dealings of the Greek-speaking men around her.[15]

The clique that Apokaukos formed around himself included a number of more or less distinguished men, some of whom

---

[15] Cantac. II, pp. 103–36; Greg. II, pp. 602–8. Cantac. II, pp. 88–103, gives a long account of the career and past misdeeds of Apokaukos. His dislike and distrust of the man were fully shared by Gregoras. Greg. II, pp. 584–95.

were easily convinced that they had personal grievances against
Cantacuzene. Among them was his wife's father, Andronikos
Asen. The Patriarch promised rewards in this world or the next
to anyone who could dispose of the wicked pretender to the
throne. The Empress set her imperial seal on letters sent out
from the palace declaring Cantacuzene to be stripped of all
his dignities and offices. He was to be deemed a prisoner in
Didymoteichon. His army must be sent post-haste to
Constantinople. A number of his supporters in the city tried
to reason with Apokaukos and the Patriarch. Apokaukos had
surrounded himself with a bodyguard, a band of desperadoes,
who whipped up the mob to chase the protesters out of town.
Their houses were ransacked. They fled to join Cantacuzene in
Thrace. Several of his relatives in the city were given the same
treatment by the angry crowd which Apokaukos had rented for
the purpose. Among them were Nikephoros, his cousin, and
Eirene, the recently married wife of his eldest son Matthew. His
mother, Theodora, who was looking after his youngest son
Andronikos, was treated with special venom. She was at first
put under house arrest. Later in the year she was imprisoned;
her house was demolished; and her property in Constantinople,
which was quite extensive, was seized. In prison she was
subjected to special forms of persecution by Apokaukos and
his agents. Her guards were barbarous, insulting her and
tampering with what little food she was given in such a manner
that she would not eat it, for she was a fastidious lady and
accustomed to civilised manners. It was a bitter winter but they
allowed her no fire. They plagued her with false reports of the
arrest or the death of her son John. They wore down her powers
of resistance. She succumbed to a fever. She was denied medical
attention. The Empress Anna was horrified when she heard of
Theodora's sufferings and sent her own doctor to the prison. He
was prevented from seeing the patient. They told him that if
he did so he would be accused of what was now coming to
be called 'Cantacuzenism', a punishable form of political
incorrectitude.

On 6 January 1342 Theodora Cantacuzene, persecuted,
starved and forbidden medical care, died in prison. Her only
comfort in her extremity had been the presence and the prayers
of another Theodora, sister of the late Andronikos III, who

had become a nun with the name of Theodosia. It was she who arranged that the corpse be buried in the family vault in the convent of Kyra Martha in Constantinople. The same brave nun rebuked the Empress Anna for her cruel neglect of Cantacuzene's mother. Anna pleaded ignorance and condemned those responsible. What was left of the property of Theodora and her son was shared among those who should have been responsible, notably Apokaukos and the Patriarch. Theodora's grandson Andronikos, who had been in her care, was not allowed his freedom for another five years.[16]

The battle lines were being drawn for a second and even more ruinous civil war. Cantacuzene and his army were in readiness at Didymoteichon. His supporters there had grown in number, swollen by a tide of political refugees from the terror in Constantinople. Neither the Empress nor the Patriarch would allow him to prevent disaster by negotiation. He was not even to be allowed to put his own case by standing trial in Constantinople, as he offered to do. Apokaukos made sure of that. He had been at Didymoteichon for only a few weeks when his army and his supporters proclaimed him as their Emperor. He must have seen that this would happen. But only with reluctance and only on certain conditions did he accept the honour. There was no coronation, merely a proclamation and an investiture. The ceremony, such as it was, is fully described in his memoirs. On 26 October 1341, the Feast of St Demetrios, in the presence of an assembly of his friends, he was robed by his nearest relatives in the vestments of an Emperor; the scarlet boots of an Emperor were put on his feet by an officer of his Latin mercenaries. He then placed on his own head a form of imperial headgear which had been lying before an icon of the Virgin. Cantors chanted the acclamation; and since Cantacuzene had declared that it must be so, they were strict in their protocol. The first to be acclaimed was the Empress Anna; the second was her son John; the third and fourth were John Cantacuzene and his wife Eirene, as Emperor and Empress. They led a procession to the church of St George in Didymoteichon to make obeisance and give thanks. The officers

---

[16] Cantac. II, pp. 163–4, 219–23; Greg. II, pp. 608–9, 617. Nicol, *Byzantine Family*, nos. 21, 26.

of the Latin troops then conferred on John the western order of knighthood, in their customary ceremony. There followed a banquet at which they were waited upon by the new Emperor's cousin John Angelos and the Empress's brothers John and Manuel Asen. The next day they exchanged their finery for white robes, which was the form for Emperors in mourning, signifying their grief for the death of Cantacuzene's 'brother' Andronikos III.[17]

The message was clear. John Cantacuzene was a secondary Emperor committed to acknowledging and protecting the rights of the legitimate heir to the throne, John Palaiologos, and his mother Anna, the son and the widow of his late lamented 'brother' Andronikos III. The pity is that there were not many there to hear his message; and those in Constantinople, when they heard of this curiously cautious ceremony, either took no notice or regarded it as hypocrisy and an open proclamation of war. It would be interesting to know if the news was ever brought to Cantacuzene's mother in her prison and whether it made her proud of her son. The ceremony was attended by various omens and portents; although whether they occurred through God's will or simply by chance is hard to tell since, as Cantacuzene humbly admits, 'The will of God in human affairs is clear only to the pure in heart and to those judged worthy of such perception by God.' One such was the Bishop of Didymoteichon, a man renowned for his prophetic gifts. He took no part in the investiture and he was aggrieved not to have been told until the day after the event. On commending the state and the Emperor to divine protection, however, he observed that 'to be Emperor of the Romans is something ordained by God; but the lips of those that eat unripe figs will surely swell up'. This cryptic remark may have implied that the new Emperor had plucked the fruits of Empire too soon and that he would be afflicted by many dangers and difficulties. Later, however, when he had recovered from his pique, the prophetic bishop was privately informed by the Holy Spirit that it was indeed God's will that John Cantacuzene should be Emperor.[18]

---

[17] Cantac. II, pp. 155–60, 166–73; Greg. II, pp. 610–12; Schreiner, *Chron. brev.*, II, pp. 252–3.
[18] Cantac. II, pp. 169–71.

But the ceremony had been marred by a more obviously ominous event. When John came to put on his imperial robes he found that, although they had been carefully made to measure, the inner garment was too tight and the outer one too loose. This led an eye-witness to predict that his reign as Emperor would be hard and troublesome at first but that later it would become easier and more relaxed. It was a fair prediction. Cantacuzene, who recalled it much later in his life, must have wondered whether and in what sense it had been fulfilled. He devoted many pages of his memoirs to justifying his action in accepting, however grudgingly, the title of Emperor. By insisting that his name should take second place after those of the Empress Anna and her son John Palaiologos, he laboured to demonstrate to the world that he was not a usurper of the throne. It might be thought that he protests too much. It might also be thought that once again he was the victim of his own diffidence and hesitation. If he had seized the occasion with more determination and less soul-searching he might have carried more conviction among those who acclaimed him as their Emperor. Some of them were in fact to desert his cause because of his lack of spirit and decisiveness.[19] From his own account he appears, as often, to be a man who had his decisions forced upon him by circumstances and yet desperately wanted all the world to know that this was so. The part of reluctant Emperor was natural to him. He categorised himself as no more than a fortress tower erected by the previous Emperor to guard the security of that Emperor's widow and her son.[20] Whatever the niceties of his constitutional position and whatever moral justification he might provide for accepting the title of Emperor, those in Constantinople interpreted his action as a declaration of war. It was a war which Apokaukos, if not the Patriarch, had hoped for and precipitated. They thought that it would not last long and Apokaukos at least foresaw a great future for himself when it was won. Victory for them and their cause was to be achieved by the simple process of capturing and silencing John Cantacuzene. The tragedy was that neither the combatants nor their partisans understood what they were setting in motion.

[19] Cantac. ii, pp. 167–8; Greg. ii, p. 615.   [20] Greg. ii, p. 612.

The war between Andronikos II and his grandson had taught
the foreign neighbours and enemies of Byzantium that they
could reap rich profits from intervening on one side or the
other. The Serbians, the Bulgarians and the Turks all saw
the advantages to themselves of participating, it mattered not
on which side. The less predictable consequence of yet another
round of civil war was the violent reaction of those over whose
land and communities it was to be waged. This came as an
unpleasant surprise to leaders of the aristocracy like John
Cantacuzene and his followers. They had assumed that their
wealth and nobility, the fact that they belonged to the 'golden
line' of landed aristocracy, gave them a prescriptive right to
govern. They expected to be obeyed, not challenged.

The first challenge came on the day after John's proclamation. On 27 October 1341 the governors of the city of
Adrianople, where John was well known, assembled the people
and read out to them an announcement of what had been
enacted at nearby Didymoteichon. The news was enthusiastically welcomed by the magnates (*dynatoi*) but the people
(*demos*) had mixed feelings, and some denounced Cantacuzene
and all that he represented. That night a few of the under-
privileged ran through the town inciting the people to rebel
against their oppressors. Rioting broke out. The houses of the
rich who had declared for Cantacuzene were plundered. Their
terrified owners fled into hiding. The people set up a revolutionary regime to protect themselves against the forces of
what they called 'Cantacuzenism'. Such behaviour on the part
of the lower orders (*demos*), was unheard of in Byzantine society.
The ruling class feared that democracy was breaking out.

'Cantacuzenism' was a term of abuse which had already
been invented by Apokaukos and his publicity agents in
Constantinople. He was quick to see its usefulness as a
propaganda slogan. He was himself a social upstart with
an inbred jealousy of the ruling class. He could turn this
unprecedented wave of social unrest to his own advantage. The
rebels could be won over to the cause of the regency in
Constantinople and the family of Palaiologos. The Empress
and the Patriarch would bless their cause. It seemed that
Cantacuzene and his aristocratic friends had unleashed social
forces which they could neither comprehend nor control. The

spirit of rebellion spread throughout Thrace and Macedonia. It took different forms in different places, but in general the *dynatoi* and propertied classes declared for Cantacuzene while the rest opted to legitimise their actions by claiming to support John Palaiologos and the regency in Constantinople. Cantacuzene recalls how the revolutionary fervour spread

like a malignant and horrible disease, producing the same forms of excess even in those who before had been moderate and sensible men . . . All the cities joined in this rebellion against the aristocracy, and those that were late in doing so made up for their lost time by exceeding the example set them by others. They perpetrated all manner of inhumanity and even massacres. Senseless impulse was glorified with the name of valour and lack of fellow feeling or human sympathy was called loyalty to the Emperor.[21]

Gregoras, in more general terms, laments how 'the whole Roman Empire was divided into two, the wise and the foolish, the distinguished and the mean, the educated and the boorish; the best people turned to Cantacuzene, the worst to those in Constantinople'. Both men were appalled at what was happening. Neither had seen it coming; neither could understand why 'The best lacked all conviction and the worst were full of passionate intensity.'[22]

The first civil war and its consequences had displayed the glaring contrast between the riches of the few and the poverty of the many. Another civil war seemed unlikely to right the balance. The people had been taken in before by promises of the remission of taxes. They did not want their land to become a battle ground yet again in a squabble between the families of the ruling class. The wealth of the Cantacuzene family was enough to condemn it in the eyes of the less privileged. The amount of gold and silver plate, jewellery, hoards of grain and provisions discovered in the house of John Cantacuzene's mother in Constantinople when she was arrested seemed to show how little the aristocracy cared for the welfare of the people. Apokaukos made the most of such discoveries for his own propaganda purposes. The extent of the Cantacuzene

---

[21] Cantac. II, pp. 175–9; Greg. II, pp. 620–2. Weiss, *Johannes Kantakuzenos*, pp. 70–85.
[22] Greg. II, p. 613. The quotation is adapted from W. B. Yeats, 'The Second Coming'.

family property in the provinces was another revelation.
Cantacuzene himself admits that when his estates in Macedonia
were expropriated in the civil war he lost 5,000 head of cattle,
1,000 draft animals, 2,500 mares, 200 camels, 300 mules, 500
asses, 50,000 pigs and 70,000 sheep. Peasants whose little
livelihood was measured and taxed in terms of the acreage of
land that could be tilled by a pair of oxen, and whose freedom
of action and movement was determined by their status as
tenant farmers on estates of such huge dimensions, were bound
to be sceptical about the motives of landowners like the
Cantacuzene family. It was difficult for the people to stage a
protest in the rural areas. But in the towns and cities where the
word of the aristocracy was also law revolt could be organised
and agitation fostered.[23]

There seems to have been no formal declaration of war. Even
after his investiture as Emperor, Cantacuzene continued to
hope that the quarrel could be settled by negotiation. All his
overtures were rejected. His envoys to Constantinople were put
in prison. The Patriarch excommunicated him and all who were
on his side. His claim to any form of imperial title was thus
denied; and the message was made still clearer when, on
19 November 1341, the boy John Palaiologos, whose inheritance
he had sworn to protect, was crowned as Emperor of the
Romans in Constantinople. The Patriarch officiated at
the coronation ceremony. John Palaiologos, hereafter known in
history as John V, was not yet ten years old; and it was observed
that 19 November was a *dies non* in the Orthodox calendar. The
Patriarch could wait no longer; and by all accounts the gravity
of the occasion and of his own part in it went to his head. He
took to robing himself in gorgeous vestments and to wearing a
mitre veiled not in the white linen customary for Patriarchs but
in cloth of gold adorned with icons of Christ, the Virgin and
St John the Baptist. Some said that he also took to signing his
documents in the red ink reserved for an Emperor.[24]

The coronation was followed, as was the tradition, by the
publication of an honours list, which must have been compiled
by the Empress mother and the Patriarch. Alexios Apokaukos

[23] Cantac. II, pp. 164–5, 184–5. Nicol, *Last Centuries of Byzantium*, p. 192.
[24] Cantac. II, p. 218; Greg. II, pp. 616, 697–9; Schreiner, *Chron. brev.*, II, pp. 253–4.

was the chief beneficiary, being reinstated in his office as Grand Duke; but several of his cronies and several known and prominent anti-Catacuzenists were promoted.[25]

The winter of 1341–2 was cold and wet. Cantacuzene was snowed up in Didymoteichon and not certain of his next step. He continued to send messages to the Empress and the Patriarch suggesting ways of making peace. The Patriarch ignored them. The Empress was distressed. It is said that she discussed her position with her companions in the ladies' quarter of the palace; she wondered whether she was right to believe all the stories she was told about the man who had been her husband's most loyal servant. She asked them if a solution could still be found through the betrothal of his daughter Helena to her son John. Some of her maidservants leaked this report to Apokaukos. He was quick to veto the idea. The Patriarch agreed with him.[26] Cantacuzene then approached the monks of Mount Athos, some of whom he knew quite well. He convinced them that it was their Christian duty to do what they could to prevent further shedding of blood. A delegation went from the Holy Mountain to Constantinople to talk to the Empress and the Patriarch. Among them were the Protos or superior of the whole community of monks, Isaac; the abbot of the monastery of the Great Lavra, Makarios; the future Patriarch of Constantinople, Kallistos; and the renowned ascetic and hermit of Vatopedi, Sabas. They soon found that their audience was not very receptive and asked leave to go back to their monasteries. The Patriarch Kalekas, however was worried that they would spread the word among their fellow monks that Cantacuzene was alone in wishing for peace. He split their ranks. The monk Makarios he appointed as Bishop of Thessalonica; the Protos Isaac he confined to a monastery near at hand; the hermit Sabas, who was known to be a close friend of Cantacuzene, was committed to another monastery in Constantinople. Only the less important of them were permitted to return to Athos.[27]

---

[25] Cantac. II, pp. 218–19.

[26] Cantac. II, pp. 199–208.

[27] Cantac. II, pp. 208–13; Greg. II, p. 620. Philotheos, *Life of Sabas*, ed. D. G. Tsamis, Φιλοθέου . . . Κοκκίνου ἁγιολογικὰ ἔργα, I (Thessaloniki, 1985), pp. 290–3.

Some of Cantacuzene's natural allies and friends in the provinces of Macedonia and Thessaly, where he was well known, were driven to take the side of his political opponents simply through fear of the reprisals that might be taken against their relatives and property in Constantinople. The one who declared himself a Cantacuzenist was his old friend Theodore Synadenos, then governor of Thessalonica, though he kept his allegiance a secret. He offered to open the gates of his city if Cantacuzene would come with an army to claim it. It was a chance not to be missed. On 5 March 1342, when the worst of the winter was over, Cantacuzene set out with his army along the road to Thessalonica. He left his brave wife Eirene in charge of the garrison at Didymoteichon, assisted by her brother Manuel Asen. Nearly two years of anxiety and misery were to pass before she saw her husband again. Her sons Matthew and Manuel went with their father. She was left with the comfort and the care of her daughters, Maria, Theodora and Helena. Good fortune was not with him. He undertook various forays along his way, but his rivals in Constantinople had forestalled him by sending troops of their own into Thrace; and Apokaukos cleverly ordered a fleet of seventy ships to get to Thessalonica before him. He was too late. The spirit of revolution which had affected Adrianople and other places had reached Thessalonica as well. The governor of the city, Cantacuzene's old comrade in arms Theodore Synadenos, had been expelled. Those of the aristocracy, who would have welcomed Cantacuzene's arrival, had been driven into hiding or escaped from the rebels who had seized power.

The revolt in Adrianople had been instigated by the mob of under-privileged workers and farmers. In Thessalonica it was organised and managed by a kind of political party. They were known as the Zealots and they established their dominance by an orgy of destruction, murder and mayhem. The regime which they set up had no real precedent in any other city in the history of the Byzantine Empire. For this, if for no other reason, contemporary historians could not understand how or why the Zealot revolution had come about. Cantacuzene in his memoirs gives a highly coloured account of the horrors and of the destruction caused. He observes that its perpetrators in their violence characterised any form of moderation and tolerance as

'Cantacuzenism'.[28] In this he was right. For the fires of the revolution in Thessalonica were fed by those who were violently opposed to John Cantacuzene, the *dynatoi* and the aristocracy and everything that he and they stood for. Apokaukos and the regency in Constantinople were quick to see that this was so and to capitalise on the fact. Cantacuzene was denied access to Thessalonica and had to retreat. His friend Synadenos just managed to escape. But he concluded that, for the safety of his own family in Constantinople, he must now desert his old comrade and join the enemy. Apokaukos reached Thessalonica with his fleet and army flying the banner of anti-Cantacuzenism. The rebels welcomed him. The fiction was thus established that the city of Thessalonica was loyal to the house of Palaiologos and the regency in Constantinople. For more than seven years it was to be maintained as a more or less independent commune by the leaders of the Zealot party.[29]

Cantacuzene was disappointed but never in despair. He remained imperturbably convinced of the justice of his own cause. He would go on fighting until the rest of the world was persuaded that justice had always been on his side. His war against the regency in Constantinople was in reality a small, if bloody, destructive and drawn-out affair. The battlefield was, as before, Thrace and Macedonia, and the battles fought were usually minor skirmishes involving hundreds rather than thousands of combatants. The troops were for the most part hastily levied on the spot or foreign mercenaries, 'Latins', Germans, and not least Turks, hired for a season and not native to the soil, though their commanders might be of professional Byzantine stock. Yet the hundreds of pages of his memoirs that Cantacuzene devoted to an almost day-by-day record of the fighting would have us believe that the petty skirmishes were epic battles fought on a scale comparable to the campaigns of Caesar in his Gallic Wars, or of Belisarius as narrated by Procopius. Unfortunately, though written in good literary Greek, his accounts lack the eloquence of the first and the interest of the second. They make tiresome reading and may,

---

[28] Cantac. II, pp. 233–5; Greg. II, pp. 634–5.
[29] On the Zealot revolution in Thessalonica, see Nicol, *Last Centuries of Byzantium*, pp. 184–5 and references.

since this is a biography of a man and not a eulogy of a hero, be abbreviated and condensed into manageable terms.

Denied access to Thessalonica and cut off from his base at Didymoteichon, he toyed with the idea of making contact with his friends in Thessaly and Epiros. The idea found little favour with his followers; and not a few absconded, feeling that his cause was now hopeless. To those who stayed, about two thousand in number, he announced his intention of taking refuge in Serbia where he could plot and plan his next move. He set much store by the friendship that he had earlier formed and cultivated with the Kral of Serbia, Stephen Dušan. He sent messengers ahead to prepare the ground and in June 1342 he began to march north over the Vardar river and made for Skopje. A Serbian noble whom he had met earlier offered to use his influence with Dušan; and due to his good offices a meeting was arranged. Dušan and his wife Helena came south to meet Cantacuzene. They entertained him in royal style for several days, and the two men signed a pact of alliance in July. Dušan had suggested as his price the cession to Serbia of a large part of Byzantine Macedonia. It was more than Cantacuzene was ready to pay and most of it was not at the time in his gift. What mattered was that Dušan now promised to assist him in every way in the fight against their common enemies in Constantinople. By the end of the summer, with a contingent of Serbian troops, he was ready to make the long march back to his headquarters at Didymoteichon where his wife Eirene with her brother Manuel Asen had been holding the fort.[30]

He got no further east than the city of Serres in eastern Macedonia. It was a vital strategic and commercial centre on the east bank of the fertile valley of the Strymon (Struma) river. Cantacuzene had hoped that its people would surrender to him, but in vain. His camp outside the walls was affected by an epidemic; and news came that Apokaukos had sent an army to block his way through to Thrace. He was thwarted at every turn. His only hope seemed to be to make his way back to Serbia. Most of his army mutinied. They said that they would rather go

---

[30] Cantac. II, pp. 237–76; Greg. II, pp. 634–40. G. C. Soulis, *The Serbs and Byzantium during the Reign of Tsar Stephen Dušan (1331–1355) and his Successors* (Washington, D.C., 1984), pp. 14–19.

to Hell than back to Serbia. They deserted to the enemy. The Serbian mercenaries who had joined him had already gone home. His numbers were reduced to not more than five hundred men. He led them in a dejected retreat back to the comfort of his friend in Serbia. There he stayed for about a month. Those in Constantinople thought that they had cornered him. Twice the Empress Anna tried to bribe Dušan into handing him over as a prisoner. But, for the moment. Dušan remained loyal to his friend.[31] It was while he was there that a deputation reached him from Thessaly inviting him to take over the province. He had for long been known to the landed gentry of Thessaly. Their submission to him was a hopeful sign indicating a turn in his fortunes. He at once accepted their offer; and since they had said that they would accept any deputy whom he might choose as their governor, he appointed his faithful cousin John Angelos. It is a measure of his self-confidence as Emperor that the appointment was enshrined in a golden bull (*chrysoboullos logos*) signed and sealed by the hand of the Emperor John Cantacuzene. It was the first such solemn document that he issued; though, ever mindful of propriety and protocol, he insisted on adding to it the names of the Empress Anna and of her son John. John Angelos was popular and successful in his term of office as governor of Thessaly. He managed to extend his authority over Epiros as well, so that his cousin the Emperor could boast that he had all of northern Greece behind him, except for Thessalonica, where the Zealots remained in power.[32]

Towards the end of 1342, encouraged by this turn of events, Cantacuzene set out from Serbia for a second time to try to reach Didymoteichon. His Serbian host went with him as far as the city of Serres, which he was still hopeful of winning over to his side. Its people, however, rejected him and he continued his march alone. Once again the Serbian troops provided for him by Dušan began to lose heart and desert. They did not know where they were and feared that they were being led not towards Thrace but to Parthia or India so that they would never see

[31] Cantac. II, pp. 292–8, 306–9.
[32] Cantac. II, pp. 309–22. H. Hunger, 'Urkunden und Memoirentext: der Chrysoboullos Logos des Johannes Kantakuzenos für Johannes Angelos', *JÖB*, 26 (1978), 107–25.

home again. Cantacuzene decided to go back to Serbia to ask his friend to supply him with a more substantial and trustworthy army. His decision provoked another threat of mutiny from his own soldiers. They had had enough of what they called the Hell of Serbia. They were constrained to change their minds and follow their leader only by the news that their route to Thrace was again blocked by an army from Constantinople and that Apokaukos was lying in wait for them with a fleet offshore. Cantacuzene and his remaining followers were soon back in the asylum if not the Hell of Serbia.[33]

His prospects seemed dismal. Gossip in Constantinople had it that he had despaired of success and had left the world to become a monk on Mount Athos.[34] He was often tempted by the appeal of the monastic life. But he still had his wife and family; and their situation was no less dismal than his own. His wife Eirene was still manfully guarding his headquarters at Didymoteichon with its garrison commanded by her brother. They were isolated and surrounded by troops from Constantinople. After so many months and so many rumours that he was on his way back, she began to lose hope that she would ever see her husband again. Towards the end of 1342 she appealed for help to her nearest foreign neighbour, John Alexander of Bulgaria. He was happy to help her but happier to help himself. A Bulgarian army arrived on the scene at Didymoteichon. Its presence merely added to the sufferings of the city by blockading it and preventing its inhabitants from getting out to find food. Their prophetic bishop urged them to hold on for he knew it to be God's will that the Bulgars would fall foul of each other and withdraw within seven days.[35] His prophecy was proved right, whether or not by the will of God. For, in his own dilemma, Cantacuzene had called on the help of his Turkish friend, Umur, Emir of Aydin. Umur was distressed to hear of the plight of his 'brother' and hurried to the rescue, sailing over from Asia Minor with a force of 380 ships and 29,000 men. He landed them at the mouth of the Marica river and marched his men up to Didymoteichon. The number of his troops must surely be exaggerated; but they were enough to

---

[33] Cantac. II, pp. 323–35.
[34] Cantac. II, p. 336.   [35] Cantac. II, pp. 336–44.

frighten the Bulgars away.[36] Eirene may have been surprised to see Umur and his hosts and, after about three months, while they devastated the coastline, she devoutly hoped that they would go. Umur finally took about 20,000 off in search of his friend Cantacuzene. He never found him. He was defeated, not by any enemy but by the weather. Another exceptionally bitter winter had closed the roads and passes to Serbia. Hundreds of the Turks died of exposure or starvation. Umur retreated, embarked the survivors and sailed over the Hellespont back to the warmth of his own country.[37]

As soon as the weather improved early in 1343 Cantacuzene set out again for Thrace. He must have been sad not to see his friend Umur; but the fact that so distant an ally had come to his aid was a form of diplomatic success for him; and word must soon have got around of the havoc created by the Turkish soldiers in Thrace. In the spring some of the towns in the south and west of Macedonia followed the lead of their neighbours in Thessaly and declared Cantacuzene as their Emperor. The first was the city of Berroia which stands some 50 kilometres west of Thessalonica. Stephen Dušan lent him a company of German mercenaries to secure its possession; and he entrusted the garrison of Berroia to his second son Manuel, who was only about seventeen.[38] Other places to the south of Thessalonica sensed a wind of change and accepted John Cantacuzene as their Emperor. He was encouraged to try again to win over Thessalonica itself. He summoned his cousin John Angelos to bring cavalry up from Thessaly to mount an attack on the city. Stephen Dušan became alarmed that his protégé was becoming too successful. He recalled the troops that he had lent him; and Apokaukos, who had always hoped that Dušan would sooner or later betray his supposed friend, brought a fleet to the defence of Thessalonica. John was blockaded and almost stranded in Macedonia. Apokaukos called on him to surrender and tried to

---

[36] The numbers are those given by Cantac. II, p. 344. Greg. gives no figures. Enveri writes of 300 ships and 15,000 men. The much later historian Doukas says that Umur led 'up to 500 Turkish horsemen and as many footsoldiers'. Enveri, *Destān*, lines 1327–1400; Doukas (Ducas), *Istoria Turco-Bizantină (1341–1462)*, ed. V. Grecu (Bucharest, 1958), p. 53.

[37] Cantac. II, pp. 344–8; Greg. II, pp. 648–52.

[38] Cantac. II, pp. 349–54; Greg. II, p. 654–6, 673.

have him assassinated in his camp. Once again his special relationship with Umur of Aydin proved its worth. Umur came to his rescue and arrived off Thessalonica with sixty ships and 6,000 men. Apokaukos and his navy melted away at the sight of this Turkish armada. But Thessalonica was not going to surrender. The fierce resolution of its Zealot leaders gave the Cantacuzenists in their city no chance to welcome their hero. Many were arrested or murdered; and the strong walls of the city could not be breached. The attempt had to be abandoned.[39]

Umur's intervention, however, and the strength of his army made it at last possible for John to break through the enemy's lines and get back to his base at Didymoteichon. His Empress Eirene, who had been marooned there for so many months, was no doubt glad to see him, as were the citizens who rejoiced 'as if their Emperor had come back to life after a long sojourn in Hades'.[40] The war was now to be fought on different terms. It was no longer a cat-and-mouse affair between the regency in Constantinople and the usurper Emperor on the run in Macedonia. John had lost the dubious alliance of his Serbian friend and protector, who now saw more profit to be gained from flattering the Empress in Constantinople. But he found that he had more powerful friends among the Turks. For at Didymoteichon he was within striking distance of Constantinople and more closely in contact with Asia Minor and his Turkish friends Umur of Aydin and Orhan, the Emir of Bithynia. The last two years of the civil war were fought in the relatively confined area of Thrace, between Didymoteichon where John had been hailed as Emperor, and Constantinople where the Empress Anna and the Patriarch, with the effective regent Apokaukos, stubbornly held on to power. Life there was not easy. Food was scarce. The Genoese, whose cargo ships kept the city supplied with wheat from the Black Sea, were engaged in fighting the Mongols of the Golden Horde over possession of the markets in the Crimea. Money was short. In August 1343 the Empress in desperation pawned the crown jewels of the Empire to the Republic of Venice. They realised a welcome sum of money, but they were never redeemed and the money did not last long.[41]

[39] Nicol, *Byzantine Family*, pp. 54–5.   [40] Cantac. II, pp. 403–4.
[41] Greg. II, pp. 683–7. Nicol, *Byzantium and Venice*, pp. 259–62.

The fighting in Thrace went on and sometimes came close to the suburbs of Constantinople. Towns and villages changed hands more than once. Farmers and citizens alike wished that it would stop. Their fields and their livelihood were ruined by the passage of armies, Greek, Serbian, Bulgarian or Turkish, living off the land; all of them had been called in by one side or the other to perpetuate a largely unnecessary conflict. For John was not the only culprit in the matter of inviting the Turks to help fight his battles, though it was becoming more difficult to get them to go home when they had fulfilled their purpose and collected their loot. There were also some independent adventurers who, in the circumstances of lawlessness, found ways of setting themselves up as condottieri. One such was Hajduk Momčilo, a Bulgarian bandit with a private army of peasants, who had deserted the service of Stephen Dušan and in 1343 joined Cantacuzene in Thrace. He changed sides in 1344 and again in 1345 and was in the end killed by Cantacuzene in one of the Thracian cities which he had taken over. Another adventurer or border-lord in the Balkan tangle was Chrelja (Chreles), who had fought for the Serbs; he too changed sides when it suited him and for a while joined Cantacuzene's cause with his private army. He died in December 1342 at the Rila monastery in southern Bulgaria, where his tomb can be seen. Such men were the products of their age, paid and flattered by both sides in the Byzantine struggle but not loyal to either unless they found it convenient.[42]

As the tide began to turn in Cantacuzene's favour, in 1343–4, Apokaukos became more desperate. When he was sure that Umur and his army of Turks had gone he launched a vain attack on Didymoteichon. He and the Patriarch then sent envoys with letters to Cantacuzene to bully him into revoking his claim to the title of Emperor. The nonsense contained in these missives amused and appalled him; and he summoned an assembly to refute all the charges contained in them. It lasted for six days. He accused Apokaukos of all manner of deceit and fraud. He

[42] On Momčilo and Chrelja: M. C. Bartusis, 'Chrelja and Momčilo: occasional servants of Byzantium in fourteenth century Macedonia', *BS*, 41 (1980), 201–21; *PLP*, VIII, no. 19255. Another Bulgarian adventurer whom Cantacuzene had to suppress in 1348 was Dobrotic, who had set himself up at Medeia on the Black Sea coast with the help of the Empress Anna. Nicol, *Byzantine Family*, pp. 68–9.

was particularly hurt by the Patriarch's accusation of perjury. He rehearsed once more the facts of what had happened in 1341, and how he had been the protector of the Empress and her son until forced to flee from Constantinople. He blamed Apokaukos and the Patriarch for having been the first to bring Turkish troops on to the scene and so ravaged Macedonia and made Thrace almost uninhabitable. It was they who had taught him to do the same. They were like men shooting arrows into the sky who, on being wounded when the arrows fell, blamed not themselves but the sky. He lectured the Patriarch on the subject of excommunication, citing numerous texts from the Fathers of the church to prove that the anathema could be laid on a man only for certain specific aberrations in his faith; and this was a charge that could never be laid against him. The Patriarch had, it seems, now relented and changed his mind on this matter. But Cantacuzene, as a deeply religious man, could clearly not have much confidence in a priest who did not know the canons of his church or interpreted them to suit his own politics. When the envoys from Constantinople were allowed to get a word in, they protested that it was the Empress Anna who was in sole charge of affairs and that she was not beholden to others. This was so manifestly untrue that Cantacuzene gave their leader a private message to be delivered to the Empress personally. If she acted upon it he would believe what they said. If she had to refer it to others then he would know that he was right. Cantacuzene was evidently in full voice at Didymoteichon. But his eloquence had little effect. The war went on.[43]

More and more places in Thrace, however, were going over to his side, some perhaps merely through despair. At the end of 1344 one John Vatatzes, a commander of one of the garrisons in Thrace, abandoned the cause of the regency. He was related to the Patriarch as well as to Apokaukos. He was a big catch and he was accordingly welcomed into the Cantacuzenist camp.[44] Before long Cantacuzene was in control of most of southern Thrace. In the towns which he captured he was careful to give no offence to those who had been appointed to their offices by the regency. He offered them safe passage to Constantinople to

[43] Cantac. II, pp. 434–6, 442–73.   [44] Cantac. II, pp. 475–6.

plead for peace. An even greater catch than John Vatatzes was Manuel, the son of Apokaukos, whom his father had installed as governor of Adrianople. The zeal of the revolutionaries who had seized power there in 1341 was fading but they were still strong enough to resist Cantacuzene's first attempt to dislodge them and Adrianople still claimed to be fiercely loyal to the Empress Anna and her son. Manuel Apokaukos, however, secretly went over to the Cantacuzenist camp claiming that he could no longer stomach his father's behaviour. Another eminent defector from Constantinople was the Patriarch of Jerusalem, Lazaros, who had fallen foul of his colleague John Kalekas.[45]

By the beginning of 1345 the gates of retribution were closing on Alexios Apokaukos and his clique in Constantinople. Another contingent of Turkish mercenaries arrived in Thrace to lend substance to Cantacuzene's success. They were sent by his friend Orhan of Bithynia. The Empress Anna had also appealed to Orhan for help but he naturally preferred to go to the aid of his older friend. Cantacuzene was consequently able to win over most of the Thracian towns as far as the Black Sea coast. Constantinople was very nearly blockaded; and it was possible for Cantacuzene to pitch camp within sight of its walls. He was encamped near the gate called Gyrolimni when a curious incident occurred. Two Franciscan friars from the Genoese colony in Galata came to see him on a fact-finding mission. One was the Provincial of his Order and came from Savoy, the home of the Empress Anna. They were educated and intelligent men and had even read some Aristotle, albeit in Latin translation, for they knew little Greek. The Genoese in Galata were not at all clear about the causes of the Byzantine civil war which seemed to be so interminable. All that they knew derived from sources in Constantinople. It was the first time that they had had a chance to hear the other side of the story. Cantacuzene was only too glad to enlighten them and did so with his customary prolixity. Their interview lasted for two days. John took pains to explain his position to them, emphasising that he had not been the first to employ the Turks on his side, for this was a point that worried the Christians of the west. He lamented the fact that his mother had been

[45] Cantac. II, pp. 485, 491. On Lazaros of Jerusalem: *PLP*, VI, no. 14350.

imprisoned and as good as murdered by his political enemies
and that his youngest son, though not then twelve years old, was
still in prison. He invited the Franciscans to act as mediators
with the Patriarch in Constantinople. He offered to go there
himself, as a private citizen and not as Emperor, to stand fair
trial by church, state and people. He even offered to abdicate
and retire to Mount Athos if it would bring peace, on condition
that all his relatives and supporters in Constantinople were set
free. The friars accepted that John was more sinned against
than sinning. They took away with them a written account of
their interview signed and sealed with his gold seal as Emperor.
Before leaving, they suggested that their task as mediators for
peace would be made easier if he withdrew his army from the
city; and to show his good intent he led his soldiers away.

The reply from Apokaukos and the Patriarch which they
finally brought to John at Didymoteichon contained no more
than a willing acceptance of John's offer to abdicate. They
would make no promises about their political prisoners. The
Franciscans, who could not read the Greek text, thought that
this offer was tantamount to peace. As John told them, they
had been deceived by the Patriarch's seal on the document,
naturally supposing that this was as trustworthy as a papal bull.
There could be no peace on these terms; and since Apokaukos
had taken unfair advantage of his withdrawal from the city,
John let his Turkish mercenaries loose on the countryside until,
as he admits, they left it almost a desert. The Franciscans came
once more to see him, but only to report that the Empress Anna
personally longed for peace but was afraid to negotiate because
she believed that she and her children would be in danger of
being murdered. He left for Adrianople, which now at last
surrendered to him.[46]

In the spring of 1345 his other Turkish ally and blood-brother
Umur of Aydin came over to join him. He was accompanied by
Suleiman, the son of Saruhan, Emir of Lydia. Together they
brought an army allegedly of 20,000 horsemen. They arrived at

---

[46] Cantac. II, pp. 498–9, 501–29. The provincial of the Franciscans, whom he calls
'Aregos' was probably Henricus, to be distinguished from Henry d'Asti, the titular
Latin Patriarch of Constantinople (1339–45). See J. Gay, *Le Pape Clément VI et les
affaires d'Orient (1342–1352)* (Paris, 1904), p. 98; K. P. Kyrris, 'John Cantacuzenus and
the Genoese 1321–1348', *Miscellanea Storica Ligure*, III (Milan, 1963), 31–2.

Didymoteichon and for a while their men enjoyed themselves raiding and plundering Bulgarian territory, until John was ready to use them for other purposes. Their first task was to clip the wings of the Slav adventurer Momčilo. He was killed in battle on 7 June 1345. Reports were then reaching John's camp that Stephen Dušan, his former protector in Serbia, was attacking the city of Serres, a stronghold which John himself had twice failed to capture. He must not let it fall into Serbian hands. As soon as he had disposed of Momčilo he set off with his allies for eastern Macedonia. They were closing in on Serres when unexpected news came from Constantinople. Alexios Apokaukos had been assassinated. John was all for pressing on to Serres. His officers, however, as well as Umur, urged him to seize the opportunity to march on Constantinople. Serres could wait. Constantinople beckoned.

Apokaukos had brought his murder on himself. As he saw his power slipping away and his ambitions being thwarted he had become ever more tyrannical. He had arrested so many political prisoners that he had to order a new dungeon to be built to hold them. When the work was nearing completion, he went to visit it. For some reason he was without his usual bodyguard. One of the prisoners snatched up a block of wood and struck him down. Others seized tools and materials that the builders had left and joined in the murder. They hacked off his head and hung it on a pole from the walls. The prison guards fled in terror when they saw what had happened. But the prisoners made no attempt to escape. They expected to be hailed as heroes who had delivered the city from a tyrant. They had miscalculated. The Empress Anna was shocked and not pleased to be so brutally deprived of her first minister and commander. She allowed the servants and followers of Apokaukos to wreak their own vengeance on the murderers of their master. About two hundred of the prisoners, many of them innocent of the crime, were slaughtered. Alexios Apokaukos was dead, but he brought many of his victims to ruin with him.[47]

The date of his assassination was 11 June 1345. It was not the

[47] Cantac. II, pp. 529–45; Greg. II, pp. 729–41; Doukas, *Istoria*, ed. Grecu, pp. 43–5; Schreiner, *Chron. brev.*, II, pp. 259–64.

end of violence and bloodshed; but it marked the beginning of
the end of the civil war. Many may also have hoped that it would
mark the end of the regency in Constantinople and the unholy
alliance that had kept it alive for four years. They were to be
disappointed. Cantacuzene had been right to be cautious about
the outcome and to be less impetuous about marching on
Constantinople. For by the time that he and his allies got near
the city he learnt that order had been restored. The Patriarch
and the Empress seemed to have everything under control. He
was cross and frustrated. He bullied his Turkish friends into a
forced march back towards Serres. On their way, however, the
young Suleiman fell ill and died. His own men accused Umur
of murdering him. Umur at once left for Smyrna, taking
his army with him. John, deserted by his allies, returned to
Didymoteichon to ponder his next move. A ray of hope seemed
to lighten his gloom, though not for long. It came from
Thessalonica. The death of Alexios Apokaukos had provoked
his son John, whom he had appointed as governor of that city, to
try to subvert the Zealots who still controlled it. His aim was
to hand over Thessalonica to Cantacuzene: and he called on his
son Manuel, then in Berroia, to come and help. The plan failed,
however, and John Apokaukos, like his father, was assassinated,
along with the other Cantacuzenists in the city. Thessalonica
was now more firmly than ever in the grip of the Zealots. A
second blow to John's hopes followed. John Vatatzes, whose
defection he had welcomed, was lured back to the side of the
Empress Anna. Some of the towns of Thrace, where he was well
known, followed his lead and changed sides. Vatatzes, however,
became the victim of his own duplicity; for some Turks whom he
had invited to serve him turned against him when called upon
to attack the territory of Cantacuzene. Vatatzes was killed.
Taking the army that he had mustered to fight the renegade,
John then marched to the walls of Constantinople. He had
hoped to make a surprise attack and he had made contact with
some of his friends inside the city. But he had misjudged the
time. He withdrew to Selymbria and, after a fruitless foray up
to the Black Sea coast, he retreated to Adrianople.

His plans and ambitions were dealt another blow in September
1345, when Stephen Dušan at last succeeded in capturing the
Macedonian city of Serres. It was, as John well knew, a key point

for the conquest of Thessalonica. Flushed with his success, Dušan now took to calling himself Emperor of the Serbs and Romans, thus declaring his intention of taking over not only Thessalonica but also Constantinople as master of the whole Byzantine Empire. On Easter Sunday in 1346 he had himself crowned as Emperor at Skopje. His coronation was a direct challenge to the claims of the regency in Constantinople and of the young Emperor John Palaiologos, but also to the titular Emperor John Cantacuzene whom he had patronised.[48]

There were now three claimants to the title of Emperor of the Romans in a world where God had ordained that one was enough. Only one of the three, however, had been properly crowned as such by the Patriarch of Constantinople in the cathedral of St Sophia, and he was John Palaiologos, son of the Empress Anna; though it was unfortunate that the real crown that had been set on his head was still, thanks to his mother's improvidence, in pawn in the treasury of Venice. The coronation of Stephen Dušan, with whatever manner of crown, had taken place on 16 April 1346. The news travelled fast and spurred Cantacuzene to action. A few weeks later on 21 May, he too was crowned, fulfilling the promise of his proclamation and investiture at Didymoteichon five years before. Nowhere does he suggest that he was influenced or prompted by the fact of Dušan's coronation, which he duly records in his memoirs. But the inference seems obvious. The day that he appointed was the feast of Saints Constantine and Helena, an auspicious choice. Crowns for himself and his wife Eirene were fashioned by local goldsmiths. The ceremony was performed by Lazaros, the Patriarch of Jerusalem, who had left Constantinople some months earlier. It took place at Adrianople. All the traditional ritual of a Byzantine coronation service was observed as far as was possible in the circumstances. After the Patriarch had crowned him, John placed the crown of Empress on Eirene's head, for it was the custom for an Emperor to perform the coronation of his Empress. Gold and silver coins were scattered among the people; and there followed several days of feasting. Some of John's officers had begged him to proclaim his eldest

[48] Cantac. ii, pp. 546–64, 568–82; Greg. ii, pp. 741–3, 746–7. O. Tafrali, *Thessalonique au quatorzième siècle* (Paris, 1913), pp. 239–49; Soulis, *The Serbs and Byzantium*, pp. 27–33.

son Matthew as his co-Emperor to ensure the succession in the Cantacuzene family. He thanked them for their loyalty but refused to consider their proposal. For, as long as the young John Palaiologos was alive, the question of the succession was not in doubt. Whenever he completed his victory by becoming Emperor in Constantinople it was his intention to uphold John in his imperial status and to give him the hand of his daughter Helena in marriage. There could be no question of nominating another heir-apparent, no suggestion that the dynasty of Palaiologos was being displaced by the family of Cantacuzene.[49]

Having done his duty at the coronation, the Patriarch of Jerusalem presided over a synod of the bishops then present at Adrianople. They discussed the case of the Patriarch of Constantinople, John Kalekas, and agreed that they could no longer keep communion with one so bold, who had clearly overstepped the line between his spiritual and temporal powers. They pronounced him to be deposed from office and, as far as they were concerned, excommunicated. Cantacuzene gave his blessing to their decision. To demonstrate that they condemned him not for political reasons but only because he had offended against the canons of the church, they charged him with ordaining heretical priests. Not many months later the bishops in Constantinople were to come to the same conclusion.[50]

When the ceremonies were over and the bishops had gone, Cantacuzene had time to consider an extraordinary proposal which had been put to him earlier. Ambassadors had come to him from Orhan of Bithynia soliciting the hand of his daughter Theodora in marriage to their Emir. They suggested that such a bond of kinship would strengthen the existing ties of friendship and alliance between the two men. Orhan would become the son and the vassal of the Emperor. John had asked for time to consider the proposal. He consulted his officers. They were all in favour of it. He also, however, consulted his old friend and blood-brother Umur, Emir of Aydin. Umur had no cause to gratify the wishes of his Muslim neighbour Orhan. He had

[49] Cantac. II, pp. 564–5; Greg. II, pp. 762–3.
[50] Cantac. II, pp. 565–8. J. Meyendorff, *Introduction à l'étude de Grégoire Palamas* (Paris, 1959), pp. 118–19.

himself earlier declined to take to wife one of John's daughters, not because she was a Christian but because the special relationship of 'brotherhood' between her father and himself made such a marriage uncanonical in Islamic law. Orhan had no such relationship and no such scruples. Once he had been assured that the proposal had the benison of so open-minded and honest a friend as Umur, John hesitated no longer. He sent envoys to Orhan to make the necessary arrangements for Theodora's marriage.[51]

This is the version of this strange affair that John gives in his own memoirs. It may be that it was he rather than Orhan who made the first move, for he knew that the Empress Anna in Constantinople was trying to bribe and persuade Orhan to put his troops at her disposal. The much later historian Doukas, who regarded the arrangement as both squalid and sacrilegious, says as much and dates the betrothal of Theodora to Orhan in January 1346.[52] Gregoras adds the romantic touch that Orhan was passionately in love with Theodora. Whether or not his love was reciprocated is immaterial, for neither she nor her mother Eirene had any say in the matter. Eirene must have found the idea of her daughter marrying a Muslim prince distasteful and distressing. Her husband reminded her that several Emperors before him had given their daughters in marriage to foreign and 'barbarian' rulers for the benefit of their Empire. This was true. Michael VIII had married off daughters to the Khans of the Mongols; Andronikos II had done much the same. But the daughters whom they exploited were born out of wedlock and it was a useful way of settling them out of reach. In John's own generation the renegade John Vatatzes had given his daughter in marriage to the Turkish Emir of Karasi. No one could claim that the wedding of Theodora Cantacuzene to the Emir Orhan was a Christian marriage; and no one pretended that it was. There is no record that the Patriarch of Jerusalem, who had crowned Theodora's father as Emperor, said anything at all.

Soon after his coronation, in the early summer of 1346, John

---

[51] Cantac. ii, pp. 585–9; Greg. ii, pp. 762–3. Nicol, *Byzantine Family*, pp. 134–5; Nicol, *The Byzantine Lady*, p. 74.

[52] Doukas, *Istoria*, ed. Grecu, pp. 57–61.

asked Orhan to send an army with a suitable escort to
Selymbria on the Thracian coast to fetch his betrothed. Thirty
Turkish ships soon arrived bringing a cavalry regiment and
several of Orhan's nobles. Orhan himself was not among them.
A somewhat bizarre ceremony was then enacted at Selymbria.
The Empress Eirene and her two other daughters, Maria and
Helena, were brought there to witness it. They were lodged in
the imperial tent while the Emperor stayed with his officers. He
had caused a large wooden platform to be erected on the plain
outside the city. It was on this that the bride-show customary at
the wedding of an Emperor's daughter was to be performed.
Theodora was to be displayed to the people. And so it was. At
the hour appointed she mounted the platform; and the silk and
cloth-of-gold curtains around it were thrown back to reveal her.
Lamps held aloft by kneeling eunuchs were lit. Trumpets and
flutes and all the musical instruments that gladden the heart of
man were played; encomia in her honour were then recited; and
when all the rites fitting for the marriage of an imperial
princess had been performed, the Emperor held a feast for
Greeks and Turks that lasted for several days. When the
ceremony was over, he sent his daughter on her way to join her
bridegroom either at the coast of Bithynia or at Brusa. He had
been the only conspicuous absentee from the festivities; but
absent from the record of the event is any mention of the dowry
which Theodora must have taken with her or of the bride-price
which Orhan, according to Muslim custom, must have paid for
her. Cantacuzene's account omits such sordid and materialistic
features. He prefers to dwell on the virtues of his daughter in a
foreign and infidel land, on her steadfast adherence to her
Christian faith despite many attempts to convert her to
Islam, and her charitable and beneficent influence among the
Christian slaves and prisoners in her husband's dominions.
That she was allowed such freedom is a measure of the great
respect in which her father was held among the Turks and of
the tolerance of the Osmanli people. For seven years after
Orhan's marriage to Theodora there were no more Turkish
incursions into Byzantine territory.[53]

[53] Only Doukas (p. 59) mentions the matters of the dowry and the bride-price. On the
marriage, see A. A. M. Bryer, 'Greek historians on the Turks: the case of the first

After the ceremony John seems to have stayed in Selymbria for a while. It was within easy reach of Constantinople and from there he could keep in touch with his spies and contacts behind the city walls. He put his eldest son Matthew, then about twenty-one, in charge at Adrianople. The Empress Anna and the Patriarch were near the end of their resources and beginning to panic. They sent agents to John's camp at Selymbria to get him murdered by a hired assassin. Some Turks whom they lured across the water went over to John's side. He sent them home, though not before they had collected much plunder. As the winter of 1346 came on and the Empress stubbornly refused to negotiate, the Cantacuzenists in Constantinople became more numerous and more confident. A conspiracy was formed to make plans for admitting their own Emperor into the city. Their leaders exchanged messages with Selymbria by boat. It was arranged that John should present himself outside the Golden Gate on a certain night. He noted the date and left Selymbria for Adrianople, partly to put his enemies off the scent, but also to recruit a troop of 1,000 picked men to fight his way into Constantinople when the moment came.[54]

It was towards the end of January 1347. The cracks in the solid wall of the regency had become apparent when Apokaukos had been murdered. The edifice collapsed when the Empress fell out with the Patriarch John Kalekas. The true reasons for their quarrel are hard to fathom. The fact remains that the Empress decided that her friend and collaborator must go. Her decision may have been an eleventh-hour attempt to conciliate the Cantacuzenists in the city. On the other hand she had been so conditioned to fear the worst from Cantacuzene in the event of his victory that she was unlikely to offer him or his supporters the palm of reconciliation. At all events, she was determined that the Patriarch must be dismissed. She had lived long enough in Byzantine society to understand that the way to get rid of a troublesome priest was to have him convicted on

Byzantine-Ottoman marriage', *The Writing of History in the Middle Ages: Essays presented to R. W. Southern*, ed. R. H. C. Davis and J. M. Wallace-Hadrill (Oxford, 1981), pp. 471–93. See also the sane remarks of Parisot, *Cantacuzène*, pp. 213–15.

[54] Cantac. II, pp. 591–6, 605; Greg. II, pp. 763–5.

theological grounds. She may have heard how he had been condemned at Adrianople. She must have known that he was not popular with his bishops and that many of them were concerned about his theology as well as his politics. She was no theologian herself and can hardly have understood the intricate traps of Christian doctrine by which he might be snared and convicted of error. At the end of January she summoned a synod of bishops in the capital, as she was entitled to do. They met in the palace on 2 February 1347. The Empress presided. The Patriarch John Kalekas was present to defend himself. He was condemned for his errors in theology and discharged from office.[55]

The meeting was in session for some hours and it was far into the night when the bishops went home. Their night's rest, already delayed, may have been disturbed by events in another part of the city. For it was the night that Cantacuzene had fixed with his conspirators to meet at the Golden Gate with his army from Adrianople. The gate had been walled up. But as arranged, the conspirators had hacked a hole through it from the inside. John and his men climbed through the breach in the dark. They met no resistance. They were, in his own words, led on by the cheers of the people. It was John's first visit to Constantinople for more than five years, but he knew where he was. He marched as far as the so-called house of the Porphyrogenitus below the Blachernai palace, where the Empress was residing. The palace was well guarded and had its own fortress behind its walls. John forbade his men to attack it or to make any disturbance. At daybreak on 3 February he went right through the city to give thanks to the Virgin in her church of the Hodegetria before returning to his camp. He was uncertain of his next move. The Empress, understandably apprehensive, barricaded herself in the palace. She summoned help from her Genoese friends in Galata, who sailed over the Golden Horn to rescue her. They were sighted and forced to turn back. John saw that she would have to be cajoled into surrender by assurances that she was in no danger. He summoned the bishops and clergy

[55] Cantac. II, pp. 602–4; Schreiner, *Chron. brev.*, II, p. 268; Greg. II, pp. 767–73, who infers that the Empress Anna fell out with the Patriarch by feigning her conversion to Palamism. See Meyendorff, *Introduction a l'étude de Grégoire Palamas*, pp. 119, 129–30.

in the city and addressed them; and after giving them his familiar apology for his own part in the civil war, with special reference to his employment of Turkish troops, he appointed two of them to go and present his respects to the Empress and ask her to negotiate. They were to warn her that the defences of the fortress in her palace were in bad repair and that she had neither the guards nor the means to hold out. Her counsellors prevailed upon her not to give in. She sent the messengers away. The gates of the palace remained barred. At this, some of John's officers became so infuriated that they disobeyed his orders, set fire to one of the gates and stormed their way in to the fortified area of the palace. In his memoirs he records that Anna was in the end persuaded to be less obstinate by her own son John who begged her to give in lest worse befall. John was then fifteen years old, 'but above his years in intelligence'. His mother listened to him and acted on his advice. She sent out two men to negotiate and discuss terms of peace. One was Cantacuzene's father-in-law Andronikos Asen; the other was the monk Gregory Palamas, whom the Patriarch Kalekas had incarcerated for his Cantacuzenism.

On 8 February 1347 an agreement was signed and sworn on the terms proposed by Cantacuzene. Its tone was pacific and conciliatory. He would take no recriminations against anyone; he would grant total amnesty to all who had wronged him over the past years; he would bear no grudge against the Empress and her son. Both sides must forget their animosities and enmities. The constitutional terms agreed were that John Cantacuzene and the young John Palaiologos should reign jointly as co-Emperors, bearing to each other the respect due between father and son, the younger yielding to the elder, for a period of ten years, at the end of which their rule should be equally shared. On these terms the gates of the Blachernai palace were opened to admit Cantacuzene as the senior Emperor.[56]

---

[56] Cantac. II, pp. 604–15; Greg. II, pp. 773–9; Schreiner, *Chron. brev.*, II, pp. 268–70. The captain Phakeolatos, one of the leaders of the pro-Cantacuzene conspiracy, was not a Genoese admiral called Fazzolati as proposed by Weiss, *Johannes Kantakuzenos*, pp. 43, 67, and by Schreiner, *Chron. brev.*, II, p. 269. He had in fact been granted a personal bodyguard to protect him from the Genoese. Greg. II, pp. 766, 773.

Some may privately have felt at the time that these were terms which could have been agreed five years before and saved the Empire so much bitterness, hatred and destruction. Most people, however, were simply relieved that it was all over. Cantacuzene, now senior Emperor in fact as well as in name, wisely ordained that the sense of relief should prevail over the feelings of bitterness. He decreed that all political prisoners were to be set free and that no reprisals should be taken against those who had persecuted them. He had already sternly forbidden his soldiers to go looting or destroying properties in the city and, with a few exceptions, they obeyed his orders. He had also restrained the people from giving vent to their feelings by causing a riot. He was intent on creating an atmosphere of order and stability, of amnesty and forgiveness. The memory of the past years must, so far as possible, be forgotten. He labours the point in his memoirs, but his sincerity is confirmed by others who were alive in 1347. The charity and generosity that he showed to his late enemies impressed them. Gregoras applauds his clemency. But his most vivid testimonial comes from a young acquaintance of his called Demetrios Kydones, who had come in his entourage from Thrace. Kydones was then about twenty-three years old. His parents and family had been made almost destitute by the Zealot revolution in Thessalonica. As a refugee he had known the horrors and terrors of intolerance and instability. For him the entry of John Cantacuzene into Constantinople in February 1347 seemed to herald the dawn of a new age, an era in which all horrors and terrors would be past history.

Before the light of day had dawned everyone in the city poured out into the streets to see the Emperor as though he were a long-lost friend, to grasp his feet and embrace him with joy; and the Emperor, though grieved to see how they had been changed by so many misfortunes, shared in the general happiness. But he resolved not be affected by the magnitude of his success; and although the crowds followed him up to the acropolis clamouring for the blood of the wild beasts who had shut themselves up inside, he was for making a settlement rather than committing murder ... At the end he pardoned all those who had so gravely wronged him, even when he had them at his mercy by right of conquest ... So, all you who have been weighed down by the burden of your sufferings ... and are now restored to life, you have your Emperor and you have your happiness. Rejoice for this day, as the Egyptians rejoiced for the rebirth of the phoenix, which should be the symbol of your better fortune.[57]

---

[57] G. Cammelli, 'Demetrii Cydonii ad Ioannem Cantacuzenum imperatorem oratio altera', *BNJ*, 4 (1923), 77–83, especially 81–3. On the early career of Demetrios Kydones: R.-J. Loenertz, 'Démétrius Cydonès, 1: De la naissance à l'année 1373', *OCP*, 36 (1970), 47–72.

5

EMPEROR OF THE ROMANS
(1347–1351)

D EMETRIOS Kydones interpreted the long struggle between
Cantacuzene and his political enemies as a conflict
between truth and falsehood, between justice and injustice,
between philanthropy and savagery, between good and evil.
Cantacuzene's victory demonstrated that the better will always
triumph over the worse and that ultimately the good will
always prevail. Kydones was a young man, full of optimism and
fond of practising his rhetoric. He entered the service of his
hero and before long became his chancellor and prime minister.
In his later years Kydones showed a capacity for political
survival unusual in a Byzantine statesman. He was to be a
guiding light in imperial policy to the very end of the fourteenth
century.

Cantacuzene's magnanimity and clemency to his former
enemies were certainly laudable and to his credit. Some of his
loyal supporters, however, wished that he would cease to be so
self-effacing and would seize the imperial authority that he had
won with a firmer hand. The settlement that he made with the
Empress Anna and her son on 8 February 1347 could have been
reached five years earlier; some thought it to be a poor prize
after so long a contest. On the following day he gave orders that
all his supporters, as well as those of the Empress, must swear
oaths of allegiance to both Emperors, to himself and to the
young John Palaiologos. Most of his own men refused. They
would swear loyalty only to John Cantacuzene. It took three
days of wrangling to make them do what they had been told to
do. It is hard to understand why their Emperor was so eager
to be seen to be sharing his imperium with a fifteen-year-old
boy, unless it were to labour the point that the boy was the
son and heir of his own late lamented 'brother', the Emperor

Andronikos III. Perhaps he wanted to lay the ghost of 'Cantacuzenism' in Constantinople and more especially in Thessalonica, where the Zealots might be prepared to do business with a government that was seen to be still in the hands of the Palaiologos family.[1]

There was a historical precedent for such an unusual constitutional arrangement. In the tenth century the usurper of the throne Romanos Lakapenos had made himself regent for the boy Emperor Constantine VII Porphyrogenitus on the pretext of safeguarding the Macedonian dynasty whose rights to the throne he claimed to uphold. Romanos gave his daughter in marriage to Constantine and in 920 was crowned as his co-Emperor.[2] But he went about his business in a more forceful and decisive manner; and Cantacuzene gives no hint that he had this precedent in mind. The similarity was, however, accentuated when Cantacuzene announced that his daughter Helena was to be betrothed to the junior Emperor John Palaiologos. The proposal had been made before Cantacuzene left Constantinople in September 1341, but the Empress Anna had turned it down. Now she had little option. In February 1347 Helena was fourteen years of age. Her fiancé was fifteen. Her mother brought her to the capital from Adrianople and her betrothal to the young John was solemnised. At the same time she was invested and proclaimed as yet another Empress of the Romans.[3]

This all but completed the constitutional arrangements which Cantacuzene had in mind. There remained, however, one odd man out who declined to be accommodated in the process of reconciliation. The Patriarch John Kalekas had been deposed from office by his own synod. The bishops in Adrianople had condemned him in 1346. His pride had been wounded. His theology had been questioned. He had hidden himself away in an apartment of the palace. Everyone knew that the Empire, though it might now have two Emperors, could not fulfil its

[1] Cantac. III (*CSHB*), pp. 8–11.

[2] S. Runciman, *The Emperor Romanus Lecapenus and his Reign. A Study of Tenth-Century Byzantium* (Cambridge, 1929), pp. 45–62; F. Dölger, 'Johannes VI. Kantakuzenos als dynastischer Legitimist', *Seminarium Kondakovianum*, 10 (1938), 19–30 (= Dölger, *ΠΑΡΑΣΠΟΡΑ* (Ettal, 1961), pp. 194–207).

[3] Cantac. III, pp. 11–12.

Christian function without a Patriarch of Constantinople.
Kalekas must either be talked into co-operation or properly
dismissed so that a successor could be appointed. Cantacuzene
went to see him. It was an embarrassing interview. Kalekas was
pleased to find that the Emperor, whose title he refused to
recognise and whom he had excommunicated, was in a
forgiving mood. He accepted an invitation to defend himself in
a fair trial against the charges of heresy that had been laid
against him. But when the day came for the trial and the synod
of bishops had gathered, he failed to present himself. A second
and a third summons went unanswered. The synod therefore
condemned him *in absentia*. He was removed from the scene
of his crimes, theological and political, and taken to
Didymoteichon. There he fell ill both physically and mentally.
He died in December of the same year.[4]

The decision of the synod that had been assembled to hear
him was made public in an imperial decree (*prostagma*) which
Cantacuzene signed as Emperor in March 1347. It was
confirmed a few weeks later by another convocation attended
by the Patriarch of Jerusalem and the bishops who had been
at Adrianople. The appointment of a new Patriarch of
Constantinople was not simple. Cantacuzene wisely decided to
offer no names and to let the bishops sort it out among themselves. In the circumstances it was not easy to find a candidate
who was theologically as well as politically sound. Several names
were considered, among them the monk Gregory Palamas, who
had suffered at the hands of the former Patriarch, and the
rather more eccentric but undeniably holy hermit Sabas of
Vatopedi. Either would have been acceptable to Cantacuzene,
for he knew them both. In the end, however, the bishops chose
another monk, Isidore, a friend of Palamas who was also known
to the senior Emperor. As soon as he had been consecrated as
Patriarch, Isidore publicly annulled the anathema of excommunication which his predecessor had imposed on
Cantacuzene. John Kalekas had already relented in this matter;
but it was better that the Emperor should be received back into
the communion by a Patriarch who was untainted. Isidore also

4 Cantac. III, pp. 20–5; Greg. II, p. 813. G. T. Dennis, 'The deposition of the Patriarch
   John Calecas', *JÖBG*, 11 (1960), 51–5.

saw to the election of a number of new bishops to the church. One of them was the Emperor's friend Gregory Palamas, who was soon to prove himself to be the leading theologian of his day. He was elevated to the See of Thessalonica.[5]

It was Isidore who had the distinction of officiating at the second coronation of John Cantacuzene. He had first been crowned as Emperor at Adrianople a year earlier. That event had no doubt been legal in the eyes of God and of those of his supporters who had witnessed it. But tradition held that the Emperor of the Romans should be crowned in his city of Constantinople by the Patriarch of that city. Michael VIII, the founder of the dynasty of Palaiologos, had been crowned as Emperor at Nicaea; but he thought it necessary to go through a second and grander ceremony after he had entered Constantinople. The second coronation of John Cantacuzene was also a grand occasion, though some of its grandeur was muted by the conditions of the time. The great cathedral of St Sophia had been dilapidated by neglect and by earthquake the year before and could not be used for the service. It had to be conducted in the church of Blachernai near the palace. The date chosen was 21 May 1347, the feast of Saints Constantine and Helena, a year to the day after Cantacuzene's first coronation at Adrianople. The ceremony was attended by three Empresses, Eirene, Anna and Helena, and two Emperors, John VI and John V. The younger John had been crowned in 1341 by the former Patriarch before he lapsed into heresy; and that coronation was thought to suffice. But after he had received his own crown from Isidore, Cantacuzene observed the tradition of placing the crown of Empress on the head of his wife Eirene. When the ceremonies were over there was a procession on horseback and a banquet in the palace. Those present on these occasions lamented past glories. For they noticed that the crown jewels were made of glass and the plate for the banquet was made of pewter and clay. The real crown jewels were still in pawn to Venice and the gold and silver plate

[5] The text of Cantacuzene's decree is in *MPG*, CLI, cols. 771–2. Cantac. III, pp. 25–8; Greg. II, pp. 785–7, 791–3; Schreiner, *Chron. brev.*, II, p. 270; Philotheos, *Life of Isidore*, ed. D. G. Tsamis, Φιλοθέου τοῦ Κοκκίνου ἁγιολογικὰ ἔργα, I (Thessaloniki, 1985), p. 393.

of the palace had long since been sold to raise money during the civil war.[6]

A week later, on 28 May 1347, the wedding of Helena Cantacuzene to John Palaiologos was celebrated in the same church at Blachernai.[7] This union between the ruling families of Cantacuzene and Palaiologos set the seal on the constitutional plans of the senior Emperor. It was supposed to symbolise the end of their feud and the beginning of the new reconciliation and harmony between them. In this it was not completely successful. Not long after his coronation Cantacuzene issued an honours list, as was the custom. His younger son Manuel, whom he had summoned from Berroia, was honoured with the title of Despot, as was his son-in-law Nikephoros of Epiros. For his eldest son Matthew, however, he devised a rank that had no title. Matthew was declared to be rather higher than a Despot and a little lower than an Emperor. It was an awkward compromise. It satisfied neither Matthew nor those loyal Cantacuzenists who believed that he should have been nominated as co-Emperor with his father and as heir to the throne. They had refused to swear allegiance to John Palaiologos until made to do so. They now felt that Matthew had been openly cheated of his rights to inherit his father's title. They urged him to proclaim his independence as a prince in his own right at Adrianople, while remaining nominally subject to his father. It was an unfortunate if not unpredictable situation. Cantacuzene confesses that it made him extremely angry. He delegated his wife Eirene to go and reason with Matthew, her first and favourite son. She succeeded where her husband, being annoyed, might have failed. Matthew was brought to see the folly of his ways and his supporters were chastised. His father tactfully consented, however, to grant him possession of Didymoteichon and a large strip of land in Thrace as an autonomous appanage for the rest of his life. Long before his life was over it became clear that this exceptional privilege was

---

[6] Cantac. iii, pp. 29–30; Greg. ii, pp. 787–91. The church of St Sophia had been damaged in May 1346. Greg. ii, p. 749. Gregoras seems to imply that Cantacuzene's second coronation was performed only to please the Palamites. Schreiner, *Chron. brev.*, ii, pp. 265, 270–1.

[7] Cantac. iii, p. 29; Greg. ii, p. 791; Doukas, *Istoria*, p. 65; Schreiner, *Chron. brev.*, ii, p. 271, dating the wedding to 24 (or 28) May.

not enough. Some of the smoke of civil war had still not been dispelled. It hung over the battlefields of Thrace. It was hard for a spirited young man like Matthew, who had been loyal to his family, to be forced by his own father to play second fiddle to a boy six years his junior. He remained loyal for a few years longer. It cannot have helped matters that Cantacuzene saw fit towards the end of 1347 to take his new son-in-law John Palaiologos on a tour of the cities of Thrace to show him off as heir to the throne.[8]

An interesting by-product of the events of February 1347 was a visit by Cantacuzene's other son-in-law, Orhan of Bithynia. He came as far as Skutari on the Asiatic side of the Bosporos, not to attend the coronation but merely to offer his congratulations and felicitations; and he brought with him his wife Theodora to wish her parents well. Cantacuzene sailed over to greet him and for some days they hunted and wined and dined together at Skutari. They dined at the same table with Orhan's four sons by his other wives while the ladies dined at another table and Orhan's nobles reclined on carpets. It might have been injudicious to invite Orhan over to Constantinople. But Cantacuzene took his sons as well as his own daughter Theodora to the city; and Theodora stayed with her mother and sisters for three days before going back to Bithynia with her husband. Such tokens of goodwill between Christians and Muslims were very much to the taste of John Cantacuzene. It was a taste not shared by many of his people.[9]

It may seem an even stranger taste when one considers the profound Christian spirituality of John Cantacuzene. The age in which he lived and which he helped to shape was one of saints and scholars, of eremitic monks and gregarious intellectuals. They did not always see eye to eye with each other. The monks were fond of saying that scholarship was not a part of their business except for study of the Holy Scriptures and the Fathers of the church. This constituted what they called 'the inner wisdom'. The scholars, such as the encyclopaedic Theodore Metochites and his pupil Nikephoros Gregoras, cultivated 'the outer wisdom' of pagan, pre-Christian philosophy and literature. They saw new meanings in the works of Plato,

---

[8] Cantac. III, pp. 33, 43–8, 52–3; Greg. II, pp. 798–812.   [9] Cantac. III, pp. 28–9.

Aristotle, Plutarch and other sages of what they termed their Hellenic legacy from antiquity. The Latin literature of the past was almost unknown to them. This intellectual movement in Byzantium had been fostered by the Emperor Andronikos II who had, like many men of his time, a foot in both camps. He held literary and philosophical soirées at his court; but he was also deeply religious and devoted to his church and his puritanical and ascetic Patriarch Athanasios.[10] His grandson Andronikos was not much interested in the culture of the mind or of the spirit. But it fell to him as Emperor to preside over a council of his argumentative bishops in Constantinople in June 1341. The point of their argument was the orthodoxy or heterodoxy of certain monks, especially on Mount Athos, who came to be known as hesychasts. They claimed to practise a method of prayer and contemplation which, in conditions of *hesychia* or stillness, could induce an awareness, however temporary, of the divine light of the Transfiguration or *theosis* (deification). The theological implications of this claim seemed to some churchmen to be verging on aberration from the received truths of Orthodoxy; others saw it as no more than a development of a strand in the long history of those truths.[11]

The first to challenge the Orthodoxy of the hesychasts was a westernised Greek monk, Barlaam of Calabria, who was staying in Constantinople in the 1330s. The man who took up the challenge was the monk Gregory Palamas who was abbot of a monastery on Mount Athos about 1335. Palamas was a leading exponent of the doctrine of hesychasm and he leapt to the defence of its Orthodoxy against the charges of Barlaam. He composed a declaration (*Tomos*) approved and signed by most of the leading monks on Mount Athos, which condemned Barlaam and all his works and sympathisers. Palamas was known to

---

[10] See, e.g., S. Runciman, *The Last Byzantine Renaissance* (Cambridge, 1970); G. Podskalsky, *Theologie und Philosophie in Byzanz: Die Streit um die theologische Methodik in der spätbyzantinischen Geistesgeschichte (14./15. Jh.)* (Munich, 1977); D. M. Nicol, *Church and Society in the Last Centuries of Byzantium* (Cambridge, 1979).

[11] On hesychasm and the hesychast controversy, see J. Meyendorff, *Introduction a l'étude de Grégoire Palamas* (Paris, 1959); S. Runciman, *The Great Church in Captivity* (Cambridge, 1968), pp. 128–58; Joan M. Hussey, *The Orthodox Church in the Byzantine Empire* (Oxford, 1986), pp. 257–60, 286–9; Nicol, *Last Centuries of Byzantium*, pp. 210–14.

Cantacuzene as well as to the Emperor Andronikos III. He was in Thessalonica in 1341 when both men were there; and he followed them to Constantinople in the spring. Barlaam was already in the capital. The Patriarch John Kalekas agreed, rather reluctantly, to summon a council to decide the issue; and on 11 June 1341 the senate, the judiciary, the bishops and abbots in Constantinople met under the presidency of the Emperor Andronikos. Their meeting lasted for only one day. The vote went in favour of Gregory Palamas and the hesychasts. Barlaam was denounced as a heretic and retired to his native Italy. It was in the course of this meeting that Andronikos III was taken ill. He died four days later.

There were few things that engaged the minds of the Byzantine people more than theology. The controversy was not over. A second council had to be called in August to stifle the opposition of some who remained in sympathy with Barlaam, notably the monk Gregory Akindynos, a former friend of Palamas. In August there was no Emperor to preside over a council. The chair was taken by John Cantacuzene. The theological issue was quickly decided. Palamas was again vindicated and his opponents condemned. In the Byzantine world, however, theology and politics were often intermingled. The fact that Cantacuzene had presided over the council in August as if he were Emperor added fuel to the fire of his rivalry with the Patriarch. It was well known that he was on friendly terms with Palamas and with other hesychast monks on Mount Athos. The Patriarch saw that there was political capital to be made out of the theological dispute. He could and did brand the cause of Palamas with the stigma of Cantacuzenism. He could and did encourage Akindynos and other anti-Palamites to disregard the rulings of the council over which Cantacuzene had presided and to spread their propaganda. In 1343 he had Palamas arrested and put in prison. In 1344 he excommunicated him.

In these matters the Patriarch John Kalekas acted on his own. No doubt he had the approval of Alexios Apokaukos, though he was not noted for his religious convictions; and it is hard to believe that the Empress Anna, dominated as she was by the Patriarch's will, could have disputed with him the theological subtleties of the nature of the divine light which

Palamas and the hesychasts claimed to apprehend. Greater minds than hers held that the hesychasts went too far in their claims. One such was the historian Gregoras, a personal friend and political admirer of Cantacuzene. It is sometimes suggested that Cantacuzene championed the cause of Palamas and his theology from purely political and private motives, to ensure that he had behind him the immense moral support of the Holy Mountain of Athos, the 'factory of virtue'. This was certainly an advantage which his political rivals, the Empress and the Patriarch, could never gain. But Cantacuzene was sincere in his religious beliefs. He had friends among the monks, including Palamas. He was greatly impressed by the holiness of Sabas of Vatopedi.[12] He was personally attracted to the monastic life; and he fully understood the theology of the hesychasts. Later in his life, when he had no more political ambitions, he was to prove his understanding in a series of learned refutations of the anti-Palamites. It was in the matter of his theology, not of his politics, that he was rebuked and disowned by his older friend Gregoras who remained loudly and violently opposed to the doctrines of Palamas until he died in 1361. Gregoras once remarked that John Cantacuzene would have been one of the best of all Emperors if only he had not allowed himself to be led astray by the theological aberrations of Palamas.[13] The statement serves to illustrate a difference between the two men. Gregoras was an intellectual and a scholar, who looked at the higher flights of spirituality from an academic and pedestrian viewpoint. Cantacuzene was a less rational and dogmatic character, who was more given to appreciating the illogicality of mystical theology.

The year 1347 was auspicious in its beginnings. Civil war was over. There was a new Emperor and a new Patriarch. The church seemed to be resolving its differences. Society was less anxious and more hopeful. Order and a measure of stability had returned to Constantinople. But it was in the summer of that year that the Black Death struck the Empire. The Empress Eirene got back to Constantinople from her mission to reason

---

[12] Philotheos, *Life of Sabas*, ed. Tsamis, pp. 308–13, who alone reports Cantacuzene's vain attempts to secure the election of Sabas as Patriarch.
[13] Greg. II, p. 589.

with her son Matthew to find that her youngest son Andronikos had died of the plague.[14] He had only recently been freed from the prison in which Apokaukos had put him five years before. He was no more than thirteen years old. He was but one of the countless victims of the disease. They are countless because no statistics were kept. A western chronicle records that eight-ninths of the population of Constantinople died. This is no doubt a wild guess. Cantacuzene gives a creditable account of the symptoms and the distressing consequences of the Black Death. But much of what he writes is modelled on if not copied from the famous account by Thucydides of the plague at Athens in the time of Pericles. Byzantine writers considered such plagiarism from 'Hellenic' models of literacy to be deserving of more praise than blame. Gregoras gives a shorter account. Both historians correctly record that the disease was carried on Genoese ships from the Crimea.[15] Demetrios Kydones vividly describes its effects in Constantinople in a letter to a friend: 'Every day', he writes, 'we bring out our friends for burial. Every day the great city becomes emptier and the number of graves increases. Men inhumanly shun each other's company for fear of contagion. Fathers do not dare to bury their own sons; sons will not perform their last duties to their fathers. The doctors that are left know not what to do.'[16]

The epidemic lasted for about a year. It did its most deadly work in the cities, especially in Constantinople, though one is left to conjecture what it may have done in Thessalonica or Adrianople. In Asia Minor it is known to have reached Trebizond in September 1347. But there is no record of how it affected the Turkish Emirates. Cantacuzene as a father mourned the death of his son Andronikos. But as a statesman he had greater cause to mourn the death of another of his relatives. His cousin John Angelos, whom he had appointed as life governor of Thessaly in 1342, died of the plague. He left the

---

[14] Nicol, *Byzantine Family*, no. 26.

[15] Cantac. III, pp. 49–52; Greg. II, pp. 797–8. *Chronicon Estense* in *Rerum Italicarum Scriptores*, XV, p. 448. H. Hunger, 'Thukydides bei Johannes Kantakuzenos. Beobachtungen zur Mimesis', *JÖB*, 25 (1976), 181–93; Nicol, *Last Centuries of Byzantium*, pp. 216–18.

[16] Demetrios Kydones, *Letters*, ed. R.-J. Loenertz, I (Vatican City, 1956), no. 88, pp. 121–2.

provinces of northern Greece open and unprotected. Stephen Dušan of Serbia marched in and occupied them. His armies had already invaded Albania and Epiros, which Cantacuzene had helped to restore to Byzantine rule seven years before. It had been his dream to add the Peloponnese to the northern provinces of the Greek peninsula to make a Greek-speaking Empire extending from the Adriatic Sea to Constantinople and the Bosporos. By 1348, when the Serbian conquest of Albania, Epiros and Thessaly was complete, it was Stephen Dušan, as Emperor of the Serbs and Romans, who had come nearer to realising that dream. He had occupied Serres in eastern Macedonia in 1345. Thessalonica continued to elude him. But he had the second city of the Byzantine Empire encircled.[17]

It might again be necessary for Cantacuzene to call on his Turkish friends for help. Umur of Aydin had troubles of his own at Smyrna and was soon to be killed fighting in its defence. But Orhan of Bithynia was still eager and ready to lend a hand when his father-in-law summoned him and even when he had not been invited. Shortly after the wedding of Helena Cantacuzene, Orhan sent a secret agent to Constantinople to murder her husband John. He was under the muddled impression that this would be a signal service to his friend the senior Emperor; for, as Cantacuzene records, it was the custom among the Turks to murder any pretender to the throne regardless of his age or kinship. The subtleties of Cantacuzene's constitutional relationship to his junior colleague were evidently lost on Orhan. But Cantacuzene made sure thereafter never to let the young John out of his sight without a bodyguard.[18] By 1348 there were Turks in large numbers raiding the coast of Thrace and marauding the countryside. They were not in the service of any of his Muslim friends in Asia Minor, and they were not always in a hurry to take their loot and go. Some were beginning to settle and put down roots on Christian territory. Cantacuzene was surprised by a band of two thousand of them who had crossed the Hellespont uninvited in 1348. He got the better of them in a battle at Mosynopolis, though in the course of it his

---

[17] On the Serbian occupation of Albania, Epiros and Thessaly: Nicol, *Despotate of Epiros*, II, pp. 128–31.
[18] Cantac. III, p. 111.

own life was endangered by the foolhardiness of his son-in-law Nikephoros. They knew who he was, for some of them had served with him during the civil war. In disentangling himself from this engagement he was able to converse with them; and this is one of the rare occasions on which he claims to have been able to speak Turkish.[19]

One day he may have hoped to expel all the Turks from European soil. But in the first year of his reign it was like swatting flies when there were lions on the prowl. The most dangerous of them was Stephen Dušan of Serbia who had almost effortlessly added most of northern Greece to his dominions. There were others closer to Constantinople. The Genoese in their colony at Galata across the Golden Horn may not have been aware that their ships had been the carriers of the Black Death down from the Crimea to the Mediterranean. But their agents were aware that the new Emperor in Constantinople was planning to reconstruct a Byzantine fleet of merchant ships as well as warships to shake off the dependence of his people on the Italian maritime Republics. It was an ambitious undertaking. It would be expensive and it would not be popular with the still wealthy bourgeoisie of the city, some of whom liked to bank their money with the Genoese. Not long after his coronation in 1347 Cantacuzene took the unusual step of calling a general assembly of all classes of citizens, merchants, soldiers, artisans, the people, abbots and leaders of the church. He gave them a long report on the current and future problems of the Empire. Once again he apologised for the excesses of the Turkish troops whom he had been forced to hire during the civil war. He emphasised the impoverished and ruined state of the Empire and of its capital, whose resources, even its crown jewels, had been spent by the regency. Taxation failed to provide revenue, for the towns of the mainland and of the islands had been reduced to penury either by enemy attacks or by revolution within their own walls. The army, though still dependable, was underfed and underpaid for lack of money. As Gregoras was to put it: 'There was nothing in the imperial treasury but air and dust and, as one might say, the atoms of Epicurus.'[20]

---

[19] Cantac. III, pp. 62–6.   [20] Greg. II, p. 790.

Cantacuzene had much experience of economic and financial affairs, acquired during his service as treasurer for Andronikos III. He had a high ideal of the role of financial administrator in the good government of Empire. He compared the position of treasurer to that of a judge in maintaining social order and respect for the law. He advocated a more equal distribution of wealth between the privileged and the poor. He expressed the ideals that he had in mind. What he asked for was that those who still had the means should pool their resources by voluntary contribution to a common fund. Some of the leading citizens agreed that this was a reasonable request and might go some way to building up the Empire's military and economic strength and restoring its former greatness. The main and most powerful opposition to the idea came from those who had made their money out of the political crisis, especially the bankers and money-changers. They whipped up the people, convincing them that they were about to be robbed. They shouted their Emperor down; he had already destroyed everything outside the walls of Constantinople and now proposed to repeat the operation inside those walls. Their arguments were not very rational but they were noisy; and they undermined Cantacuzene's resolution to instil some patriotism into the selfish elements of the population.[21]

What he could not achieve by voluntary means he would have to enforce by compulsion. The immediate enemy of the economic recovery of Constantinople was plainly visible to its people in the Genoese colony at Galata across the water. They could see that its inhabitants were engaged in extending and fortifying their colony. The rumour that the new Emperor was determined to build ships of his own to challenge Genoese dominance over the Bosporos had stirred them to action. The Emperor too was stirred. But he must find the money to build the ships. It was a race for time. The Genoese were further infuriated when the Emperor deliberately lowered the tariffs payable by ships unloading their wares at Constantinople, so that traffic and revenues were diverted from Galata. To raise

---

[21] Cantac. III, pp. 33–42. D. A. Zakythinos, 'Crise monétaire et crise économique à Byzance du XIIIᵉ au XVᵉ siècle', *L'Hellénisme Contemporaine* (Athens, 1948: reprinted in Zakythinos, *Byzance: Etat-Société-Economie* [London, 1973], no. XI), pp. 92–6.

the money Cantacuzene appointed a special commissioner to supervise and enforce the collection of funds and ordered the wealthy to contribute. They were now more ready to do so, though many complained of extortion. The Genoese saw that their bluff had been called. Cantacuzene told them that there could be no discussion until they had dismantled the fortifications that they were building. Meanwhile a Byzantine fleet was in the making in the docks at Constantinople. A number of incidents occurred to aggravate the tension. In the middle of August the Genoese sailed over in force and attacked the sea walls, the docks and quays, setting fire to whatever ships they could find. They chose their moment well, for the Emperor was in Thrace and had been taken ill at Didymoteichon. The defence of the city was in the hands of his wife Eirene, with her son Manuel and her son-in-law Nikephoros. She must have been reminded of the long months that she had spent holding the fort in Thrace in the early days of the civil war. The Genoese were surprised to find such strong resistance. They asked for talks to be held. But the citizens of Constantinople were in no mood for peace.

On 1 October the Emperor, ill though he was, came back to take command. He ordered the construction and equipment of ships to proceed as fast as possible. More money was collected, some of it, as Gregoras says, willingly given, but most of it with a bad grace. It all took time, for the timber for shipbuilding had to be dragged by oxen from the mountains of Thrace, since the Genoese controlled the sea route. By the beginning of March 1349 the moment seemed to have come to engage the fleet from Galata in a sea battle in the Golden Horn. Simultaneously an army was to march round and lay siege to the Genoese by land. The combined operation ended in total disaster for the Byzantines. On 6 March their fleet, of nine large warships and about 100 smaller vessels, sailing round from the harbours on the south of the city, foundered or were captured by the enemy. Cantacuzene is not alone in attributing the catastrophe to a sudden gale which blew them off course and caused their crews to panic. The Genoese could hardly believe what they were witnessing. It must have looked like mass suicide. The simple explanation for the behaviour of the Byzantine sailors is that they were not sailors at all: most of them had never manned a battleship before and had no experience of seafaring or naval tactics. When the wind blew up they lost control of themselves and of their ships and plunged into the sea in terror. Another and even simpler explanation was that the sudden gust of wind was an act of God, a punishment to the Byzantines for their sins. The soldiers who were supposed to attack Galata from behind also panicked when they saw what was happening to the fleet. They abandoned their weapons and ran as fast as they could back to the safety of the city walls. They too sensed the wrath of God.

The Genoese on the other hand knew that God had been on their side. On the next day they sailed along the sea walls of Constantinople in sight of the Blachernai palace dragging the imperial standards in the water. Before they were able to enforce their own terms for a settlement, however, a ship arrived from their masters in Genoa carrying ambassadors who were empowered to make a formal treaty. They found that their men in Galata were in the wrong in strengthening the fortifications around their colony. They were obliged to pay a large indemnity to the Emperor for the cost of the war that they had provoked and to swear that they would never again attack Constantinople.[22] Cantacuzene was luckier than he can have hoped. He was more than ever determined to build on that luck, to make sure that the city of Constantinople at least should become self-sufficient for its trade and its defence. He found once again that his hardest task in this respect was to coerce its citizens into helping him. He admits that there was uproar in the streets after allegations that the commissioner appointed to raise money for the building of ships had over-played his hand or helped himself, and most of the ships were now at the bottom of the sea. To counter these charges Cantacuzene again summoned an assembly of the citizens so that the commissioner could render an account. He was able to show that the amount collected and spent on the fleet was nowhere near the millions alleged by the trouble-makers

---

[22] On the war with Galata in 1348–9: Cantac. III, pp. 68–80; Greg. II, pp. 841–67; Alexios Makrembolites, *Historical Discourse on the Genoese*, ed. A. Papadopoulos-Kerameus, Ἀνάλεκτα Ἱεροσολυμιτικῆς Σταχυολογίας, I (St Petersburg, 1891), pp. 144–59; Schreiner, *Chron. brev.*, II, pp. 273–5. Kyrris, 'John Cantacuzenus and the Genoese', 8–48; Nicol, *Last Centuries of Byzantium*, pp. 220–6.

and that it was all properly accounted for. The trouble died down.[23]

But in the longer term stricter measures would have to be enforced if Constantinople, let alone the rest of the Empire, was ever to become independent of the Italian Republics for its defence, its economy and its very subsistence. The rot had set in when the Emperor Andronikos II had feebly decided to disband the Byzantine navy towards the end of the thirteenth century. That fatal mistake had ever since left the Byzantine seas open to exploitation and appropriation by the Venetians, the Genoese and latterly the Turks. The sins of the fathers had been visited on their successors for all too long by the time of John Cantacuzene. Gregoras computed that in his day the revenue accruing from customs dues at Constantinople was only about one-third of that collected at Galata.[24] It is true that Alexios Apokaukos, for all his faults, had tried to build up the maritime strength of Constantinople, but mainly for purposes of war. Cantacuzene deserves the credit for introducing what were for him uncharacteristically strong and decisive measures to solve the problem. He called for a series of taxes which had never before been levied. Their interpretation and indeed their date of imposition have prompted philological and chronological disagreements among scholars. But their general intention is clear. The new taxes fell mainly on those who could afford to pay them. They were special measures designed to bring badly-needed revenue to the imperial treasury. One was a tax on all cereals imported from abroad. Another was a tax on the export of wine. The producers of the wine had to pay a small duty on their sales; but the middlemen who made an easy profit from their exports were to pay double this amount to the treasury. The duty payable by merchants bringing their goods to the docks at Constantinople rather than to Galata was lowered from 10 per cent to 2 per cent of the value of their cargoes.[25]

---

[23] Cantac. III, p. 80.

[24] Greg. III, p. 842.

[25] Cantac. III, pp. 80–1; Greg. II, pp. 869–70. Zakythinos, 'Crise monétaire', 94–5; G. Ostrogorsky, *History of the Byzantine State*, translated by Joan Hussey (Oxford, 1968), p. 528; N. Oikonomides, *Hommes d'affaires grecs et latins à Constantinople (XIIIᵉ–XVᵉ siècles)* (Montreal, 1979), pp. 46–8.

Cantacuzene can not have hoped to win popularity by these unprecedented measures. New taxes are never popular. But, if his own account is to be believed, the money came in and Byzantium was, as never before, on the way to becoming a maritime power. Before long 200 cargo ships had been built. The number may be optimistic. But other contemporary sources testify to the resurgence of Byzantine naval strength; and the Genoese became so anxious about the competition that they tried to close the ports of the Black Sea to Byzantine as well as Venetian ships and to impose a heavy toll on all vessels plying up and down the Bosporos. Cantacuzene, however, felt confident enough in his dealings with the Genoese to request their rulers in Italy to hand back the island of Chios, which had been reoccupied by some Genoese sailors in 1346. It was agreed that the island should revert to Byzantine rule in ten years' time; the Republic of Genoa would meanwhile pay an annual rent to the Emperor and protect the rights of all his subjects on Chios.[26] At the same time Cantacuzene resumed diplomatic relationships with Venice. The Venetians had formally recognised the joint rule of the two Emperors in Constantinople. They still maintained their commercial quarter in the city, though they had been careful to take no sides in the conflict with the Genoese at Galata. They were, however, concerned as always about the activities of Genoese merchants in Byzantine waters; and in March 1349, at the Emperor's request, they had authorised the dispatch to Constantinople of arms and equipment for the new Byzantine fleet. The embassy that he sent to Venice in the same year was instructed to renegotiate the treaty between Constantinople and the Republic. It had last been renewed in 1342 and had run its seven-year course. To renew it seemed sensible to the Venetians and advantageous to the Empire. It might have been straightforward had there not been the matter of large sums of money owing to Venice from the previous government of Constantinople. There was the question of the crown jewels and the payment of accumulated interest on that account, and there had been other loans which the Empress Anna had incurred during her regency. The

[26] Greg. II, pp. 842, 877; Cantac. III, pp. 81–7.

jewels were still in Venice and no interest had been paid. There was even talk in Venetian circles about putting them on the market and pocketing the proceeds. Cantacuzene must have been annoyed to be landed with the bill for the mistakes of the Empress Anna. Her son John as co-Emperor was no less responsible. But both found themselves faced with a demand for full repayment as the price of renewing their treaty with Venice. After much discussion with Venetian ambassadors in Constantinople the treaty was renewed for another five years. The Emperors paid one-sixth of the sum stipulated. They would pay the rest in equal instalments. The document was signed and sealed with gold bulls by both Emperors on 9 September 1349. It would hardly have been tactful to ask the Empress Anna to sign it as well.[27]

In the summer of that year Cantacuzene extended his diplomacy still further afield. He sent Lazaros, the Patriarch of Jerusalem, on a mission to the Sultan of Egypt, Malik Nasir Hasan. Lazaros had been canonically elected as their Patriarch by the Christians in Jerusalem, but he had been evicted by a rival. He had taken refuge in Constantinople where, after the outbreak of the civil war, he was suspected of Cantacuzenism and fled to Didymoteichon and Adrianople. There he performed the first coronation of Cantacuzene in 1346. Lazaros was assuredly a Cantacuzenist and he was willing to act as the Emperor's agent in Egypt and the Holy Land. He did his job well. The Sultan reinstated him in his See as Patriarch of Jerusalem. Better still, the Sultan wrote a letter to Cantacuzene, fulsome in its praise of his talents and titles and its congratulations on his accession. It was dated 30 October 1349 and written in demotic Greek. Cantacuzene was so proud of it that he reproduced its full text in his memoirs. The Sultan addressed him as Emperor of the Hellenes, the Bulgars, the Asans, the Alans, the Vlachs and the Russians, and as the pillar of the Christian faith. In particular he granted his request that the Orthodox churches in Jerusalem should be freely open to their faithful and that pilgrims, including the Emperor himself, should be given the protection of the local Emir on their visits

---

[27] Nicol, *Byzantium and Venice*, pp. 268–71.

there at Easter. It was as if Cantacuzene had been appointed as
Christian protector of the Holy Land. His friend Lazaros the
Patriarch and all the Christians of Jerusalem, apart from the
heretical Jacobites, had cause to be grateful to him.[28]

His dealings with the Christians of the Latin west were not
quite so successful. He gives a long account of his correspondence with Pope Clement VI.[29] It began in the autumn
of 1347 when he sent three ambassadors to Avignon. One was
a Latin knight who was known to the Pope. Another was
the priest Bartholomew of Rome whom he had met at
Didymoteichon. They took with them a letter sealed with a
golden bull explaining why Cantacuzene had found it necessary
to employ Turkish soldiers in the civil war that had brought him
to the throne in Constantinople with John V. They were
surprised to find that the Pope was well briefed on the circumstances. An Italian lady-in-waiting of the Empress Anna had
given him her version of events. Cantacuzene and his advisers
knew that Clement VI was hoping to reconstitute a league of
western Christian powers against the Turks. Its purpose was to
protect the interests, the trade and the commerce of western
Christians on the coast of Asia Minor and in the islands such as
Lesbos and Chios. One of its main targets was Cantacuzene's
friend and ally Umur of Aydin and the city and harbour of
Smyrna from which he operated. It is therefore hard to explain
why the Emperor offered the Pope and his league his whole-
hearted support in the war against the 'barbarians' which he
knew was being planned against the Turks. He offered not only
to assist the passage of their armies over to Asia but also to lend
them substantial help with his own troops. 'For he would yield
to no one in his zeal to make the barbarians suffer the equal of
the sufferings that they had inflicted on the Christians for so
long.'[30]

Clement VI may or may not have seen through this hypocrisy.

[28] Cantac. III, pp. 90–9. Nicol, *Byzantine Family*, pp. 70–1.
[29] Cantacuzene's own account of his dealings with Clement VI is in Cantac. III,
pp. 53–62. See also: J. Gay, *Le Pape Clément VI et les affaires d'Orient (1342–1352)*,
pp. 94–118; R.-J. Loenertz, 'Ambassadeurs grecs auprès du Pape Clément VI (1348)',
OCP, 19 (1953), 178–96 (= Loenertz, *BFG*, I, pp. 285–302); Nicol, *Byzantine Family*,
pp. 66–7.
[30] Cantac. III, p. 54.

But it was soon put to the test. Cantacuzene's envoys with his letter reached the Pope early in March 1348. In April he appealed to Umur for support against the Serbians. In May Umur was killed defending Smyrna against the forces of the Pope's league. Cantacuzene makes no mention of the loss of his close friend and 'barbarian' ally. Only from Gregoras do we learn of the grief which he suffered on the death of Umur, one whose friendship he had cherished all his life.[31] The language of diplomacy must often trade in hypocrisy and falsehood. But there were matters which he held to be even more true and dear than his relationship with Umur; and on these Cantacuzene spoke with sincerity. The Pope had answered him graciously and sent him two legates, a Franciscan and a Dominican. He had suggested that they might have discussions in Constantinople on the union of the eastern and western churches. This was a matter on which Cantacuzene knew his mind. He did not have to veil his true thoughts in the mists of rhetoric. He felt with a passionate sense of the history of his own Orthodox church that the only way to achieve a true union of the Christian communities was through the medium of a truly oecumenical council.

The text of the letter that he sent to Pope Clement VI in 1350 is known only from his memoirs. But its words and sentiments testify to its authenticity. So great and wonderful an event as the healing of the schism between the churches, he said, could not come about easily or in a haphazard manner, but only after much serious inquiry and earnest endeavour to arrive at a correct definition of the faith. This was the prime cause of the separation. For if those who had first introduced the doctrine now held by the Roman church had put the matter forward for discussion with the leaders of the other churches, then the evil would not have grown so great, nor would the members of Christ have been so torn apart. Only common debate could lead to common consent. For these reasons he would never let himself be persuaded, nor would he bully others, into accepting or condoning alterations in the faith unless an oecumenical council has assembled and revealed the universal truth. 'I myself', he went on,

[31] Greg. ɪɪ, p. 835.

am ready to subscribe to whatever is agreed about the faith by the common judgement of the bishops, but without that I shall offer myself to no kind of innovation. And I believe that all the bishops and other contributors to the doctrine of the church would be eager for this; but not if they are dragooned into it by an imperial ordinance, for at that they will stop up their ears and no one will break the silence. I do not suppose that I would really inspire you with much confidence for the future if I were to accept your doctrine easily and uncritically; for the man who readily abandons the faith in which he was reared instead of safeguarding it cannot truly be faithful to more recent doctrines. It is therefore my opinion that with your approval an oecumenical council should be summoned about matters of such great moment at which the eastern and western bishops must be present. When this happens, God will not suffer us to deviate from the truth. If Asia and Europe were still, as once they were, subject to the Roman Empire, then the council might be held on our territory. But this is now impossible, for the Pope cannot come here and I cannot for so long desert my Empire, beset as it is by enemies and barbarians. However, if the Pope agrees, we could meet halfway, at some point on the coast, to which he could bring the western clergy and I the Patriarchs and their bishops. I believe that God would then guide us to the truth.[32]

Nothing came of these fine words. The Popes could never understand why the Orthodox Byzantine Christians insisted so strongly on the necessity of holding an oecumenical council to define or even discuss matters of faith which had long since been defined by the supreme authority of the See of Rome. Clement VI died in 1352. Cantacuzene politely sent congratulations to his successor Innocent VI on his election. But no more was said about a council.

As Emperor of the Romans, Cantacuzene was on surer ground when dealing with his fellow Orthodox Christians in the church of Russia. In September 1347 he wrote to Symeon, Grand Prince of Moscow, reminding him that the Empire of the Romans, together with the most holy great church of God, the Patriarchate of Constantinople, constituted the source of all piety and holiness. He exploited this evident historical truth to undo some of the muddle which the Patriarch John Kalekas

---

[32] Cantac. III, pp. 59–60. The 'alteration' to the faith of which Cantacuzene complained was of course the addition of the *Filioque* clause to the Roman Creed.

had made of the affairs in the Russian church. He had the backing of his new Patriarch Isidore; and in August 1347 he issued an imperial chrysobull confirming all the arrangements that they had made. It says much for Cantacuzene's diplomatic talents that he could exert pressure on the secular and ecclesiastical authorities in Russia. The appointment of a unified Bishopric of Kiev was in no small part his achievement.[33]

A greater achievement, however, for the future of the Empire was his decision to build upon the Byzantine province in Greece. The north of the peninsula had been occupied by the Serbians in 1348. The Catalans still held possession of Athens and Thebes; while the northern Peloponnese or the Morea remained in the hands of the French Princes of Achaia. To the south of that Principality, however, the country was still a Byzantine province governed by officials sent out from Constantinople. It was an unruly province and its links with the government in the capital were tenuous. By land it was cut off from Catalans and Serbs; by sea Turkish pirate ships made the voyage to and from Constantinople hazardous. At the start of the civil war in 1341 Cantacuzene had hoped to capitalise on the offer of some of the Latin lords of the Morea to come to an arrangement with him. By 1347 that chance had been lost. But he had not abandoned his hope that one day the Empire might again stretch in an unbroken line from Greece to Constantinople. The Peloponnese was in his blood. It was there that his father had died as governor. In 1349, as soon as the trouble with Genoa seemed to be over, he appointed his second son Manuel to take over its administration. Manuel Cantacuzene was only twenty-three years old. But his father had already placed much confidence in his ability. He had made him governor of Berroia in Macedonia when he was still in his teens. In 1348 Manuel had found himself entrusted with the defence of Constantinople against the Genoese. By then his father had dignified him with the rank and title of Despot. It was an honour more recognisable than that bestowed on his older brother Matthew at the

[33] The documents are published in F. Miklosich and J. Müller, *Acta et Diplomata Graeca Medii Aevi*, I (Vienna, 1860) (= *MM*), pp. 261–71. F. Dölger, *Regesten der Kaiserurkunden des oströmischen Reiches* (= *DR*), v (Munich and Berlin, 1965), nos. 2925–9. D. Obolensky, *The Byzantine Commonwealth* (London, 1971), p. 265; J. Meyendorff, *Byzantium and the Rise of Russia* (Cambridge, 1981), pp. 155, 160.

same time, for everyone knew that the Byzantine *cursus honorum* placed a Despot second in rank only to an Emperor. Matthew's honour, for all that his father had intended, was less clearly defined. It was as Despot, as the Emperor's deputy, that Manuel was sent to govern the Peloponnese or the Morea with his capital at Mistra. He arrived there on 25 October 1349.[34]

Manuel's tenure as Despot in the Morea was long and successful. The original terms of his appointment, however, are nowhere very clearly expressed. When Cantacuzene appointed his cousin John Angelos as governor of the province of Thessaly in 1342 he had defined the terms and tenure of his appointment by a chrysobull. John Angelos had been made governor for life. No such document exists in the case of Manuel. The province prospered so much under his rule, however, that it came to be assumed that he too had been appointed for life; and it came to be known as the Despotate of the Morea in recognition of the title of its governor. He held office at Mistra until his death in 1380. Cantacuzene adopted this method of administering the remaining fragments of his Empire by design more than by accident. By parcelling them out as more or less autonomous appanages to members of his own family or relatives he hoped that they would be controlled and unified under the senior Emperor in Constantinople. His eldest son Matthew had his portion in Thrace. Manuel held the Morea. His son-in-law Nikephoros, also with the title of Despot, was set to govern the Thracian cities on the Hellespont with his headquarters at the port of Ainos. His other son-in-law John Palaiologos was his own co-Emperor. Even the Turkish Emir Orhan of Bithynia could be thought to fit into this convenient jig-saw of family government; for he too was Cantacuzene's son-in-law. It was a system that much diminished the status and the supreme autocratic authority of the Emperor of the Romans. The old Emperor Andronikos II had been horrified when his western wife suggested that her sons might be accommodated by partitioning the Empire among them as appanages. He had protested that this would turn the monarchy into a

---

[34] Cantac. III, pp. 85–90; Schreiner, *Chron. brev.*, II, pp. 275–6. On Manuel Cantacuzene: Nicol, *Byzantine Family of Kantakouzenos*, no. 25, pp. 122–8; Zakythinos, *Le Despotat grec de Morée*, I, pp. 94–113.

polyarchy.[35] But John Cantacuzene was sensible enough to see that those days were over and that not even a senior Emperor could gather all the reins of power into his own hands. Government through a family network was a workable compromise when the Empire was so much a thing of shreds and patches, at least so long as the members of the family held together.

The Patriarch Isidore after his election in May 1347 had consecrated a number of new bishops in the church. Among them was Cantacuzene's friend Gregory Palamas, who was appointed as Metropolitan of Thessalonica. The city remained under the control of the Zealot party. Their revolutionary fervour and their tyranny had somewhat abated, but they still claimed to owe their primary allegiance to the house of Palaiologos. They refused to accept as their bishop a man whom they knew to be a Cantacuzenist. They barred their doors to Gregory Palamas. Cantacuzene, without much conviction, wrote to their leaders commanding them to receive their canonically elected bishop. He also tried to win them over by conferring on them a number of personal and public privileges. They were not impressed. They burnt his document in the middle of the city. These were the events that turned the scale in Cantacuzene's favour in Thessalonica. They led to a long-awaited rift between the leaders of the Zealots. The moment came for the second city of the Empire, which had led a detached existence for eight years, to be restored to the fold. The rift in the city had reduced the leadership of the Zealots to one man. He was Alexios Metochites. As a son of Theodore Metochites, that pillar of the old establishment of the *ancien régime*, it may seem strange that he should have associated himself with any revolutionary movement such as the Zealots. The truth is that his allegiance to the house of Palaiologos and hence to the Emperor John V was real and not fictitious. Above all, he was fearful that Stephen Dušan of Serbia was about to close in on Thessalonica. It was already all but surrounded by Serbian armies; and some of the diehard revolutionaries in the city were in touch with Dušan. Metochites and the more 'patriotic' of the people therefore wrote to Cantacuzene urging him to come to their help without delay. He wrote back telling

---

[35] Nicol, *Last Centuries of Byzantium*, pp. 151–2.

them to hold on; help was on its way. He could not bear, as he put it, to think of the Empire of the Romans being deprived of the sight of one of its eyes. He must lose no time, for it was already September and it would be well to seize the opportunity before the Macedonian winter came on. He sent messengers to his son-in-law Orhan, who at once provided a company of 20,000 horsemen under the command of his son Suleiman. He met them when they reached the Hellespont. Matthew Cantacuzene was instructed to join them in Thrace and to lead them on to Thessalonica, while his father sailed along the coast taking with him his co-Emperor John V, whose arrival might help to pacify the Palaiologan party in the city. The plan was nearly wrecked when the Turks were suddenly ordered by Orhan to hurry back to Bithynia. Suleiman and his cavalry withdrew. Matthew, deprived of their support and harassed by Serbian ambushes, was forced to turn back. His father, possibly unaware of these misfortunes, continued his voyage along the Thracian coast. Good luck was with him. He had anchored his ships for a night off Amphipolis. It was at the time occupied by a Serbian commander whom Cantacuzene had known in earlier days. Once more he played the card of past friendship. He sailed over on a raft by night and persuaded his Serbian acquaintance to change sides. The next morning he came across twenty-two Turkish pirate ships at the mouth of the Strymon river. He invited their captains to join him. They were happy to do so; and together they sailed on to reach Thessalonica.[36]

Such is the substance of Cantacuzene's own account of this adventure. He cannot have had many soldiers with him. But it seems that he met little opposition. The citizens of Thessalonica were busy fighting each other. It came to a stop when the two Emperors appeared at their gates. They were received with acclamation. The Zealot revolution had run its course and most of the people were only thankful that they had been rescued from what had seemed to be certain conquest by the Serbs. Cantacuzene had been wise to bring with him his junior Emperor John Palaiologos, whose title as Emperor so many of the citizens of Thessalonica claimed to acknowledge.

[36] Cantac. III, pp. 104–5, 108–18.

He called an assembly of them to explain his own position and to paint the Zealots in their true colours, not as loyalist patriots but as destructive revolutionaries, plunderers of the rich and traitors ready to sell their city to the Serbs. He ordered that their surviving ringleaders be rounded up and sent to Constantinople or chased out of the city. The Serbian troops who were encamped around its walls were driven away. The second eye of the Empire of the Romans had been saved.[37]

The official verdict on the barbarous regime of the Zealots in Thessalonica was reinforced soon afterwards when Gregory Palamas was at last received into his city as its bishop. Three days after his entry he preached a sermon in the church of St Demetrios. With indignation he condemned the savagery of the wicked Zealots and their leaders, who had made Thessalonica like a city under enemy occupation, wrecking its houses and slaughtering its inhabitants without pity or mercy. But with Christian forbearance he called, as his Emperor had called in Constantinople, not for revenge or recrimination but for peace, forgiveness and tolerance.[38] His tolerance did not, however, extend towards the Serbians. They had tried to win Thessalonica by force or by intrigue. They had failed. Their moment of truth had now come. Cantacuzene spent the next few months dislodging the garrisons of troops which Dušan had placed in various towns in the neighbourhood. A few of their commanders surrendered of their own accord. In his memoirs this campaign reads like a triumphal progress resulting in the Byzantine recovery of most of Macedonia. In fact it was accomplished while Dušan was otherwise occupied in war against Hungary at the other end of his extensive Serbian Empire. As soon as he heard of Cantacuzene's activities he hurried south. The two men arranged to meet near Thessalonica, each accompanied by armed guards. It might have been a historic meeting, and Cantacuzene describes it as if it were. But in fact it was an occasion for mutual accusations of bad faith and it achieved nothing of lasting memory or consequence.

---

[37] Greg. II, pp. 876–7; Schreiner, *Chron. brev.*, II, pp. 277–8.
[38] Gregory Palamas, *Homilies*, in *MPG*, CLI, cols. 12–13. Meyendorff, *Introduction*, pp. 138–9.

Cantacuzene records or invents the speeches delivered by each party. Dušan accused him of base ingratitude in biting the hand that had fed him in his hour of need. Cantacuzene apologised for giving such an impression but reminded Dušan of the original terms of the treaty between them and the many occasions on which he had broken them. If he would now restore to the Empire the provinces of Epiros and Thessaly and numerous towns in Macedonia which he had taken in defiance of that treaty then they could rewrite it and remain friends. Dušan then asked that they could continue their discussion without witnesses. Their guards withdrew. He then confessed that he had been partly in the wrong and proposed certain compromises. These were quite unacceptable to Cantacuzene, who threatened to terminate the meeting and go back to Thessalonica to prepare for war. It would be 'a war of liberation of the Greek cities enslaved by the Serbs'. It is hard to believe that this threat frightened Dušan into submission and to the signing of a new treaty. It is even harder to believe Cantacuzene's story that the great Serbian Emperor was so anxious about his future that he could no longer sleep at night. His main anxiety, if he felt any at all, was that Cantacuzene might turn his 'barbarian' Turkish allies on him.[39]

The treaty was patched up in December 1350. It is said to have been celebrated by a dinner party at which the young John Palaiologos was present. The dinner party as well as the treaty may well be no more than a fabrication. For as soon as Cantacuzene left for Thessalonica, Dušan resumed hostilities in Macedonia, capturing the city of Edessa. If there was no real treaty, there was at least a stalemate; and Cantacuzene was saved by the onset of another severe Macedonian winter which caused Dušan to return to the comfort of Skopje. Cantacuzene felt that, having safely mastered Thessalonica, he could go back to Constantinople. He had been absent for nearly three months. He sailed away in January 1351. He left the junior Emperor John V behind him, to fly the flag in the second city of the Empire.[40] This was a dangerous move that might lead to trouble. The Zealots had traded on their loyalty to the

---

[39] Cantac. III, pp. 118–36, 137–60. On the treaty of December 1350: *DR*, v, no. 2967.
[40] Cantac. III, pp. 161–2.

Palaiologos family in Thessalonica. On the other hand it was consistent with the policy of farming out portions of the Empire among members of the imperial family. Thessalonica was to be regarded as an appanage ruled by the son-in-law of the senior Emperor, an element in the structure of government by the imperial family. Cantacuzene failed to foresee that Stephen Dušan of Serbia, who was far from satisfied with a patched-up treaty, would work on the young Emperor's friends in Thessalonica and try to stir up another round of civil war in Byzantium.

Cantacuzene returned to Constantinople to find that the church was in turmoil. The Patriarch Isidore who had crowned him as Emperor had just died. His successor was Kallistos, another hesychast monk from Mount Athos, a friend of Palamas and of the Emperor. The dissension among the clergy was now less coloured by political considerations. The matter over which they bickered was theological. It had become so divisive a matter that Emperor and Patriarch agreed that it must be settled once for all at another council of bishops. The division between them was the same as it had been in 1341 and 1347. The opposing camps took their stand on the acceptance or rejection of the theology of Gregory Palamas and the hesychasts; for some had refused to bow to the rulings on the subject by the two previous councils. Barlaam of Calabria and his acolyte Gregory Akindynos were both dead. But their ghosts stalked the church and many still believed that they had been nearer the truths of Orthodoxy than the Palamite innovators and heretics. Prominently vociferous among the dissidents was Nikephoros Gregoras whose disaffection on theological grounds was a source of grief to his friend John Cantacuzene.[41]

The members of the council convened on 28 May 1351 in the Blachernai palace. Cantacuzene as Emperor presided. No one could now dispute his right to do so. His junior Emperor was in Thessalonica. The debates went on at different sessions for four days. Their concern was not to cover new ground but to

---

[41] It is at this point that the rational historian in Gregoras gives way to the ranting theologian. He describes the new Patriarch, the Palamite Kallistos, as a man 'with a natural aptitude for persecution, this being his substitute for scholarship and education'. Greg. II, p. 873.

examine and reaffirm the decisions already made at the councils of 1341 and 1347, at which the doctrines of Palamas and the hesychasts had been approved as Orthodox. In case it might appear that the verdict had been predetermined, Cantacuzene made sure that the anti-Palamites there present, among them Gregoras, should be given time and freedom to voice their views. Gregoras made the most of it. The matter affected him deeply. He devotes most of the 200 pages of the second volume of his *History* to his own part in the defence of what he believed to be the received and immutable truths of his Orthodox faith. Gregory Palamas, who was at the council, was very patient with him, as was the Emperor, who had talked to him beforehand as a friend and tried to calm him down. For all the Emperor's efforts to ensure fair play and impartiality, the result of the council's debates was almost a foregone conclusion. At the final session, on 9 June 1351, the decree (*Tomos*) of the council of 1341 was read out and, after a last appeal to the anti-Palamites, that of the council of 1347. In July 1351 another council was assembled; and there the Emperor pronounced the final verdict; Palamas was declared to be fully Orthodox in his beliefs and his doctrine fully in keeping with the teachings and traditions of the Fathers of the church. Finally, on 15 August 1351, the feast of the Dormition of the Virgin, Cantacuzene solemnly presented the council's decree, now signed by himself and the Patriarch Kallistos, in the sanctuary of the cathedral of St Sophia. It was recited three times; and it became and remains binding truth for the whole Orthodox church. In this sense it was perhaps the most monumental of all the achievements of John Cantacuzene. It exists in what is probably a contemporary copy in the monastery of St John on Patmos; and its influence on the Orthodox world in Greece, Serbia, Bulgaria and Russia has been immense. Gregory Palamas, who had inspired it, was to be canonised as a saint by his church in 1368. Gregoras would have been appalled. But he had died, still protesting, seven years earlier.[42]

---

[42] Cantac. III, pp. 166–72; Greg. II, pp. 869–1031. Meyendorff, *Introduction*, pp. 141–51, 406.

6

EMPEROR OF THE ROMANS
(1351–1354)

O N 6 August 1350 Venice had declared war on Genoa. A Venetian delegation had gone to visit Cantacuzene while he was in Thessalonica. They hoped that he would join in the war as their ally against the Genoese who had given him so much trouble. He was very reluctant to be drawn into a conflict which was almost bound to be fought in Byzantine waters and might be prolonged as well as expensive. He politely told the Venetians that he would rather not be involved.[1] But it was hard to remain neutral when the cause of the war was control of the trade route through the Bosporos to the Black Sea which the Genoese, still firmly entrenched in Galata, were trying to monopolise. The war was indeed to be prolonged. It went on for five years, from 1350 to 1355; and for all their wish to stay out of it, the Byzantines could not avoid becoming its victims. It was especially galling for the Emperor at a time when he was labouring to build up the size and strength of his own fleet, with some success. In January 1351 he received complaints from John Alexander of Bulgaria about the damage done to his territory by Turkish soldiers. Cantacuzene apologised without admitting any responsibility. But he cleverly hinted that it would help matters if the Bulgarians would contribute towards the cost of building ships to patrol the passage of the Hellespont, thus deterring the Turks from crossing over to Thrace whenever they felt like it. John Alexander thought this was a good idea, but there is no sign that he acted on it.[2]

As Cantacuzene had feared, the conflict between Venice and

---

[1] Cantac. III, pp. 118, 185–200, 209–37; Greg. III, pp. 46–51, 77–92, 106–7. Nicol, *Byzantium and Venice*, pp. 271–6.

[2] Cantac. III, pp. 162–5.

Genoa soon came to his own doorstep. In March 1351 a flotilla of
Venetian warships sailed into the Golden Horn and attacked
Galata in full view of Constantinople. The ambassador whom
they had brought with them had been briefed to twist the
Emperor's arm and make him join their side. He refused to be
bullied. He quickly changed his mind when the Genoese in
Galata responded by catapulting rocks over the sea walls of
Constantinople in broad daylight. He was thus forced into
taking sides, into making an alliance with Venice which he did
not want. Its text was enshrined in a chrysobull signed and
sealed by Cantacuzene as Emperor.[3] It was a treaty of war, not
of commerce; and it committed the Emperor to providing ships,
men and money for up to four years for the sole purpose of
annihilating the Genoese. Their merchants in Galata were
given eight days to pack their bags and go. This and other great
plans outlined in the treaty hardly materialised. The men of
Galata refused to budge, although blockaded by the Byzantine
army from the land and by the Venetians from the sea. In
October 1351 a large Genoese fleet from Italy sailed to the
relief of Galata. The news of its impending arrival caused
Cantacuzene's Venetian allies to withdraw. He was left to face
a war which he had neither planned nor desired. To make
matters worse, the Genoese ships on their way stormed and
pillaged the Thracian port of Herakleia. Before they reached
Constantinople, the Emperor ordered all his own ships to be
withdrawn to the harbour, that repairs be made to the defences
and that all the inhabitants be brought inside the walls. There
was little that the Genoese fleet could do. But the final
reckoning was yet to come.

A more substantial fleet from Venice, joined by ships
supplied by King Peter of Aragon, was on its way from Italy. Not
until early in 1352 did it reach Constantinople. Its commander
Nicolò Pisani joined forces with Cantacuzene's ships and men
according to the terms of their treaty; and on 13 February the
Genoese sailed out from Galata to do battle. The fighting went
on until nightfall. The casualties were many. But the issue was
not decided. Cantacuzene was later to claim that it was a victory

---

[3] Cantac. III, pp. 190–1. Of the treaty of May 1351 only the Latin text survives: *DR*, v,
no. 2795.

1 John VI Cantacuzene as Emperor and monk

2 John VI Cantacuzene presiding over a synod of bishops

3 The Emperor Manuel II Palaiologos

4 Alexios Apokaukos as Grand Duke

5   The Emperors Andronikos III, John VI Cantacuzene and John V Palaiologos

6 Stephen Dušan of Serbia and his wife Helena

7 The Transfiguration

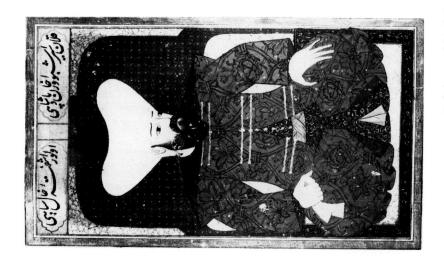

8 Orhan and his father Osman, Emirs of Bithynia

for his own people, or that it would have been so but for the craven cowardice of the Venetian admiral. For Nicolò Pisani refused to listen to the Emperor and led his remaining ships away. Cantacuzene was thus left to fight alone or to make what terms he could with the Genoese. He had no option. On 6 May 1352 he signed a treaty with them. It was not in his favour. He was made to pay for the error that had been forced upon him by siding with the Venetians. He had to agree that the men of Galata could extend and fortify their settlement as they wished. Nor could he object to the continuing Genoese occupation of the island of Chios. The battle in the Bosporos, however, was, as he knew, only a marginal incident in the larger war between the two Italian republics. The rest of the battles were to be fought in the waters of the western Mediterranean, far from Constantinople. For that he was grateful. What must have distressed him in particular was the fact that the Genoese had sought and obtained the help of his son-in-law Orhan of Bithynia. They promised him money as well as a place of honour in the roll of benefactors to the Genoese people. Orhan had his own grievances against Venice; and in spite of his father-in-law's protests, he sent infantry and cavalry over to support the defence of Galata.[4]

It was in the summer of 1351, when he had been forced into signing his fateful treaty with Venice, that reports began to reach the Emperor that all was not well in Thessalonica. That which he had failed to foresee was being plotted. John Palaiologos, whom he had left there as Emperor, was a susceptible youth of nineteen. He was easy prey to those who wished to manipulate him. Some of his friends took to convincing him that he had been pushed into exile by the senior Emperor and that he was being excluded from his patrimony in Constantinople. He should stand up for his rights and if necessary fight for them. The ruler of Serbia would gladly support him. They persuaded him to dismiss his uncle Andronikos Asen who had been deputed to keep an eye on him

---

[4] Cantac. III, pp. 193–200, 228–9; Greg. III, pp. 84–90, 99–100; Schreiner, *Chron. brev.*, II, pp. 279–80. M. Balard, 'A propos de la bataille du Bosphore. L'expédition génoise de Paganino Doria à Constantinople (1351–1352)', *Travaux et Mémoires*, 4 (1970), 431–69. The terms of the treaty of May 1352 are outlined in *DR*, V, no. 2991.

in Thessalonica. It was from Andronikos that Cantacuzene got the first substantial report of what seemed to amount to the opening of another chapter of civil war. He learnt that John had been in touch with Stephen Dušan, who had enthusiastically agreed to lend him every assistance towards what he called the restoration of the young Emperor to his rightful throne. He even proposed that John should repudiate his Cantacuzene wife Helena, send her as a hostage to Serbia and take another wife generously provided from Dušan's own family. It was impossible for Cantacuzene to leave Constantinople at the time, beset as he was by the machinations of the Genoese and the Venetians. But something must be done. He prevailed upon John's mother, the Dowager Empress Anna, to go to Thessalonica to scold and reason with her son. She told Cantacuzene that she had always been against leaving the poor boy alone in Thessalonica at the mercy of unscrupulous plotters. But she rose to the occasion and sailed off to see him. She found that the rumours were true. Preparations for war were in hand. Dušan and his wife were encamped near Thessalonica. She was cross with her son and with those who had led him astray. She went straight to Dušan's camp and talked to his wife and persuaded both of them to go away. It was no mean diplomatic achievement. Some months later, no doubt under his mother's influence, John asked the senior Emperor if he could leave the conspiratorial atmosphere of Thessalonica and make himself Emperor in a principality in Thrace, rather nearer to Constantinople. Cantacuzene was surprised that he should want to exchange an Empire for a principality. But he granted him an appanage to call his own. It was centred on Didymoteichon, which was the capital of the portion of Empire that had been allotted to Matthew Cantacuzene. Matthew was transferred to Adrianople.[5]

This may have appeared to be a convenient arrangement. But it was almost bound to lead to trouble and friction between Matthew and John. Matthew had been a patient and obedient son; but he was beginning to feel that his father had gone too far in his favouritism towards his son-in-law. He had his own partisans ready to support him in his grievance. The rivalry

[5] Cantac. III, pp. 200–8; Greg. III, pp. 147–50.

between the two men might well become uncontainable when they were asked to live as such near neighbours in Thrace. Trouble was not long in coming. The Empress Anna, who had played her diplomatic role in re-arranging the pieces of the imperial pattern, took her son's place in Thessalonica. She never returned to Constantinople. Thessalonica was recognised as being the portion of Empire that belonged to her; and there she stayed as Empress in her own right until her death some fourteen years later. This too may have seemed to be a convenient arrangement in 1351; and no doubt Cantacuzene was glad to have her out of the way. But it proved to be more than a mere convenience. Anna's management of the second city of the Empire was more forceful and more successful than that of her son John. Her reign there was later to be remembered as an era of peace after the social and political upheavals which had afflicted Thessalonica in the years before.[6]

John Palaiologos spent some time with his father-in-law in Constantinople in the early months of 1352 before going to take over his new principality in Thrace. There were now signs that Cantacuzene had lost his grip on the political situation which he had helped to create. It may be that his unwanted and expensive involvement in the conflict between the Venetians and the Genoese had unnerved him. He began to look back with longing, or so he says, to the time many years before when he had seriously contemplated abandoning the pomp and glory as well as the troubles of his life. He would retreat to the peace and quiet of a monastery on Mount Athos, whose monks, 'like Atlas, carry the burden of the world on their shoulders through their prayers'. He had picked on the monastery of Vatopedi and paid its monks to build him a place to live. His own account is that he was dissuaded from his purpose only by the entreaties of the Emperor Andronikos III and of his wife the Empress Anna. Both thought that it would be selfish of him as well as unfriendly. So he abandoned the idea, after promising the monks of Vatopedi that one day he would come to join them on Athos. This was most likely in 1340 when he and Andronikos III were in Thessalonica.[7] It may have been then that he first

---

[6] On Anna as Empress in Thessalonica: Nicol, *The Byzantine Lady*, pp. 91–5.
[7] Cantac. III, pp. 175–7.

met the saintly hermit Sabas who had settled, after many
wanderings, in the monastery of Vatopedi. Sabas was much
admired by Cantacuzene, who later wanted to make him
Patriarch of Constantinople.[8] Ten years afterwards, when he
was again in Thessalonica in 1350, Cantacuzene returned to
Mount Athos, taking the young John Palaiologos with him on
pilgrimage. The story of their visit is not to be found in his
memoirs. It is recorded only in the *Life* of an eccentric anchorite
called Maximos Kapsokalyvis, so-called from his propensity
for burning down his hermitage (*kalyve*) and moving on. His
fame was widespread; and it was to seek his blessing that
Cantacuzene went out of his way on the Holy Mountain. The
holy man imparted words of wisdom to his imperial visitors,
counselling them to shun injustice and greed, to forgive those
who offended them, to comfort the poor, and to care for the
needs of their monks, for the monks are as the soldiers and
friends of Christ, the ruler of all. Maximos was endowed with
prophetic gifts. He foretold that Cantacuzene would one day
become abbot of a monastery and that John Palaiologos would
have a long and stormy reign as Emperor. When they had gone
he sent after Cantacuzene a parcel containing some dry bread,
some garlic and an onion, symbolising the daily fare of a monk.
This was his sign that his prophecy would be fulfilled and that
the Emperor was destined to become a monk.[9]

The cares of the world were to be with him for a while longer
before he realised this dream; and they came upon him thick
and fast after 1352. He became more and more deeply immersed
in a sea of troubles, some of which he had undoubtedly brought
on himself. He seemed unable to appreciate that his treatment
of his eldest son Matthew was a source of bitterness and
violence. Matthew was not alone in feeling that his father had
forced him into a secondary if not a subordinate position to the
young John Palaiologos; and that he had done this merely
so that posterity could never accuse him of obstructing

---

[8] Philotheos, *Life of Sabas*, ed. Tsamis, pp. 307–13.
[9] *Lives of Maximos* by Niphon and Theophanes, ed. F. Halkin, 'Deux vies de S. Maxime
le Kausokalybe, ermite au Mont Athos (XIVᵉ siècle)', *Analecta Bollandiana*, 54 (1936),
38–112, especially 46–8, 21–2; Kallistos Ware, 'St Maximos of Kapsokalyvia and
fourteenth-century Athonite hesychasm', *ΚΑΘΗΓΗΤΡΙΑ. Essays Presented to Joan
Hussey for her 80th Birthday* (Camberley, 1988), pp. 409–30, especially 420.

John's legitimate right to inherit the throne. In a panegyric of Matthew written in 1353 Nicholas Kabasilas praises his filial piety, obedience and patience and recalls how easily he might have been vexed by a father who seemed to hold his enemies in higher esteem than his own son.[10] The moment came when Matthew's patience broke. He had established himself in Adrianople in the autumn of 1351. John Palaiologos took over Didymoteichon soon afterwards. The senior Emperor seems to have been so obsessed with the Genoese affairs in Constantinople that he had not properly considered the danger of stationing the two men in such close geographical proximity. When he began to see trouble brewing he summoned Matthew to come and see him in Constantinople. Matthew claimed that he was too busy. Once again the Empress Eirene, Matthew's mother, was invited to act as a mediator. In the spring of 1352 she travelled to Didymoteichon with a small delegation, including two bishops to add moral force to her persuasions. Her mission was to reconcile the two men to the arrangements that her husband had made. She met them both, though separately. John was amenable in principle, but he would not commit himself by signing any document of agreement with Matthew. Eirene and her bishops went back to Constantinople with little accomplished. As soon as she had gone John attacked Adrianople. Civil war broke out in earnest.[11]

Many of the people of Adrianople were put in mind of their glorious revolution of 1341. They gladly opened their gates to John Palaiologos. Matthew and his men were driven to the citadel in the upper part of the city, where they were besieged and subjected to abuse as the representatives of Cantacuzenism. Matthew's father, to whom he sent urgent messages for help, at once led an army to his relief. Among his troops were some Turks supplied by Orhan but also some Aragonese or Catalan mercenaries who had survived the fiasco of the Venetian war against the Genoese. When they had fought their way through to Adrianople the Catalans excelled themselves in burning and

---

[10] Nicholas Kabasilas, ed. M. Jugie, 'Nicolas Cabasilas, Panégyriques inédits de Mathieu Cantacuzène et d'Anne Paléologine', *Izvestija Russkago Archeologičeskago Instituta v Konstantinopole*, 15 (1911), 112–21, especially 115. Nicol, *Byzantine Family*, pp. 111–12.

[11] Cantac. III, pp. 238–41; Greg. III, pp. 150–71.

destruction. Thrace again became a battlefield. Some sort of
order was restored in Matthew's principality by allowing the
Turks to terrorise the nearby towns. But John too had foreign
friends who were keen to stir the pot of another civil war and
take their profits. The Serbians eagerly answered his call.
Stephen Dušan sent him a troop of cavalry. John Alexander of
Bulgaria also obliged him; and in October he went down to the
coast to meet a deputation from the Venetians at the port of
Ainos. They tendered him a loan of 20,000 ducats in exchange
for possession of the island of Tenedos offshore, which they
could use in their war against the Genoese. The Serbs, the
Bulgars and the Venetians all saw John Palaiologos either as
the next Emperor or simply as a pawn in their own games of
power politics or commercial profit.

Cantacuzene may have heard the call of Mount Athos
growing louder in his mind. Faced with such opposition from
his son-in-law John Palaiologos he had, in his own words, no
alternative but to call again on the help of his other son-in-law,
Orhan of Bithynia. A huge Turkish cavalry force arrived in
Thrace. They were commanded by Orhan's son Suleiman. On
their march up the Marica river to Adrianople they happened to
encounter the Serbian and Bulgarian allies of John Palaiologos
and inflicted on them a crushing defeat. They went on to
plunder Bulgarian territory to the north of Adrianople before
going back to Asia Minor. But they put the fear of God into
the young Emperor and his allies. In the midst of the melée the
Patriarch Kallistos thought that he might be able to put a more
Christian fear of God into the combatants before matters went
any further. In October 1352 he went to talk to Cantacuzene
in Adrianople in an effort to avert further bloodshed.
Cantacuzene sent him down to Didymoteichon to reason with
John Palaiologos. John was no longer open to reason. The
Patriarch's mission failed and he went back to Constantinople.
Cantacuzene made one more effort to bring John to heel. When
that too failed, he declared open war. At the end of the year
John was forced to come to terms.[12]

His father-in-law, the senior Emperor, interviewed him and
lectured him as if he were a naughty and ungrateful child. He

12 Cantac. III, pp. 242–52; Greg. III, pp. 178–82; Kydones, *Letters*, I, no. 64, pp. 96–8.

emphasised that a lasting peace could be achieved only if the causes of war and rebellion were removed. Without clearly explaining what he thought those causes might be, he at first proposed that John should keep control of the appanage allotted to him in Thrace, including the city of Didymoteichon. The condition was that his supporters, on whom he laid most of the blame, must change their rebellious mood and pay homage to the senior Emperor. John accepted these terms; but his friends were not ready to forsake his cause. They were now fired by the single-minded ambition of placing their hero John Palaiologos on the throne in Constantinople. Cantacuzenism was dead. It was time for the house of Palaiologos to assert its right to the Empire of the Romans. Cantacuzene read the danger signs. At the end of the year he turned the screw on the rebels by forcing John to leave Didymoteichon and sail over from Ainos to the island of Tenedos, there to take up residence with his wife and family. The island was legitimately a part of his principality. It is ironical, however, that he had so recently contracted to sell it to the Venetians.[13]

This was a desperate measure and by no means a solution to the problem. Matthew Cantacuzene was no doubt pleased. John's friends, however, were infuriated. In March 1353, while Cantacuzene was still in Adrianople, they encouraged their champion to play mouse while the cat was away. On Palm Sunday he sailed up the Hellespont from Tenedos and tried to burst his way into Constantinople. He had only one warship and a few rowing boats. He hoped that his supporters in the city would rally to his call. But the Empress Eirene was too quick for him. She set her closest relatives and trusted guards to man the gates and walls; and she ordered her soldiers to keep the people quiet. John was thwarted. He cruised around the walls and spent the night near Galata before sailing back to Tenedos at dawn. His sailors hurled abuse at the city as they left. Yet again Eirene had saved the day for her husband's cause.[14] He arrived back in Constantinople ten days later. He found a state of confusion and uncertainty. He knew, and he admits, that the

---

[13] Cantac. III, pp. 252–4; Greg. III, pp. 182–3 (who states that John V was sent to the island of Lemnos rather than Tenedos); Schreiner, *Chron. brev.*, II, pp. 281–2.
[14] Cantac. III, pp. 255–6; Greg. III, pp. 187–8.

people in the capital as in many other cities were well disposed
to the Emperor John. Eirene had done well to get her soldiers to
see that they did not rebel. The upper classes, however, were
bewildered. Three days after his return Cantacuzene invited
them all to the palace to hear their views. They complained, not
without reason, that they were mystified by the turn of events.
They wanted reassurance and guidance. Were they now to
regard John Palaiologos as their Emperor and heir to the throne
or as their enemy? If the latter was the case then Matthew
Cantacuzene should be proclaimed as co-Emperor in his place
without delay. Cantacuzene reminded them of the solemn
agreement that he had made with John's mother the Empress
Anna and with John himself in 1347. The prevailing confusion
was not of his making, although he appreciated their bewilder-
ment. Above all, he counselled them not to act rashly but to give
the matter time and thought.[15]

As so often in his life, he found himself in a dilemma and
unable or unwilling to make a firm and rapid decision. He went
to seek the advice of the Patriarch Kallistos. The Patriarch
promised to think about it. He would report to the palace within
three days. Seven days later he shut himself in a monastery
and let it be known that he would not come to the palace nor
go back to his Patriarchate if there was to be any question of
proclaiming Matthew as Emperor in place of John. He would
discuss the matter no further.[16] It was this bold statement
that cleared the air. The senators, the aristocracy and the
officers of the army approached Cantacuzene and with one
voice urged him now to nominate Matthew as Emperor and heir
presumptive. He was comforted, as he had frequently been
comforted before, by the thought that his mind was being made
up for him. He addressed them at considerable length. Yet
again he delivered his own version of events, recapitulating his
attempts to abide by the terms of his agreement with the
Empress Anna and dwelling on the provocation he had suffered
from her son, not least in his latest attempt to push his way into
the city. Having laboured to make it clear that his hand was
being forced, he yielded to the unanimous voice of the senate
and the army. He was careful not to call on the voice of the

---

[15] Cantac. III, pp. 255–69.   [16] Cantac. III, pp. 259–60.

people, for he knew that their hopes and loyalties lay elsewhere. A few days later, Matthew, who had been summoned from Adrianople, was proclaimed as Emperor in a ceremony in the palace. He was invested with all the imperial trappings and a hat adorned with precious stones and jewels was set on his head. It was declared that henceforth his name was to be recited in the acclamations of Emperors at court and in the churches. The name of John Palaiologos was to be omitted. But the names of his mother the Empress Anna and of his son Andronikos, Cantacuzene's grandchild, would continue to be remembered.[17]

Matthew, at last solaced with a proper imperial title and proclaimed as lawful heir to his father's throne, went back to Adrianople. The date of his coronation had yet to be fixed, for everything must be done according to the book. A coronation required a Patriarch qualified and willing to perform it. Kallistos, who had withdrawn to his monastery, would have no part in it. He seems to have convinced himself that it would be unconstitutional. There were, however, other reasons for his displeasure, for Cantacuzene had committed the sin, unpardonable in the eyes of many churchmen, of sequestering treasures from monasteries and churches to help him pay his troops, including his Turkish allies.[18] Emperors in the past had learnt that laying their hands on church property was bound to lead to trouble; and although Kallistos was theologically impeccable as a Palamite and a friend of the Emperor who had helped to appoint him, he felt that John Palaiologos had been crowned as Emperor in Constantinople in 1341 and that Matthew had no right to supersede him.

Cantacuzene called together all the bishops whom he could find for consultation. A few of them went to see Kallistos. He was adamant. His response was to pronounce anathema on the man who had caused this problem. He would not go against his conscience; but he would be content to see them find themselves another Patriarch. Since he had volunteered to resign, a successor could legally be appointed. This too must be done by the book; and Cantacuzene was ready to remind the bishops of

---

[17] Cantac. III, pp. 261–9; Greg. III, p. 188; Schreiner, *Chron. brev.*, II, pp. 282–3 (where for 'Krönung' read 'Proklamation').

[18] Greg. III, pp. 179–80.

the rules. Assembled in synod, they must call on the Holy Spirit and pray to God to reveal to them His chosen leader of the church. They should then nominate three candidates from whom the Emperor would select one. 'Human frailty being what it was, however, there was sometimes a tendency in these cases to select a candidate in advance and then to call on the Holy Spirit to ratify a choice that had already been made.' This was wrong procedure, although it had been adopted in the past, in error and in sin, by Cantacuzene himself and by many of his predecessors. For this he could only beg God's mercy and forgiveness and grant the bishops their traditional freedom of choice to proceed to the nomination of three candidates for the office of Patriarch. Of the names put forward to him, the Emperor selected Philotheos Kokkinos, the Bishop of Herakleia in Thrace; and he was at once enthroned with all the customary rites and ceremonial in September 1353. Kallistos stayed for a while in his monastery before going by way of Galata to join John Palaiologos on Tenedos.[19] In February 1354 Philotheos as Patriarch performed the coronation of Matthew Cantacuzene in the church of the Virgin at Blachernai. Matthew then placed the crown of Empress on the head of his wife, according to custom. She was Eirene Palaiologina, a grand-daughter of Andronikos II, whom he had married in 1341. She was the fourth among the ladies of the court to bear the title of Empress. Anna of Savoy reigned as such in her own right in Thessalonica. Cantacuzene's wife and Empress Eirene reigned with her husband in Constantinople. The status of their daughter Helena, whose husband John had now been struck off the register, is not clearly stated; though her father had insisted that the name of her young son Andronikos, then six years old, should be commemorated as an heir to the throne.[20]

Matthew's coronation as Emperor in name and title ended the elaborate façade which his father had tried to present for so long. It was now to be accepted as a fact that the dynasty of Cantacuzene had superseded that of Palaiologos. Whether this

[19] Cantac. III, pp. 269–75. A. Failler, 'La déposition du patriarche Calliste I (1353)', *REB*, 31 (1973), 5–163; P. Charanis, 'Imperial coronation in Byzantium: some new evidence', *Byzantina*, 8 (1979), 39–46.
[20] Cantac. III, p. 276; Greg. III, p. 204.

would be welcomed or even recognised by the Byzantine people remained to be seen. The sins of the fathers continued to be visited upon their children. The first official document on which Matthew was required to put his signature as Emperor was the decree of the church council of 1351 which had pronounced Gregory Palamas and his hesychasts to be Orthodox. This may seem an odd perversion of priorities. But to the Patriarch Philotheos who had crowned him and who was himself a fervent Palamite, it was a necessary testimony to the new Emperor's right belief. Even John Palaiologos, who had not been present at the council in 1351, had to sign its decree at a later date.[21] Every newly acclaimed Emperor was required to make a *confessio fidei* to his bishops. Yet all the protestations and declarations of Christian Orthodoxy made by all the Emperors were not, it seemed, enough in the sight of God to purge the Empire of its sins. On 2 March 1354, a few weeks after Matthew's coronation, the coastline of Thrace was shaken by a terrible earthquake. Its epicentre was the city of Gallipoli (Kallioupolis). Cantacuzene vividly describes its effects. It struck at night. Some places simply disappeared into the ground. Houses and city walls collapsed. Survivors of the wreckage, fearful of being left without shelter or protection, fled with their belongings to take refuge in the towns that had been spared. Many, especially the women and children, died of exposure, for the night brought torrents of rain and blizzards. Many more were captured by Turkish soldiers who descended on the ruins at the break of day. Gallipoli was almost completely destroyed. Some of its inhabitants got away safely in their boats; a few were rescued by a ship that was on its way to the Peloponnese. It was a catastrophe on a vast scale exceeding all the man-made disasters which had devastated Thrace. The Byzantines might well have attributed it to the wrath of God. The earthquake had struck on the Feast of Orthodoxy. Gregoras could well have cited it as another indication of divine displeasure at the 'blasphemous' doctrine of Palamas. But it was not the Lord that people blamed. It was the Turks and so, by implication, the Emperor John Cantacuzene.[22]

---

[21] Meyendorff, *Introduction*, pp. 148–51.
[22] Cantac. III, pp. 277–8; Greg. III, pp. 220–3; Schreiner, *Chron brev.*, II, pp. 283–4.

One distinguished victim of the disaster was Gregory Palamas himself, a fact which gave Gregoras some wicked satisfaction. He was not killed but he was taken prisoner by the Turks. He had been sailing from Thessalonica to Constantinople when the earthquake happened. His ship had put in to shore at Gallipoli and he and his fellow passengers were captured by the Turks who were already moving into the ruins of the city. Gregoras writes of the captivity of Palamas with unconcealed glee. He was carried off to Bithynia and it was over a year before he was ransomed and set free. It was perhaps not in his nature to blame the Turks. He had lost only his liberty. Others had lost their all, their families and their property; and they were less tolerant of the 'barbarians' who traded on their misfortune. What God abandoned the Turks defended.[23] The dust had barely settled on the ruins of Gallipoli when Suleiman, the son of Orhan, Cantacuzene's friend and relative, crossed the Hellespont with crowds of soldiers and squatters to take their pickings of what was left. Just before the earthquake Cantacuzene had been in touch with Suleiman and his father. Somewhat late in the day the Emperor had realised that the Turkish troops whom he and his opponents had invited to Thrace had come to stay. John Palaiologos had employed them in his war against Matthew in 1352. Thousands more had been brought over to relieve the siege of Adrianople in the same year. Suleiman was their commander. He did not share his father's special relationship with Cantacuzene and saw no reason why he should. Gentleman's agreements about the division of spoils and territory seemed to him irrelevant and inapplicable between Muslims and Christians. In the course of his campaigns in Thrace in 1352 Suleiman had captured a fortress called Tzympe near Gallipoli. When the fighting was over he refused to evacuate it. He claimed that it was his by right of conquest. Cantacuzene sent to Orhan to protest and offered to compensate Suleiman if he would surrender Tzympe and take his soldiers home. The negotiations were still in progress when the earthquake shattered Gallipoli and the

---

[23] Greg. III, pp. 226–36. Meyendorff, *Introduction*, pp. 157–64; Anna Philippides-Braat, 'La captivité de Palamas chez les Turcs. Dossier et Commentaire', *Travaux et Mémoires*, VII (1979), 109–22.

neighbouring district. To the Osmanli leaders, at least to Suleiman, it seemed like divine intervention. There could now be no question of surrendering any of the towns in Thrace that had come their way. They had come, as Suleiman explained, if not by conquest then simply as piles of ruins deserted by their inhabitants. They had come in fact by the will of Allah.[24]

Orhan was not so sure that his son was in the right. He proposed that all three parties should meet somewhere near Nikomedia to discuss the problem. The meeting never took place, however. Orhan, claiming to be unwell, failed to appear at the appointed time. The meeting was postponed *sine die*. It is not surprising that Cantacuzene began to think again about retiring from public affairs and opting for the peace and quiet of the monastic life. Perhaps it would have been a good moment to act on that thought. He seemed to have lost his self-confidence. The aristocracy were divided in their minds about the new arrangements which he had made for the constitution and the succession to the throne. The people had lost all trust in him after his appeasement of the Turks. As Gregoras says, they believed that he had trampled on the faith of their fathers and given them over as slaves to the impious infidel.[25]

The Patriarch Philotheos offered to go to Tenedos and to act as a mediator with John Palaiologos. It was too late. John was nursing his grievances and plotting his own coup. He had been back to Thessalonica to seek his mother's comfort and counsel. We are not told what she said. In the summer of 1354 Cantacuzene announced that he would go to Tenedos in person to settle his differences with his son-in-law. Rather unwisely he took with him his son Matthew. This fact, it was later alleged, made John determined to ignore them. Cantacuzene claimed that his voyage to Tenedos was a mission of peace not of war. He would not invade the island. His ships anchored for the night at an uninhabited island nearby. He confesses that some of his own officers treacherously sent messages to John Palaiologos. He alleges that John's soldiers prevented them from drawing water for their ships on the other side of the island. The fact remains that there was no meeting and no discussion. Cantacuzene sailed back to Constantinople leaving his son Matthew at Ainos

[24] Cantac. III, pp. 278–9.   [25] Cantac. III, pp. 279–81; Greg. III, p. 242.

on the Thracian coast to make his way up to Adrianople.
Gregoras has a different interpretation of this supposed
mission of peace. His story is that Cantacuzene intended to
arrest John and his men and that he was driven away by the
garrison. He suffered the same setback at the island of Imbros.
It may be as well that the mission failed; for if he had contrived
to meet John he would have been unable to resist inserting into
his memoirs another long speech in justification of his actions.[26]

The play was drawing to its close. There was but one last
dramatic scene to be enacted. It is a celebrated scene which has
had many versions and interpretations in many languages from
the fourteenth to the sixteenth centuries. It is best, though not
necessarily most reliably told by Cantacuzene, who was one
of the two leading dramatis personae. On a stormy night on
29 November 1354 John Palaiologos surprised everyone, as he
had done before, by slipping across from Tenedos and up the
Hellespont to Constantinople. He had only one or two armed
ships and a few smaller boats. A much later account has it that
he was assisted by a Genoese adventurer who became the hero
of the hour.[27] This may or may not be true. In the dark they
crept into the harbour of the Heptaskalon on the southern side
of the city, eluded the guards and found their way in. The word
was quickly passed around that the Emperor John Palaiologos
was back. At dawn the people were eager to join him; but
they feared that they would become involved in fighting.
Fighting was the last thing in the mind of the Emperor John
Cantacuzene when he heard the news. He held a hurried
consultation with the Empress Eirene and his first minister
Demetrios Kydones. To his wife he confessed that he was in a
quandary, between the devil of resistance and the deep sea of
submission. Eirene must have heard this cry before in their long
years of marriage. The more militant of his advisers and officers
urged him to take immediate action. His Catalan mercenaries
in particular were longing for a fight. To satisfy them he

---

[26] Cantac. III, pp. 256, 276, 282–3; Greg. III, pp. 236–7.
[27] The Genoese adventurer was called Francesco Gattilusio, who later married a sister
of John V and was made lord of Lesbos. His part in the exploit is told only by Doukas,
Istoria, ed. Grecu, pp. 67–71. See D. M. Nicol, 'The Abdication of John VI
Cantacuzene', *Polychordia: Festschrift Franz Dölger zum 75. Geburtstag* (= *Byzantinische
Forschungen*, 2 (1967)), 269–83.

sent for reinforcements to his son Matthew, his son-in-law Nikephoros and others. He also appealed to some of the Turkish leaders in Thrace. All this, however, was by his own account mere bluff; for he had already made his plans to give in and to abdicate. John Palaiologos took heart at the apparent lack of resistance. The people, no longer deterred by fear of fighting in the streets, took to destroying the houses of known Cantacuzenists, seized control of the arsenal at the harbour and armed themselves for battle. John, much encouraged advanced on the palace at Blachernai and encamped by the house of Porphyrogenitus, exactly as Cantacuzene had done in 1347. On the next day, 30 November, the city mob enthusiastically joined in attacking the fortified area of the palace. The Emperor's Catalan guards drove them back with several casualties and set fire to some of the buildings in front of the palace. At the height of the confusion the Patriarch Philotheos, afraid of the frenzy of the mob, fled into hiding in a secret recess of St Sophia.[28]

On 1 December, the third day after his entry into the city, John Palaiologos sent to the palace a negotiator who was acceptable to both parties. Cantacuzene risked the displeasure of his civil and military advisers and gratefully agreed to a settlement. The agreement, to which both men swore solemn oaths, provided that they should reign together as joint Emperors, the junior giving precedence to the senior. It was the mixture as before; and it was no more promising as a constitutional settlement than it had been in 1347. It was not likely that Matthew Cantacuzene, the third Emperor in the equation, would be happy to accept it, though it was agreed that he should retain his appanage at Adrianople with the title of Emperor for the rest of his life; and John vowed never to go to war with him again. Finally, Cantacuzene promised to hand over the fortress at the Golden Gate which he had renovated and refortified. It was almost impregnable and garrisoned by another unit of his Catalan guards. The settlement left much to be desired. But at least it prevented more bloodshed. Cantacuzene sent messages to his relatives and friends to say that their help was no longer

---

[28] Cantac. III, pp. 284–91; Greg. III, pp. 241–3; Schreiner, *Chron. brev.*, II, pp. 284–5. E. Frances, 'Narodnie dviženija osenju 1354 g. v Konstantinopole i otrečenie Joanna Kantakuzina', *Vizantijskij Vremennik*, 25 (1964), 142–7.

required. Some of the Turks in Thrace, however, had antici-
pated their summons and were waiting outside the walls. They
could only be convinced that they were not needed when
Cantacuzene showed himself to them from the ramparts by
the light of lamps. The thought of missing a unique chance
of plundering the great city of Constantinople must have
disappointed them. The question of how to deal with the Turks
in Thrace was indeed the first main item on the agenda of the
revived joint government of the two Emperors. On 5 December
the first, and as it turned out the last and only meeting of
that government was held in the house of the late Theodore
Metochites, still one of the most sumptuous and palatial
buildings in the city. There the Emperors together presided
over a gathering of the senators and the great and the good of
Constantinople. The people were not invited. The matter for
debate was the occupation of Gallipoli and parts of Thrace by
the 'barbarians'. Was it a matter for war or for diplomacy?[29]

The only record of this debate is that in the memoirs of
John Cantacuzene in which, as might be expected, his own
contribution takes pride of place. The speech that he made,
however, is interesting because it is in part, and perhaps
unconsciously, an indictment of his own government of the
Empire for close on seven years. He was strongly against
going to war against the Turks in Thrace or anywhere else.
'Intelligent men', he said,

do not go to war without first weighing the strength of their own forces
against those of their enemy. Good luck is never enough. These
barbarians have great experience, great numbers and great enthusiasm. They can draw on their resources in Asia Minor as well as in
Europe. Our resources are by comparison minimal. Our army, once so
brilliant and celebrated, is now poor and small; our public revenues
are reduced to poverty and insignificance. Our own stupidity and
thoughtlessness, our own selfishness and failure to put our individual
interests second to the common good have brought us to this pass. It
is not cowardice that makes me advise you against going to war
against the Turks. No one hates them more than I, not only because
of their religion but also because of all the wrongs that they have done
us over so many years. On the other hand, I do not suggest that we

[29] Cantac. III, pp. 291–5.

should passively submit to their wickedness. But we cannot do it on our own. What we need is money and the help of some foreign army equivalent in strength to theirs, since our own forces in their present condition, though brave, are not equally matched. We also need a fleet to control the sea and prevent them from getting help from elsewhere. For if they master the waves we shall be up against not only Orhan and his men in Thrace but all the barbarian hordes in Asia who will come to fight for him. For their arch-heretic Mahomet offered the prize of immortality to all who die in battle against us and kill as many Christians as they can. Therefore instead of going to war I propose that we should send ambassadors to them to make peace and persuade them to hand back the places which they have stolen in Thrace; for this can still be achieved. Once we have expelled them beyond our frontiers then we can contemplate going to war with them, provided that we have a fleet. We can also then consider forcing the Bulgarians and the Serbians to restore the lands of ours which they have appropriated.[30]

Such was the substance of Cantacuzene's speech. It was, as he says, somewhat enigmatically expressed; for he was still withholding the secret of his own intentions. Most of his audience kept quiet. Only the younger and more impetuous of them reproached him for his lack of spirit and accused him of evading the issue because his own daughter was married to a barbarian. They were all for war. John Palaiologos remained pensive and expressed no opinion. Cantacuzene therefore dismissed the meeting. There seemed no point in trying any further to swing the vote in his favour. His secret, which he had not revealed to them, was that he was on the point of leaving them to their own devices by abdicating his throne and responsibilities. Not long afterwards he had the satisfaction of knowing that the young and impetuous trouble-makers got their way. They incited war against the Turks and it brought them nothing but disaster.

Three days later, on 8 December, he went to the Golden Gate to hand over its fortress to John Palaiologos as he had promised. They went together, but he left John in a church along the way. The garrison of Catalan soldiers in the fortress welcomed him and offered him their services. They were under the impression

---

[30] Cantac. III, pp. 295–300.

that he had come to order them to join the fighting. They were looking forward to it. They said that they had supplies enough to hold out for three years. They were crestfallen when their Emperor explained that there would be no fighting and that he had come only to hand over their fortress to the man whom they had thought to be his rival and enemy. Their commander was particularly upset. He was a man called Juan Peralta and he had served Cantacuzene with unswerving loyalty throughout the civil war. He protested that he and his men could easily clear the city of any number of enemies. Cantacuzene was furious at their obstinacy. He bullied them into obeying his orders by threatening to write to their own king in Spain denouncing them as mutineers so that they would for ever be dishonoured. He harangued them in a Latin tongue in which he claims to have been proficient. The threat of these denunciations and of the loss of their honour changed their minds. They handed over the keys of their castle. On the next day John Palaiologos took it over, dismissed the Catalans and installed a garrison of his own.[31]

Barely a week had passed since John had entered Constantinople. The two Emperors lived apart, Cantacuzene and his wife in the palace, John in a separate private residence called Aetos. This seemed to be a rather unsociable arrangement, since they had sworn to be joint Emperors; and the people, who were expecting great things of John Palaiologos, thought it outrageous. They were in rebellious mood. Some of them staged a noisy disturbance outside the Aetos while the two Emperors were breakfasting together. Cantacuzene consulted his wife and they invited the young Emperor and his suite to move into the palace. He now had nothing further to lose. He had made up his mind that he must abdicate. It was on 9 December that he first formally announced his intention to John, a secret which he claims to have kept from all the world until that moment. The next day, in a simple ceremony at the palace, he discarded all his imperial insignia and put on the habit of a simple monk. The whole world now knew his well-kept secret. He adopted the monastic name of Joasaph;

---

[31] Cantac. III, pp. 300–4. On Juan Peralta, an engineer as well as a soldier, see *PLP*, IX, no. 22404.

and henceforth the Emperor of the Romans, John Angelos Palaiologos Cantacuzene, was to be known as the Emperor-monk Joasaph. The prophecy of Maximos the Hut-burner had been fulfilled. We are not told who tonsured him and invested him with the 'angelic habit'. Nor are we told whether his son Matthew, who still held the title of Emperor, had been privy to his father's secret. Matthew had for long been the odd man out in his father's arrangements. But the Empress Eirene certainly knew the secret, for her husband had discussed it with her four years before. Eirene did what a dutiful wife was expected to do in such cases. On 11 December she too left the palace, became a nun and retired behind the walls of the fashionable convent of Kyra Martha in Constantinople taking the monastic name of Eugenia. It was in that convent that her mother-in-law Theodora Cantacuzene lay buried.[32]

It is perhaps as well not to know what passed between husband and wife before they went their separate holy ways in December 1354. Eirene may have talked to him about the succession of their son Matthew which seemed to have been left undefined. She may have considered whether she would ever again see their daughter Theodora, lost in a harem in Turkey. It is most improbable, however, that she chastised him for his feebleness and lack of spirit by saying: 'If I had guarded Didymoteichon as you have guarded Constantinople, we would have said our farewells twelve years ago.'[33] She was far too obedient and supportive a wife to utter such a rebuke to her husband. Perhaps, as he suggests, she too had a longing for a life of holy peace and quiet. They were not young lovers torn apart by cruel fate. He was about sixty. They had been married for more than thirty years. They had produced three daughters and three sons. It may be that she was quietly relieved to see him go, for he must have been difficult to live with and tiresome to listen to.

---

[32] Cantac. III, pp. 106, 304–7. The chronology of these events has been established by A. Failler, 'Note sur la chronologie du règne de Jean Cantacuzène', *REB*, 29 (1971), 293–302, and Failler, 'Nouvelle note', *REB*, 34 (1976), 119–24; Nicol, 'The abdication of John VI', 270–4.

[33] Parisot, *Cantacuzène*, p. 298; Nicol, *The Byzantine Lady*, pp. 79–81.

7

MONK, HISTORIAN AND THEOLOGIAN
(1354–1383)

THE new age which Demetrios Kydones had hailed when John Cantacuzene entered Constantinople in 1347 had dawned, shone briefly, flickered and then died. Its creator had, as he put it, 'despaired of the Romans ever being able to think or to act intelligently or in their own best interests'.[1] It was Edward Gibbon's opinion that the Emperor John VI had been forced to abdicate his throne by his son-in-law John Palaiologos. 'He asserts in his history (does he hope for belief?) that, in free obedience to the voice of religion and philosophy, he descended from the throne and embraced with pleasure the monastic habit. So soon as he ceased to be a prince, his successor was not unwilling that he should be a saint.'[2] George Finlay pretends that John Palaiologos 'gave him to understand that his life could only be preserved by an immediate abdication and by taking the monastic vows'.[3] Both historians are in good company, for Nikephoros Gregoras also implies that Cantacuzene's abdication was forced upon him. Gregoras, however, was almost as prejudiced against his former friend as Gibbon and Finlay; and his prejudices, being stoked by religious bigotry, were if anything less rational than either.[4]

There is no reason other than prejudice to doubt Cantacuzene's own words on the subject. It is probably true that John Palaiologos was astonished when he was first let into the

---

[1] Cantac. III, p. 308.
[2] Gibbon, *Decline and Fall of the Roman Empire*, ed. Bury, VI, p. 505.
[3] G. Finlay, *A History of Greece from its conquest by the Romans to the present time, B.C. 146 to A.D. 1864*, ed. H. F. Tozer, III (Oxford, 1877), p. 246.
[4] Greg. III, p. 243. On the political role of Cantacuzene in Byzantine affairs after his abdication: Lj. Maksimović, 'Politička uloga Jovana Kantakuzina posle abdikacije (1354–1383)', *ZRVI*, 9 (1966), 120–93.

secret of Cantacuzene's plans for his abdication and that he put pressure on him to stay. In the years to come he was often glad to have his father-in-law at hand as a guide, comforter and friend. His combined qualities of an experienced statesman and respected monk were to give Cantacuzene a moral authority and even a popularity greater than he had enjoyed as Emperor. In Byzantine society monks commanded a deeper respect than statesmen or politicians. The Patriarch Philotheos, who knew him well, observed that when he was Emperor his subordinates prostrated themselves before him as their lord, though for some this was merely a formality. After he had resigned and become a monk, however, everyone respected him with honest affection; and all the imperial family, all the Emperors and Empresses, became devoted to him as children to a father.[5] Philotheos knew that Cantacuzene had for long been considering retiring into the monastic life with two of his colleagues, Demetrios Kydones and Nicholas Kabasilas. Philotheos, before he became Patriarch, was to be their spiritual director; and the place of their retreat was to be either the monastery of St Mamas or that of St George of the Mangana. Both were monasteries in the city of Constantinople.[6] It was for this reason that John Palaiologos dissuaded Cantacuzene from his idea of disappearing to the distant monastic seclusion of the Holy Mountain of Athos. John needed him in the capital as an elder statesman. More immediately, he needed him to help deal with the still awkward problem of what to do with his son Matthew. Cantacuzene therefore retired as a monk not to Mount Athos but to the monastery of the Mangana which he had discreetly endowed a few years before. It was there that he began his religious life as the monk Joasaph in the winter of 1354–5.

During that winter John Palaiologos and Matthew Cantacuzene lived well apart from one another but in peace. As time went on, however, John came increasingly under pressure

---

[5] Philotheos, *Refutations (Antirretika) of Nikephoros Gregoras*, ed. B. Kaimakis, Φιλοθέου . . . Κοκκίνου, Δογματικὰ ἔργα, I (Thessaloniki, 1983), pp. 503–4. As early as September 1355 John V referred to Cantacuzene as his 'father': *DR*, v, no. 3048; Dölger, 'Johannes VI. Kantakuzenos als dynastischer Legitimist', p. 197.

[6] Cantac. III, pp. 107–8.

from his followers to put an end to the farce by declaring
Matthew to be no better than a usurper with no real right to his
imperial title. This opinion may have been upheld by the
Patriarch Kallistos who had refused to ratify Matthew's title by
crowning him, and who had now reclaimed his office in defiance
of the absent Philotheos. John and Matthew met in Thrace to
try to settle their differences. They agreed that each should
retain his title of Emperor. But since what was left of Byzantine
territory was not extensive enough to support two Emperors of
the Romans, Matthew should relinquish his appanage in
Thrace and move to the Peloponnese where he could rule over
the cities of Greece. This was a new attempt to shift the pieces
on the imperial board. It was a mistake. Manuel Cantacuzene
had been successfully administering, defending and expanding
his Despotate of the Peloponnese or the Morea for five years.
He had no wish to be posted elsewhere to suit the political
whims of John V. The plan had been that Matthew was to take
over the island of Lemnos until such time as his brother vacated
his post in Greece. But the garrison on Lemnos refused to have
a Cantacuzene at their head; and he discovered that there was
a plot to assassinate him.[7]

The last phase of the dynastic conflict between the families
of Palaiologos and Cantacuzene had now to be played out. It is
a sordid tale. Fighting began early in 1356. Matthew advanced
on Constantinople from Thrace. He was embarrassed to find
that the Serbian commanders of some of the towns in western
Thrace wanted to join in on his side. The Serbian Emperor
Stephen Dušan had died in December 1355 and his great
Empire at once disintegrated, as Cantacuzene reports, into
ten thousand fragments. Matthew's embarrassments were
multiplied when Orhan's Turkish soldiers took to fighting the
Serbians who had come to help him. The Turks had seen that
the collapse of the Serbian Empire offered them new scope for
conquest in eastern Europe. Matthew was taken prisoner by one
of the Serbian commanders, who offered him to John V on
payment of a huge ransom, with the threat that he might be
blinded. Matthew was, however, delivered unharmed to
Constantinople and shipped to custody on the island of Lesbos

---

[7] Cantac. III, pp. 309–14.

until new arrangements were made for his future.[8] Towards the end of 1357 he was released. A conference was planned between the two men. It was held at Epibatai on the Sea of Marmora, where Alexios Apokaukos had once had his castle. It was proposed that Matthew should now forfeit his imperial title and accept the status of a private citizen, though ranking above all members of the imperial family except the young Andronikos, the Emperor's son. Matthew at first objected to being so treated. He declared that he would rather remain imprisoned for life than have to renounce his title as Emperor. Matthew's father had much to answer for in creating this constitutional muddle. It was fitting therefore that he should be called in to unravel it. In December 1357, dressed not as Emperor of the Romans but in the angelic habit of a monk, he went to Epibatai to talk to his son and persuaded him to accept the terms offered to him. His mother too may well have used her influence; for she was among the witnesses at a ceremony at Epibatai at which Matthew swore allegiance to John V and disclaimed all his pretensions to the name of Emperor. It was a solemn occasion, for it was attended by the Patriarch Kallistos, who had declined to officiate at Matthew's coronation in the first place, and by the Patriarch of Jerusalem, who had performed the first coronation of Matthew's father in May 1346.[9]

The ceremony at Epibatai at the end of 1357 marked the formal conclusion of the feud between the house of Palaiologos and the house of Cantacuzene which had begun on the death of Andronikos III sixteen years before. No other member of the Cantacuzene family ever again aspired to call himself Emperor. After that ceremony the house of Palaiologos supplied all the Emperors of the Romans in unchallenged succession until the end of the Empire in 1453. Matthew continued to honour his oath of allegiance. For a few years he stayed in Constantinople without making his presence felt and on amicable terms with the Emperor John. In 1361, when there was another outbreak of the plague, he accompanied his father to the Peloponnese to join his brother Manuel at Mistra. Manuel was afraid that Matthew had come to take his place as Despot of the Morea, as

---

[8] Cantac. III, pp. 314–15, 319–40; Greg. III, pp. 503–4, 564–6.
[9] Cantac. III, pp. 345–60. Nicol, *Byzantine Family*, pp. 116–18.

had formerly been proposed. Once assured that this was not so, he settled down happily enough with his brother; and Matthew, briefly and reluctantly, succeeded to the government of the Despotate when Manuel died in 1380.

Their father, Joasaph the monk, returned to Constantinople in 1362. He was certainly there in April of the following year when envoys from the Emperor of Trebizond were in the capital. The chronicler of Trebizond mentions that they had audience of John V Palaiologos and of 'the Emperor Joasaph Cantacuzene the monk', as well as the Patriarch Kallistos, the Empresses and the Emperor's sons.[10] For the rest of his life, as a mark of deference, people continued to style him Emperor. As late as 1375, Dorotheos, then Bishop of Thessalonica, cited a document referred to him by 'our most pious Emperor and lord the Monk Joasaph Cantacuzene'.[11] The last event that he recorded in his memoirs occurred in the year 1364. It was the return to office of the Patriarch Philotheos in October of that year. Kallistos died the year before. The continuous narrative of his life and achievements comes to an abrupt end at this point. Not all biographers of famous men are fortunate enough to have such detailed if sometimes contentious and prolix autobiographies of their subjects. This makes it all the harder for a biographer when that precious source of first-hand information dries up and he is suddenly launched into an uncharted sea for the last thirty years of his subject's existence. For John-Joasaph Cantacuzene lived on as a monk, as a writer, as a theologian and a grey eminence in the political and ecclesiastical affairs of the Byzantine Empire until his death in 1383.[12]

A fruitful source of information for a biographer is the private correspondence of his subject. For Cantacuzene there is none, or none that has survived. That he wrote letters to his friends and colleagues, probably in great numbers and at great length, is evident from their replies. Many of these date from

[10] Michael Panaretos, *Chronicle of the Empire of Trebizond*, ed. O. Lampsides (Athens, 1958), p. 74.
[11] Document of Dorotheos in G. I. Theocharides, *Makedonika*, 2 (1962), 42–9. See Nicol, *Byzantine Family*, p. 90.
[12] The latest event in his memoirs: Cantac. III, p. 363. The only study of his life after his abdication is that by Lj. Maksimović in *ZRVI*, 9 (1966), 120–93.

the period while he was still Grand Domestic, between 1325 and 1347. Michael Gabras, a tedious pedant, addressed eight letters to him in those years.[13] Theodore Hyrtakenos, a depressed schoolmaster in Constantinople, whose pupils included Alexios Apokaukos, wrote two letters to him before 1328.[14] Matthew Gabalas, who became Bishop of Ephesos in 1329, wrote three letters to him before that date.[15] Nikephoros Choumnos, statesman and scholar of the court of Andronikos II, is known to have corresponded with him when he was Grand Domestic;[16] and from the pen of Nikephoros Gregoras no less than twenty-two letters to Cantacuzene survive, all of them written before the year 1345, when their friendship cooled.[17] His principal correspondent while he was Emperor was Demetrios Kydones, who wrote him eleven letters between 1347 and 1352.[18] His correspondents after his abdication were fewer in number. One of Kydones's letters written about 1372 survives; and Manuel Raoul, a scholar who lived in the Morea in the time of Manuel Cantacuzene, wrote two letters to him.[19]

Out of so much correspondence one might hope to extract much historical material. It is not so. Some of the letters reveal a few facts, notably those written by Gregoras and Kydones. But most of them are obscured in the mists of rhetoric, the besetting sin of Byzantine epistolography. A love of rhetoric for its own sake was instilled into every educated Byzantine. Letters ornamented by rhetorical artifice and all but devoid of factual content were cherished as works of art; the more abstruse the style and language the greater was the admiration and joy of the recipient. By reading between the lines of such letters and struggling to interpret some of the deliberately

---

[13] Michael Gabras, ed. G. Fatouros, *Die Briefe des Michael Gabras (ca. 1290–nach 1350)* (Wiener byzantinische Studien, XI/1–2: Vienna, 1973), nos. 351, 368, 370, 386, 403, 411, 421, 456.

[14] Theodore Hyrtakenos, *Correspondence*, ed. F. J. G. La Porte-du Theil, *Notices et extraits des manuscrits de la Bibliothèque Nationale*, 6 (1980), nos. 54, 55, pp. 17–20.

[15] Matthew Gabalas, ed. D. Reinsch, *Die Briefe des Matthaios von Ephesos im Codex Vindobonensis Theol. Gr. 174* (Berlin, 1974), nos. 50, 51, 54.

[16] Nikephoros Choumnos, *Letters*, ed. J. F. Boissonade, *Anecdota nova* (Paris, 1844), no. 129.

[17] Gregoras: see Nicol, *Byzantine Family*, p. 97 n. 156.

[18] Kydones, *Letters*, I, nos. 6–16.

[19] Kydones, *Letters*, II, no. 400; Manuel Raoul, *Letters*, ed. R.-J. Loenertz, 'Emmanuelis Raoul Epistulae XII', *EEBS*, 26 (1956), nos. 1 and 2.

obscure literary allusions, the historian can sometimes detect a
fact or two. But they are a disappointing source of information;
and since Cantacuzene's own private correspondence is lost, his
biographer has to depend for further information on isolated
official documents or on the evidence sparsely provided by
much later Byzantine historians, most of whom lost interest in
him after he ceased to be Emperor.

His first monastic retreat after his abdication was the
monastery of St George of the Mangana in Constantinople. It
was a large and wealthy foundation dating from the eleventh
century, centrally situated in the district of that name on the
eastern side of the city.[20] At some unspecified date, however, he
moved to the smaller monastery of Charsianites, also known
as the Theotokos Nea Peribleptos. Here he had a proprietary
interest, for he had endowed it while he was Emperor. It was
a comparatively recent foundation initiated by one John
Charsianites who became the monk Job. He and Cantacuzene
were friends and he was evidently known as a 'Cantacuzenist';
for his house was one of those looted and destroyed by the mob
when John Palaiologos entered Constantinople in November
1354. His monastery also suffered, losing some of the property
which Cantacuzene had given to it. Cantacuzene's patronage,
however, helped to revive its fortunes; and his decision to settle
there as a monk added very considerably to its prestige. He put
himself under the spiritual direction of Markos, the monastery's
abbot, for he was determined to abide by the rules of monastic
discipline. But he enjoyed some preferential treatment. He was
lodged in the abbot's quarters, there being no ordinary monk's
cell thought grand enough to sustain his dignity as ex-Emperor.
He rewarded the monks and their abbot by building a loggia
and balcony for them and paying for some interior decoration of
their living quarters. It is said that he recorded these
benefactions in a document written by his own hand. It may well
have been here, in the monastery of Charsianites, the Nea
Peribleptos, that he completed the four books of his memoirs.
At the very end of them he notes that he finished writing
during the second Patriarchate of Philotheos, between 1364 and

---

[20] R. Janin, *Le géographie ecclésiastique de l'Empire byzantin*, I: *Le Siège de Constantinople et le
patriarcat oecuménique*, III: *Les églises et les monastères*, 2nd edn (Paris, 1969), pp. 75–81.

1376; and the earliest known manuscript of the text bears the date December 1369. The later Patriarch Matthew I (1397–1410) had formerly been abbot of the Charsianites monastery; and it is he who, in his Testament, records what little is known about the residence there of its most distinguished monk, the former Emperor Joasaph Cantacuzene.[21]

Much earlier in his career, in his capacity as Grand Domestic and as Emperor, he had shown his interest in other monastic foundations in the Empire. It was the Christian duty of a nobleman and still more of an Emperor to protect, support and endow the monasteries. Mention has been made of his particular concern for the monastery of Vatopedi on Mount Athos, where he paid the monks to build him a place of retirement. His wish in this respect was never realised. But his special interest in that monastery is revealed in a number of his private and official documents. Some time before May 1329, when he was still Grand Domestic, he partnered his mother Theodora in making over to the monks of Vatopedi a small monastic dependency of St Demetrios situated in the city of Serres in Macedonia. Theodora and her family owned considerable property in the district.[22] In the first year of his reign as Emperor the monks of Vatopedi asked him to provide them with a hostelry in Constantinople at which they could stay when visiting the capital. He granted their request by a decree (*prostagma*) in October 1347; and two years later he gave them some more property in the city by a chrysobull dated and signed by his own hand in December 1349. He is also known to have given some manuscripts to the library of their monastery. But Vatopedi was not the only foundation on Mount Athos to benefit from his generosity. About 1350 he confirmed the privileges which his 'grandfather' (Andronikos II) and his 'brother' (Andronikos III) had granted to the monastery of Alypiou; and in July 1351 he did the same for the monastery

---

[21] H. Hunger, 'Das Testament des Patriarchen Matthaios I (1397–1410)', *BZ*, 51 (1958), 288–309; Nicol, *Byzantine Family*, pp. 94–5.

[22] Cantac. II, p. 192. In 1338 Theodora was again joined by her son in granting a small estate in that district to the monastery of Koutloumousiou. P. Lemerle, *Actes de Kutlumus* (*Archives de l'Athos*, II: Paris, 1946), no. 18. In 1332–4, as Grand Domestic of Andronikos III, he was named as a lay patron and protector of the monastery of St John Prodromos in the hills above Serres. A. Guillou, *Les Archives de Saint-Jean-Prodrome sur le Mont Ménécée* (Paris, 1955), pp. 8–11, nos. 26 and 32.

of Iviron on Mount Athos. The great monastery of Megaspelaion in the Peloponnese also received his attentions in a chrysobull dated April 1348, a time when he may have been contemplating the appointment of his son Manuel as Despot of the Morea.[23]

After he had himself become a monk such largesse was no longer expected of him nor was it within his means, although he did some service in paying for the repair and renovation of his own monastery of Charsianites in Constantinople. Retreat to a monastery did not, however, imply total withdrawal from public life. In the long span of Byzantine history many Emperors before him had ended their days as monks, not always by their own volition. Andronikos II, against whom Cantacuzene had waged war, had been obliged to resign and enter a monastery where he lived the last four years of his life. Long before him, the Emperor Romanos Lakapenos, having been violently deposed by his own sons, was exiled to an island monastery where he passed his days as a monk happily repenting of his sins. An Emperor rather more like John in character was Nikephoros II Phokas (963-9). Nikephoros was covered in glory as a soldier and yet periodically smitten with the desire to abandon the world for the higher calling of the ascetic life. He too was a friend of holy men; he too had reserved a place for himself on Mount Athos; but his habit of wearing a hair shirt and indulging in other eccentric austerities proved too much for his wife, who arranged for him to be murdered. It was thought quite acceptable for Emperors to be tonsured as monks when they felt the moment of death approaching. Andronikos III had asked to be made a monk prematurely in 1330, much to Cantacuzene's annoyance.[24] John-Joasaph, however, was unique in abdicating his throne voluntarily and then spending the remaining thirty years of his life as a monk. He was not, so

---

[23] *DR*, v, no. 2939. Nicol, *Byzantine Family*, p. 93. An eighteenth-century copy exists of what purports to be a chrysobull of John Cantacuzene in favour of the church of Monemvasia. I. P. Medvedev, 'Pozdnie kopii Vizantijskich dokumentov v sobranii Biblioteki Akademii Nauk SSSR', *Vizantijskij Vremennik*, 32 (1971), 223-31, no. 9 (227-30). It seems likely to be a forgery, though its authenticity has been defended by Haris A. Kalligas, *Byzantine Monemvasia. The Sources* (Monemvasia–Athens, 1990), pp. 243-7.

[24] See above, p. 34. R. Guilland, 'Les Empereurs de Byzance et l'attrait du monastère', in Guilland, *Etudes Byzantines* (Paris, 1959), pp. 33-51; Rosemary Morris, 'The two faces of Nikephoros Phokas', *Byzantine and Modern Greek Studies*, 12 (1988), 83-115.

far as we know, given to wearing hair shirts. Nor did he indulge himself in extravagant gestures of repentance. But he was deeply and sincerely religious in his Orthodox fashion. He did not discredit the possibility of miracles and the powers of prophecy; and he enjoyed the company of the saints who worked the miracles and made the prophecies. He named three of them whom he had known in person. One was the fanatical Patriarch Athanasios who had mesmerised the Emperor Andronikos II; another was Hilarion, the prophetic bishop of Didymoteichon.[25] He was also impressed by the holy eccentricities of such saints as Sabas of Vatopedi and Maximos Kapsokalyvis on Mount Athos. But he was not, it seems, given to astrology and superstition; and he would probably not have followed the example of Andronikos II who, in moments of crisis, would open his Bible at random to see what the future might hold.[26]

One of his closest associates in the early years of his retirement was the Patriarch Philotheos whom he had called upon to crown Matthew in 1354. Philotheos had been upstaged when his predecessor Kallistos came back to reclaim his office following the change of Emperors in that year. But when Kallistos died in 1363 he was reinstated. Philotheos was a convinced adherent and missionary of the theology of Gregory Palamas, whose life he wrote. Both as an Emperor and as a highly influential monk, Cantacuzene was the Patriarch's natural ally in the propagation of the Palamite doctrine of hesychasm which he had helped to establish as an essential element in the Orthodox faith in 1351. It has often been suggested that he embraced the cause of the hesychast monks of Athos and of Palamas mainly in order to win their moral support for his political advancement. This is manifestly a misunderstanding of the man and of the cause which he continued to defend and expound long after he had any personal political drum to beat. It was a cause that lost him the friendship of some of his oldest and dearest acquaintances and therefore must have hurt him. Nikephoros Gregoras was never going to be consoled about what he considered to be

---

[25] Cantac. II, pp. 169–71. Nicol, *Church and Society in the Last Centuries of Byzantium* (Cambridge, 1979), p. 45.
[26] Greg. I, p. 358.

Cantacuzene's lapse into a blasphemous form of theological error. Demetrios Kydones, whom he had befriended as a young man and then employed as a minister of state, retired from public affairs for a time in 1354. He was anxious to resume his studies, which had already begun to lead him down a scholarly path almost untrodden by Byzantine intellectuals of the time. In the course of his duties at court, Kydones had acquired a knowledge of Latin and learnt to speak, read and write it well. He was prompted to learn more about Latin theology, particularly about St Thomas Aquinas, and to open the eyes of his compatriots to a new field of vision by translating some of it into Greek. Cantacuzene had encouraged him in his Latin studies and read some Thomist literature himself; and when Kydones entered the service of John V, as he soon did, he remained friendly with his former employer. On the other hand, he found himself unable or unwilling to follow him into the higher flights of Palamite theology. He preferred the more logical and intelligible ground of Thomism. His brother Prochoros Kydones was a monk on Mount Athos. He too learnt Latin, though he did not follow Demetrios on the road to Rome. He admired and translated some of the works of St Augustine as well as St Thomas. But he parted company with Cantacuzene by becoming argumentatively anti-Palamite.[27]

Another of Cantacuzene's personal friends who served at his court was Nicholas Kabasilas who, though one of the leading spiritual lights of Orthodoxy and even proposed as a Patriarch, seems to have been a layman all his life. It was in company with Demetrios Kydones and Nicholas Kabasilas that Cantacuzene had once proposed retiring to the Mangana monastery under the spiritual direction of Philotheos.[28] Kabasilas was slow to be convinced of the truth of Palamite doctrine. Kydones rejected it. It is not easy to categorise those who were for and those who were against it in the fourteenth century. John Cantacuzene, however, did not have to advertise his theological position. He had done more than anyone else to bring his church to a firm decision on spiritual matters which are by their nature indefinable. His successor John Palaiologos thought it wise to

27 On Demetrios and Prochoros Kydones: *PLP*, vi, nos. 13876, 13883.
28 Cantac. iii, p. 108.

leave well alone in the church for fear of stirring up a hornet's nest of bishops. No doubt he accepted Cantacuzene's advice and judgment in these matters and was glad to be relieved of the burden; for he was not much interested in the transcendental heights of apophatic theology. He wore his religion more lightly than his father-in-law.

That the Emperor-monk Joasaph Cantacuzene pondered deeply on these matters is evident from his many writings on the teaching of his friend Palamas and the practices of the hesychasts composed during the years of his monastic life. Some of them he wrote, for reasons unknown, under the pseudonym of Christodoulos the monk. Most of them are extensive refutations of the polemical works of the anti-Palamites. One is directed against a treatise composed by the monk Prochoros Kydones, which he wrote in 1368–9. Other opponents of Palamas who incurred his reasoned invective were Isaac Argyros, a mathematician and astronomer as well as a monk, who had been a pupil of Nikephoros Gregoras; and John Kyparissiotes, a philosopher and a friend of both Gregoras and Demetrios Kydones. Under the name of Christodoulos he wrote a shorter work against the heretical teachings of Barlaam and Gregory Akindynos, the two 'arch-heretics' of his demonology. In less polemical vein he composed an essay on the light of Mount Tabor, the divine light of the Transfiguration so central to the doctrine of Palamas; and a series of scholia on the hesychasts.[29]

His principal theological interest lay in the defence and justification of a doctrine in whose universal acceptance by the Orthodox church he had played so important a part, especially in presiding over the council of 1351. But he also composed polemical works of a more traditional and general interest to Christian readers. One was a treatise against the Jews, in nine chapters.[30] Another and rather more interesting work was his Defence of Christianity against Islam, divided into four

---

[29] Nicol, *Byzantine Family*, pp. 99–100. His two treatises against Prochoros Kydones are edited by E. Voordeckers and F. Tinnefeld, *Johannis Cantacuzeni Refutationes duae Prochori Cydonii et Disputatio cum Paulo Patriarcha Latino Epistulis Septem Tradita* (Corpus Christianorum, Series Graeca, 16: Turnhout and Louvain, 1987).

[30] *Treatise* against the Jews: Ἰωάννου Στ' Καντακουζηνοῦ κατὰ Ἰουδαίων Λόγοι ἐννέα, ed. C. G. Sotiropoulos (Athens, 1983).

chapters, and four Orations against Mahomet. In this he was heavily indebted to the treatise against the Koran written in Latin much earlier in the century by the Dominican Ricoldo da Monte Croce, which Demetrios Kydones had rendered into Greek.[31] To Kydones this may have been little more than a literary exercise to improve his knowledge of Latin. For Cantacuzene, however, it must have meant rather more; for he had maintained close relationships with several Muslim leaders, especially with Umur, the Emir of Aydin, and Orhan, the Emir of Bithynia, who had married his daughter Theodora. Orhan died in 1362 and Theodora came back to Constantinople to live in the palace with her sister the Empress Helena. It is hard to believe that her father would have written such anti-Islamic tracts while his Muslim son-in-law was still alive. But his personal dealings with the Turks did not necessarily accord with his public pronouncements about their religion. Gregory Palamas, when held captive by them in Asia Minor in 1355, had occasion to discuss and dispute with Muslim theologians; and he was sometimes pleasantly surprised by the tolerance shown by the conquering Turks towards the Christian people. By the norms of Byzantine literary convention the Turks had, of course, to be designated as 'barbarians'; and by the norms of Christian usage they had to be described as 'impious' or 'atheists'. It might none the less be possible for Christians and Muslims to live as neighbours in peace and mutual tolerance. Both John Cantacuzene and Gregory Palamas seem now and then to have glimpsed this possibility.

If the controversy between Palamites and anti-Palamites in his day expressed itself as a difference between monks and scholars, theologians and humanists, Cantacuzene was on the side of the theologians. He was well versed in the grammar, rhetoric and literature of classical antiquity and in what was known in monastic circles as the 'outer learning'. He seldom pretended, however, to make ostentatious display of his classical or Hellenic erudition in his writings. He adhered to the Byzantine convention of referring to the neighbours and enemies of his Empire by their classical names. He calls the

---

[31] *Treatises* against the Muslims: in *MPG*, CLIV, cols. 371–584, 583–692. Nicol, *Church and Society*, p. 79.

Turks the 'Persians', the Bulgars the 'Mysians', the Serbs the 'Triballi'. But he does not often deliberately introduce obscure allusions to ancient authors simply to advertise his scholarship, as was the way with so many of his contemporaries. His friend Demetrios Kydones was a master of this art. Nikephoros Gregoras too was eager to display his wide reading of the Hellenic sages of the past. Cantacuzene's own literary master in style and expression was Thucydides. His language is simple and subtle. He does not strain to find recherché words and contrived phrases to express his thoughts. He may occasionally introduce references to ancient myths and heroes such as Atlas or Odysseus, Lycurgus or Solon, and also to Romans such as Scipio Africanus, Pompey or Sulla.[32] But he was not obsessed with antiquity like some of his literary friends; and he would not have shared the pessimistic view of Theodore Metochites, the master of Gregoras, that the great men of antiquity said it all to perfection and there is nothing left for us to say.[33] On the other hand, he would not have gone so far as Palamas who, after an early grounding in ancient Greek grammar and philosophy, concluded when he became a monk that such profane studies were not merely irrelevant to the spiritual life of a Christian but positively dangerous. In this he exaggerated the incompatibility of the 'inner' with the 'outer' wisdom. It could be said that Cantacuzene strove to find a balance between the two, always bearing in mind that the wisdom of the Hellenes of old could never be more than the servant and handmaid of the true wisdom of theology or the knowledge of God. He was more on the side of the angels than of the philosophers, of the theologians rather than the humanists.[34]

He never set his hand to writing commentaries on the ancient philosophers, an exercise much in vogue in the fourteenth century. Nor does he seem to have been excited by the rediscovery of ancient astronomy and mathematics, which so

[32] A. P. Kazhdan, 'L'*Histoire* de Cantacuzène en tant qu'oeuvre littéraire', *B*, 50 (1980), 279–335. It has been suggested that Cantacuzene had read Caesar and been influenced by his style. R. Guilland, *La Correspondance de Nicéphore Grégoras* (Paris, 1927), p. 309.

[33] Theodore Metochites, *Miscellanea philosophica et historica*, ed. C. G. Müller and T. Kiessling (Leipzig, 1821), pp. 14–16.

[34] Nicol, *Church and Society*, pp. 50–1.

delighted Gregoras. It was for long believed that he was the author of a Paraphrase of the Nicomachean Ethics of Aristotle. This ghost has now been laid. It would not have been to his taste to compile a learned work so redolent of the wisdom 'beyond the door'. The Paraphrase, whose author remains unknown, was merely transcribed at his expense in 1366.[35] He has further been credited with copying many manuscripts with his own hand under the name of Joasaph, among them the sumptuous collection of his theological and polemical compositions contained in a manuscript in Paris written between 1370 and 1375. This is the manuscript which contains the well-known portraits of Cantacuzene as Emperor and monk. But he did not write or illustrate it himself. It was the work of another monk and scribe with the name of Joasaph who belonged to another monastery in Constantinople.[36] He did, however, take an active interest in the translation of Thomas Aquinas by Demetrios Kydones, for the transcription of which he commissioned his own scribe, Manuel Tzykandyles. To understand the arguments of western churchmen and theologians Aquinas was required reading.[37]

Relations with the Roman church became a matter of some urgency almost as soon as Cantacuzene abdicated, for the new Emperor John V was convinced that what was left of the Byzantine Empire could only be rescued or saved with the active military and economic aid of the western Christian powers. Cantacuzene had said much the same in his speech of resignation. Constantinople could not go it alone in controlling or mastering all the barbarian hordes of Asia. But he differed profoundly from John V on the ways in which the help and co-operation of the western Christian world was to be sought and obtained. He understood that the idea of a crusade against the Saracens was dear to the minds of the Popes. He also understood that his Empire could not be invited to participate in such a venture so long as his church remained in schism from the

[35] D. M. Nicol, 'A paraphrase of the Nicomachean Ethics attributed to the Emperor John VI Cantacuzene', *BS*, 29 (1968), 1–16.

[36] L. Politis, 'Jean-Joasaph Cantacuzène fut-il copiste?', *REB*, 14 (1956), 195–9; L. Politis, 'Eine Schreiberschule im Kloster τῶν 'Οδηγῶν', *BZ*, 51 (1958), 17–36, 261–87.

[37] Meyendorff, *Introduction à l'étude de Grégoire Palamas*, p. 331; Nicol, *Byzantine Family of Kantakouzenos*, pp. 99, 100. On Manuel Tzykandyles, who did much of his work at Mistra: *PLP*, xi, no. 28129, and below, p. 155.

church of Rome. The way to the hearts and minds of the Popes was to renounce the schism and pretend that the whole of Christendom, east and west, Greek and Latin, was under the supremacy of the Bishop of Rome. In December 1355 John V sent a list of proposals to Pope Innocent VI at Avignon, outlining the benefits that would accrue to the Roman church if the Pope could see his way to sending military and naval reinforcements to Constantinople. They were extravagant proposals; and the young Emperor did not conceal the fact that the Byzantine church and people would find them unpalatable if not completely unacceptable. But he emphasised that they would be impressed and perhaps persuaded if they saw with their own eyes some material evidence of the concern of the western world for their defence and salvation.[38]

John's letter was composed with the help and advice of a western bishop who understood something of the Orthodox mentality and of the political and military realities of the time. He was Paul, whom Pope Clement VI had sent as Latin Archbishop of Smyrna after its capture from Umur of Aydin in 1345. He happened to be in Constantinople in 1355. Paul of Smyrna was acquainted with the Emperor John and also with the ex-Emperor and monk Joasaph; and it was he who presented the Emperor's letter to Pope Innocent VI in 1356.[39] The Pope was not much impressed by the wild and unrealistic proposals of a young man in Constantinople. Twelve years later the same young man, then older if not much wiser, and humiliated by his Orthodox neighbours as well as by the Turks, returned to the subject of coming to terms with the Christians of the west. The Pope was then Urban V. It was he who sent Paul of Smyrna, whom he had elevated to the position of titular Latin Patriarch of Constantinople, as his legate to the Emperor in 1367. The true Patriarch Philotheos, the friend of Cantacuzene and of the late Gregory Palamas, politely refused to talk to this emissary from the west, except in private. The Emperor was embarrassed. Some other authoritative

---

[38] Nicol, *Last Centuries of Byzantium*, pp. 258–9.
[39] On Paul of Smyrna: *PLP*, IX, no. 22143; K. M. Setton, *The Papacy and the Levant (1204–1571)*, I: *The Thirteenth and Fourteenth Centuries* (Philadelphia, 1976), pp. 216–17, 225–9, 298, 301–12, 457–9; Maksimović, 'Politička uloga', 157–70.

spokesman must be found for the Byzantine point of view in the
discussions about the union of the churches which he was
determined to hold in Constantinople. There was no better
person than his father-in-law, the Emperor and monk Joasaph
Cantacuzene. He was invited to lead the debate with Paul. They
had already had some correspondence, for Paul had asked him
for clarification on certain points of Palamite theology; and he
had addressed him not as Joasaph the monk but as 'the most
exalted and sagacious Emperor'.[40]

A detailed report survives of what was said on both sides in
the debate. It took place in the palace in June 1367.[41] It was
attended by the Emperor John V, his wife Helena Cantacuzene,
their sons Andronikos and Manuel, some civic functionaries,
Joasaph's own confessor Markos and three bishops. The
Patriarch Philotheos declined to appear. He was content to
leave the defence of the Orthodox faith in the capable hands of
his old friend, the monk Joasaph. The subject of the debate was
simply the ways and means of achieving a true and lasting
reunion of the sundered parts of the Christian church. It was a
subject on which Cantacuzene had expressed his views to Pope
Clement VI nearly twenty years earlier. Even before then, when
he was still Grand Domestic, he had held a number of amicable
discussions at Didymoteichon on theology and the union of the
churches with an Italian priest called Bartholomew of Rome.
His name was not unknown in the offices of the Curia and his
views might even command respect. They had not changed
since his dealings with Clement VI in 1350. They were those
held by the majority of the Byzantine church and people. His
opening speech to the Pope's legate may be summarised as
follows:

People are reluctant to obey God's command to keep the peace. There
are those, the infidels, the disciples of Mahomet, who hate the
Christians and want to deprive them of their spiritual as well as their
material possessions. There are those, like the Bulgars and the Serbs,

---

[40] Parisot, *Cantacuzène*, Annexe E, pp. 231–2; Meyendorff, *Introduction*, p. 412; Maksimović,
'Politička uloga', 145; and see above, n. 29.
[41] Text, introduction and analysis in J. Meyendorff, 'Projets de concile oecuménique en
1367: un dialogue inédit entre Jean Cantacuzène et le légat Paul', *DOP*, 14 (1960),
149–77 (reprinted in J. Meyendorff, *Byzantine Hesychasm: Historical, Theological and
Social Problems. Collected Studies* (London, 1974), no. XI).

who want only their material goods and sometimes their very lives by provoking war, although they are Orthodox Christians by faith. Others, while being similar in race and appearing to live in friendship, are in truth like dishonest merchants who, having deceptively acquired a precious object for next to nothing, rejoice in their theft as a triumph and provoke conflict. These are the divisions among enemies. There are on the other hand things that unite people. You Paul come from Italy. I come from Constantinople. Yet we meet together in an amicable spirit. Some are united by such bonds of friendship; some by ties of family or blood, as a father and son, a brother and his sibling. A wife is not merely the friend of her husband; they are of one flesh. But none of these relationships can be compared with the spiritual unity and love of the church. For an individual human being cannot be united in himself in spirit except through the church, which is the body of our Lord, whose head is Christ. This is why he who divides the church divides the very body of our Lord and identifies himself with the crucifier of Christ who pierced his side with a lance.

He made many protestations of his lifelong desire for the union of the churches and confessed that he would face death or trial by fire in defence of the truth. But he complained that the church of Rome had never, since the time of the schism, sought to re-establish unity on fraternal and friendly terms but only through the magisterial authority which it claimed to exercise over the eastern church.

No one is allowed to contest or contradict what the Pope has said or may say, for he is the successor of Peter and his words must be accepted as the words of Christ himself. Union is not possible on these terms . . . In an army, when generals plan to invade an enemy's territory, they do not rely entirely on their own judgment; they consult their soldiers at the frontier posts even if their own intelligence is superior to theirs; for the frontier troops are what we call 'the eyes of the army'. In like manner, I know better than you the lie of the land here. So take my advice. What we must do is convene a universal and oecumenical council here at Constantinople. All the bishops under the jurisdiction of our Oecumenical Patriarch from far and near should attend, from as far afield as Russia, Trebizond, Alania and Zecchia; and also the other Patriarchs of Alexandria, Antioch and Jerusalem, the Catholicos of Georgia, the Patriarch of Trnovo in Bulgaria and the Archbishop of Serbia. The Pope must send his legates, as Popes have done in the past in accord with ancient tradition. These are the ways in which, inspired by our love of the Holy Spirit and our sense of brotherhood, we must examine the causes of the stumbling-block between us. If we go about it in this fashion, God will not suffer his will and the truth to lie hidden from us . . . If, however, we adopt the proposal of the Roman church, I fear that we shall create a division worse than before . . . The people of Constantinople will be divided among themselves. Some will take refuge elsewhere; some will submit to your will; some will endure persecution and martyrdom for their faith, as they did in the days of my ancestor Michael [VIII] Palaiologos.[42]

Such was the tenor of Cantacuzene's address to the Pope's legate. He said nothing new, for indeed there was nothing new to say. The views that he expressed and the plan that he proposed might have come from the lips of many a Byzantine Emperor or Patriarch before him. The fact that in 1367 he was neither an Emperor nor a Patriarch but rather a much-respected monk of great political and ecclesiastical experience only added weight to his words. The legate Paul, who had earlier addressed him as Emperor, clearly thought that he still possessed a certain imperial authority. He compared Cantacuzene to a skewer of meat. If the skewer turned on the spit, all the chunks of meat turned with it. So it was with an Emperor and his people.[43] This, as Cantacuzene had to point out, was one of the common misconceptions in the western world about the relations between a Byzantine Emperor and his church. An Emperor had no authority to control the souls as well as the bodies of his people. In that sense he was not the arbiter of the people's faith. The legate Paul fell back on the argument that the only permissible faith was that judged to be true by the Pope; and the proof of this lay in the evident fact that, since they left the communion of Rome, the Byzantines had been persistently defeated and conquered by their enemies. This was an easy jibe and easy to answer. The Christians of the east had suffered their worst defeats and losses long before the schism occurred. After a further exchange of similar banalities and some tactless remarks by the legate on the infidelity of those poor Christians already living under the rule of the Turks, Cantacuzene concluded the debate by repeating

[42] Meyendorff, 'Projets', 170–4.   [43] Meyendorff, 'Projets', 174.

his call for a council of the whole church in the style and tradition of the early oecumenical councils. He warned that nothing would result from it if the Latins came to sit in judgment or to instruct and talk down to the Orthodox from magisterial heights. They must come as friends and brothers in search of truth, peace and harmony. 'If as a consequence a spirit of unity was engendered, the glory would be to God. If no reconciliation proved to be possible, then each church should continue in its own ways and beliefs for fear of making matters worse, leaving it to God to mend the schism according to his own will.'[44]

If the Greek record of this extraordinary encounter is to be believed, the papal legate was in the end convinced that a council of the church should be held at Constantinople within the next two years. The Orthodox church certainly believed that this had been agreed; and the Patriarch Philotheos at once began to send out invitations to his fellow Patriarchs and bishops. This then was the last diplomatic triumph of John Cantacuzene, the Emperor among monks. It would be pleasant to suppose that once again his eloquence had won the day. It was not so. But what marked him out as the man of God more than the calculating statesman was his insistence that union with the church of Rome, whatever material advantages it might bring, could never be achieved by compromising one jot or one tittle of the Orthodox faith. That faith, for those with ears to hear, must somehow reconcile the theology of St Thomas Aquinas with that of St Gregory Palamas, which, in fairness to Cantacuzene, he had tried to explain to the Pope's legate and committed to writing for him. The tragedy was that he had spent his time and his eloquence in vain.

Pope Urban V, like Clement VI before him, could see no point in holding a council to dispute the eternal verities of the Roman church. He paid no heed to the words of the ex-Emperor or to his own legate. No council of the church was ever mentioned in his correspondence. No council was ever called. The main outcome of the debate in Constantinople in 1367 was that it helped the Emperor John V to make up his mind. He had promised that he would go to see the Pope in person. Two years

[44] Meyendorff, 'Projets', 175–7.

later he fulfilled that promise. In October 1369 he met Urban V in Rome; and in a ceremony in St Peter's he declared his conversion to the Roman faith and submission to the Roman obedience.[45] No one pretended that this act symbolised the end of the schism. It was a purely private initiative on the Emperor's part; and it attracted little comment in the Byzantine world, except among those who approved of it and shared the Emperor's feelings. One such in particular was Cantacuzene's old friend and former supporter, Demetrios Kydones. It was he who had helped to bring it about, translated the necessary documents into Latin, and accompanied John V to Rome. Kydones had been so carried away by Latin theology that he had announced his own personal conversion to the Roman faith. His was an intellectual conversion and as such was to have a profound influence among a small circle of Byzantine scholars. His Emperor on the other hand had undergone what might be called a political conversion in the hope that his reward would be a generous military and economic rescue operation by the grateful Christians of the west. His hope was to be deceived.

There is no record of what his father-in-law, the Emperor-monk, may have said or thought about this betrayal of his own ideals. It was clearly not a path that he himself would ever follow. The Patriarch Philotheos too must have been bewildered. But so long as it remained only a matter for the Emperor's own conscience and not a policy to be forced upon his people and his bishops it was wiser to say nothing about it. Cantacuzene at least was more interested in spreading the light of Palamite theology. About 1371 he wrote from Constantinople to a bishop in Cyprus. It is one of the very few of his letters that survives, though it is more official than personal in tone and he signed it as 'John Cantacuzene, true Emperor of the Romans, and monk'. The signature is in fact more interesting and significant than the content; for it proves yet again that he felt entitled to call himself Emperor in matters which were of little concern to John V. His letter expounds to the good bishop in Cyprus the past history of the successive condemnations of the anti-Palamites, Barlaam, Akindynos and the rest; and it

---

[45] Nicol, *Last Centuries of Byzantium*, pp. 267–70.

includes his refutation of an anti-Palamite tract which seems to have been circulating in Cyprus. Its other interest lies in the statement that he had been away from Constantinople for some time on certain unspecified business.[46] There is evidence for believing that he had been staying with his sons Manuel and Matthew at Mistra. For in 1370 Demetrios Kydones wrote a letter from Venice, whither he had gone from Rome, addressed to one Constantine Asen in Mistra. He had been in the service of John V in Rome in 1369 and he was an uncle of the Despot Manuel Cantacuzene. Kydones counts him lucky to have the chance to meet at Mistra a 'learned Emperor' who will be worth listening to for his memories alone, though he may get excited on the subject of Palamism.[47] Constantine Asen is known to have been an anti-Palamite. There can be little doubt that the learned Emperor whose company he was to enjoy, however much he disliked his theology, at Mistra in 1370 was John Cantacuzene.[48] For about that time he was working on his monumental refutation of the theological errors of the monk Prochoros Kydones, who had written his own version of the nature of the light of the Transfiguration, of its essence and the 'energies' emanating from it.[49] This was the very stuff of Palamism; the attainment of *theosis* or deification through the divine light was the goal of every hesychast. One of the manuscripts of Cantacuzene's refutation of Prochoros was in fact written at Mistra in 1370 by his own scribe and secretary Manuel Tzykandyles. Prochoros's brother Demetrios Kydones had by then embraced the more rational and intelligible theology of Thomas Aquinas; and he wrote to Cantacuzene accusing him of disseminating his polemical work as far afield as Cyprus, Crete, Palestine, Egypt and Trebizond.[50] This may well be true, for the good news of hesychasm travelled far and fast by word of mouth and by example among the monks of the Orthodox world.

[46] J. Darrouzès, 'Lettre inédite de Jean Cantacuzène relative à la controverse palamite', *REB*, 17 (1959), 7–27.

[47] Kydones, *Letters*, I, no. 71, pp. 102–3.

[48] E. Voordeckers, 'Un Empereur Palamite à Mistra en 1370', *RESEE*, 9 (1971), 607–15. On Constantine Asen: *PLP*, I, no. 1503.

[49] Nicol, *Byzantine Family*, p. 99.

[50] Kydones, *Letters*, II, no. 400, pp. 355–6.

The Popes did not despair that the ex-Emperor might yet be influential in steering the Byzantine church and state towards a union of the churches on their terms. If Urban V had ever read his predecessor's correspondence with Cantacuzene he would have known that this was most unlikely. He was pleased to have secured the conversion of the Emperor. But there had been no oecumenical council; the Turks had felt free to advance deeper into eastern Europe; and John V had been forced to acknowledge that he was their vassal. In July 1374 Pope Gregory XI, Urban's successor, sent two legates to Constantinople. They went armed with recommendations to several influential persons in the east. One of them was John Cantacuzene, the monk 'of the Order of St Basil'. A few months later Gregory addressed a personal appeal to Cantacuzene. He also wrote to his son Manuel at Mistra.[51] Both of these distinguished men might be able to further the cause of the union of the churches and, as a result, stimulate common action against the Turks. The Popes always insisted that the union of Christendom must be achieved before common action could be taken. They should have learnt that in the view of Byzantines like John Cantacuzene the order of priorities was reversed. The Popes, however, were not alone in believing that the Emperor-monk Joasaph could still exercise some political power in the land. In March 1376 the government of Venice sent a special commission to Constantinople to demand a renewal of their trade agreement with the Byzantine Empire. John V had been slow to see to the matter. The Venetian commissioners therefore were instructed to approach the former Emperor John Cantacuzene if all else failed. It is not known whether they did so. But they were well aware that the Emperor John V was in deep trouble.[52]

In 1373 his son Andronikos had rebelled against him. A feud between father and son of the ruling family of Byzantium was an event to be exploited by the Italians as well as the Turks. It developed into another chapter in the perennial conflict between Venice and Genoa. The Genoese took the side of Andronikos, the Venetians that of his father. In 1376 the

---

[51] Nicol, *Byzantine Family*, pp. 90, 127.   [52] Nicol *Byzantium and Venice*, pp. 310–11.

Genoese engineered Andronikos's escape from the prison in which his father had put him and spirited him over the Golden Horn to their colony at Galata. A few months later, with the help of the Turks as well as his Genoese friends, he fought his way back into Constantinople, arrested his father John, and had himself crowned as the Emperor Andronikos IV. For three years he pretended to reign as such. But he was heavily indebted to the Genoese and for that reason if for no other the Venetians would never let him rest. In 1379 John V escaped from prison and made his way over the sea to the court of the Ottoman Sultan Murad I, whose vassal he was. In July of that year he in his turn fought his way back into Constantinople. The Turks provided him with soldiers, the Venetians with ships. His rebellious son Andronikos fled to take refuge with his Genoese friends at Galata.[53] This was the beginning of one of the saddest episodes in the long life of John Cantacuzene. For Andronikos took with him to Galata some distinguished hostages. Among them were his mother the Empress Helena and her father the monk John-Joasaph. They were the miserable victims of the frustrated ambitions of the failed usurper Andronikos IV. They were also helpless pawns in the continuing game of war between Venice and Genoa. For more than a year Cantacuzene, the blameless monk Joasaph, was held as a prisoner in Galata. He was over eighty years of age. He was accustomed to the sparse fare and meagre comforts of the monastic life. Now he was denied his freedom as well; and worse still, warfare raged around his prison. For John V and his Venetian allies laid siege to the Genoese fortress of Galata in which he lay captive. It was the fortress which, in his days as Emperor, he had commanded them to demolish. Some of the misery and suffering of the royal prisoners can be deduced from a letter which Demetrios Kydones later wrote to the Empress Helena. Not only were they under siege; they were also hungry and in danger of catching the plague which was sweeping through Galata. The fighting went on until April 1381. In May an agreement of sorts was reached and the hostages were released to go back to

---

[53] J. W. Barker, *Manuel II Palaeologus (1391–1425): A Study in Late Byzantine Statesman-ship* (New Brunswick, N.J., 1969), pp. 30–40; Nicol, *Last Centuries of Byzantium*, pp. 276–82.

Constantinople. Joasaph Cantacuzene must have welcomed the peace and quiet of his monastic cell.[54]

It was while he was in prison in Galata that his second son Manuel died at Mistra, on 10 April 1380.[55] His brother Matthew had shown no further ambition for power since he disclaimed his imperial title in 1357. He had enjoyed a life of tranquil scholarship at Mistra, writing philosophical treatises and commentaries on the Scriptures. Manuel had no children and died without an heir; and Matthew, rather reluctantly, took over the administration of the Despotate of the Morea until a successor was appointed. His father John, the monk Joasaph, came to join him. No doubt he had been enfeebled by his harrowing experience as a prisoner. The plague had spread from Galata to Constantinople in 1381.[56] He felt that the time had come to leave the noisy and dangerous environment of the capital and retire to end his days in the scholarly and peaceful atmosphere of Mistra. His last act on the political scene in Constantinople was to approve a proposal that the Emperor John V had made. Now that Manuel Cantacuzene was dead, the Emperor wished his own son Theodore Palaiologos to succeed as Despot of the Morea. In the meanwhile Matthew could, as Demetrios Kydones wrote to him in the autumn of 1382, benefit from the wise counsel of his father who had joined him at Mistra.[57]

Even in his last years John seemed destined to find no rest. Matthew had two sons, John and Demetrios Cantacuzene, both aged about forty. Demetrios resented the appointment of Theodore Palaiologos to the position of Despot which he had expected to inherit. He raised a rebellion of the local lords. It was history repeating itself. It must have reminded Matthew of his own stormy past in Thrace. The last embers of the feud between the 'golden lines' of the house of Cantacuzene and the house of Palaiologos were briefly rekindled in the Morea. When Theodore Palaiologos arrived there in December

[54] Kydones, *Letters*, II, no. 222, pp. 103–10. G. T. Dennis, *The Reign of Manuel II Palaeologus in Thessalonica, 1382–1387* (Rome, 1960), pp. 41–6; Nicol, *Byzantine Family*, p. 91.

[55] Nicol, *Byzantine Family*, p. 127. Schreiner, *Chron. brev.*, II, p. 323.

[56] Schreiner, *Chron. brev.*, II, p. 324.

[57] Kydones, *Letters*, II, no. 241, p. 145.

1382 he saw that he was going to have to fight to assert his rights.[58]

It was in the course of this unseemly squabble, of a kind that he had known all too well, that the Emperor John Cantacuzene, known as the monk Joasaph, died, on 15 June 1383. He was about eighty-eight years of age. Only one chronicler records the date of his death and his burial in the Morea. His son Matthew died in the same year.[59] His rebellious grandson Demetrios died in 1384. The way was clear for Theodore Palaiologos to take over the Despotate in the name of his own family. He ruled it as Despot until 1407 without any further challenge or interference from the family of Cantacuzene. There is no record of where John-Joasaph was buried. He may have been laid to rest in the church of the Holy Wisdom in Mistra which his son Manuel had built. There was once an inscription carved on the columns of the portico of this church glorifying the deeds of both of Manuel's parents and of Manuel himself as its founder.[60] It is sad that there was no one at hand at Mistra in 1383 to pronounce the epitaph which he so richly deserved. He had enjoyed the flattering rhetoric of many encomiasts in his lifetime. His own daughter Helena, whose beauty, culture and learning were much praised by Demetrios Kydones, composed some eulogies of his military prowess.[61] The scholar Thomas Magister, who died about 1347, wrote an elaborate address to him when he was Grand Domestic, trumpeting his triumphs as a soldier.[62] The court poet of Andronikos II, Manuel Philes, played with the fancy that Hermes and Mars vied with one another to call Cantacuzene his own. He also put together a dramatic characterisation of 'the celebrated Grand Domestic Charitonymos [i.e. John] Cantacuzene' in the form of a dialogue between the poet and his own mind. In 966 lines of

[58] The appointment of Theodore Palaiologos as Despot in the Morea is recorded in the Epitaph which his brother Manuel composed for him after his death. J. Chrysostomides, *Manuel II Palaeologus, Funeral Oration on his brother Theodore* (*CFHB*, xxvi: Thessaloniki, 1985), pp. 111–13. On John and Demetrios Cantacuzene: Nicol, *Byzantine Family*, nos. 49, 50, pp. 157–60; *PLP*, v, nos. 10961, 10972.

[59] Schreiner, *Chron. brev.*, i, no. 7/24; ii, p. 325.

[60] G. Millet, 'Les inscriptions byzantines de Mistra', *Bulletin de Correspondance hellénique*, 23 (1899), 144–5; Nicol, *Byzantine Family*, pp 127–8.

[61] Kydones, *Letters*, ii, no. 389, p. 340.

[62] F. W. Lenz, *Fünf Reden Thomas Magisters* (Leiden, 1963), pp. 91–5.

indifferent versification Philes runs through the multifarious virtues of his hero without enlarging on any of the facts of his career.[63] Such effusions were part of the stock-in-trade of Byzantine poets. Rarely do they add much to our historical perception of the persons concerned. An anonymous poem in praise of John as Emperor, monk and defender of Orthodox faith and doctrine comes in thirty-two verses written at the end of his polemic against the anti-Palamite John Kyparissiotes; and he was not without his western admirers. Simon Atumano, who became Catholic Archbishop of Thebes in 1355 and participated in the talks about the union of the churches in Constantinople in 1374, wrote fourteen iambic verses in Greek in praise of John as a soldier and commander. He was the most admirable of Emperors and no less admirable of monks. He excelled in every rank which he assumed.[64]

---

[63] Manuel Philes, *Poems*, ed. E. Miller, *Manuelis Philae Carmina* (Paris, 1855–7), I, pp. 143–84, 323–30; II, p. 58.
[64] Nicol, *Byzantine Family*, pp. 96–8 and references.

8

HIS CHARACTER,
ACHIEVEMENTS AND FAILURES

Few Emperors of Constantinople had such long and varied careers as John Cantacuzene. Few had so many natural gifts and talents. Demetrios Kydones once congratulated him on his ability to fit into the space of one day the functions of a soldier, a judge, a statesman, a man of letters and a theologian.[1] His older friend Gregoras applauded him for being at once a savant, a great general of his army and a just and modest leader of men.[2] He had a charming manner and his company was always a source of joy and pleasure. Different people admired his different qualities. Some praised his energy, others his faithfulness, others his mild humour; while the affection which he inspired in his soldiers was known to everyone.[3] Gregoras, himself a scholar, was particularly pleased by Cantacuzene's devotion to learning. Hector had been famous for his bravery, Aeneas for his wisdom. Cantacuzene had both of these qualities.[4] All these eulogies by Gregoras were written before his friend became Emperor and before he openly espoused the abominable heresy of Palamism. Gregoras felt this lapse on the part of a man whom he much admired as a personal affront and the end of a long-standing and sincere friendship. Long before Cantacuzene came to the throne Gregoras had observed the qualities with which nature had endowed him; and he hoped that once he became Emperor he would see the folly of fighting against the immutable truths of Orthodoxy.[5]

For all his breadth of vision, Cantacuzene lived all his eighty-

[1] Demetrios Kydones, *Letters*, I, no. 12, pp. 38–40.
[2] Nikephoros Gregoras, ed. R. Guilland, *Correspondance*, nos. 39, 40, 80.
[3] Gregoras, *Correspondance*, no. 147.
[4] Gregoras, *Correspondance*, no. 83. [5] Greg. II, p. 821.

eight years in the narrow world of the dwindling Byzantine
Empire. He never ventured as far as Italy or the west. He knew
his friends and enemies in Asia Minor better than he
knew those in western Europe. Perhaps he understood the mind
of a Turkish Emir better than the mind of a Latin ruler. He
exchanged little correspondence with the kings and princes of
the west except for the Popes at Avignon and Rome. The Latins
who forced their attentions upon him were the greedy business
men of Venice and Genoa; and their representatives with whom
he had to deal were hardly the cream of western culture and
society in the fourteenth century. He was once credited as
author of a letter written by an 'Emperor of Constantinople' to
Cola di Rienzo congratulating him on his *coup d'état* in Rome in
1347. This never seemed very probable and it has now been
shown to be a fiction.[6] He corresponded with the Orthodox
rulers of Russia, of Serbia and of Bulgaria, and with the Muslim
Sultan of Egypt. But the only western monarch with whom he
is known to have exchanged official letters was Peter III of
Aragon, though he seems to have thought that Aragon and
Ravenna were the same place.[7]

It is sad that he never knew or corresponded with his
contemporary Andrea Dandolo, the great Doge of Venice, for
Dandolo too was a historian and scholar. He died in 1354, three
months after Cantacuzene's abdication. Neither mentions the
other in his work. They never met. The histories that they
wrote were very different in style and purpose. That of Dandolo
was a comparatively simple chronicle in the form of annals.
Cantacuzene's *Histories* or memoirs are a personal record of the
events that shaped his life between the years 1321 and 1354.
They assume the sophisticated style of an *apologia pro vita sua*.
Neither was a man of the people. Both were wealthy members
of a gilded aristocracy.[8] But what Cantacuzene could never have
condoned was the form of government over which Dandolo
presided. For as a Byzantine born into the ruling class he was
irremediably committed to the ideology of *imperium*, *basileia*, or

---

[6] E. de Vries-Van der Velden, 'A propos d'une lettre inexistante de Jean VI
Cantacuzène', *B*, 46 (1976), 330–53.

[7] Cantac. III, p. 186. Nicol, *Byzantine Family*, p. 76 n. 108.

[8] Nicol, *Byzantium and Venice*, pp. 280–2.

Empire. He knew about and disapproved of the revolutionary democratic antics of Simone Boccanegra in Genoa in the 1340s and 1350s.[9] They put him in mind of the deplorable activities of the disorderly citizens of Adrianople and Thessalonica at about the same time. Such disrespect for the order of society was symptomatic of the times. As Gregoras observed, the 1340s witnessed civil wars and disturbances the world over, in Italy, in Egypt, in Spain and in Asia, and even in the far west, where the Britons invaded the mainland of the Celts and fought a great battle.[10] The western world was seldom uppermost in the mind of a Byzantine like Cantacuzene, though where there was a monarchy he found it to be more intelligible. This was no doubt why he assured the Pope that he would be prepared to respect the See of Rome in much the same way as did the King of France.[11]

Cantacuzene's aversion to visiting western Europe was partly a fear of tarnishing the radiance of his imperial dignity. In times past it had been unthinkable for an Emperor of the Romans to leave his capital to visit a foreign monarch. It had been assumed that it was the part of lesser princes to come to Constantinople to pay their respects to the one true Emperor. Times had changed. But the first precedent in this matter was set not by Cantacuzene but by his son-in-law who, as the Emperor John V, debased himself and his dignity by travelling to Hungary to beg the help of its King Louis the Great in 1365.[12] The title and style of Emperor of the Romans meant a lot to John Cantacuzene. As early in his career as November 1347 he issued a chrysobull rewarding one of his supporters. The document is boldly signed with his full title of 'John in Christ God true Emperor and Autokrator of the Romans Kantakouzenos'. In his correspondence with Pope Clement VI he had to bear the impropriety of being addressed as 'Emperor of the Greeks'. But in his own letter to the Pope he righted the wrong by signing himself in Latin as 'Iohannes in Christo Deo fidelis imperator et moderator Romanorum Canthacusinos'.

---

[9] On Simone Boccanegra: Cantac. III, pp. 197, 235–7.
[10] He refers to the battle of Crécy, 1346: Greg. II, pp. 687–9.
[11] R.-J. Loenertz, 'Ambassadeurs grecs auprès du Pape Clément VI (1348)', *OCP*, 19 (1953), 182: 'sicut Rex francie' (= Loenertz, *BFG*, I, p. 288).
[12] Nicol, *Last Centuries of Byzantium*, pp. 263–5.

He made reference to the King of France ('Rex francie'), but he made no mention of the only western monarch who claimed the title of Emperor.[13] The ideological quarrel between the Holy Roman Emperor in Germany and the Emperor of the Romans in Constantinople had been simmering for at least five hundred years by the time Cantacuzene was crowned in 1347. There were by then others nearer to Constantinople who claimed the title of Emperor, in Serbia and Bulgaria. They were an embarrassment to the Byzantine view of the world. They had the merit of being Orthodox Christians by faith. But Cantacuzene could never bring himself to dignify Stephen Dušan with the name of Emperor which he had appropriated in 1346. Dušan was, and remained in his view, no more than a Serbian Kral. The rulers of Bulgaria too, although distantly related to his wife Eirene, had to be content to be known as Tsars of the Mysians.[14]

Even in the fourteenth century the myth lingered on in Constantinople that the Byzantine Empire of the Romans was God's last word on the order of the world. The western world was not immune to the mystique of Byzantium. Cantacuzene was happy to note, when writing of the marriage of Anna of Savoy to Andronikos III in 1325, that the lady's father much preferred that she should marry the Emperor than the King of France, who was also in the running for her hand. 'For not only the barbarians but also the Italians and other rulers considered the Empire of the Romans to be greater and more prestigious than any other state.'[15] Cantacuzene saw his Empire as the direct successor and continuation of the Roman Empire of old, whose armies 'had conquered all the peoples of Europe as well as those of Asia'.[16] The ancient Greeks, the Hellenes, had provided the stuff of the 'outer wisdom' of pagan philosophy. But it was the ancient Romans who provided the military enterprise. They were never fainthearted in adversity. They mastered almost all the world. As a soldier he appreciated

[13] Chrysobull of November 1347 in favour of Demetrios Kabasilas: *Actes de Dionysiou*, ed. N. Oikonomides (*Archives de l'Athos*, IV: Paris, 1968), no. 2, pp. 42–7; Loenertz, 'Ambassadeurs grecs', *BFG*, I, pp. 287, 288, 291, 295.
[14] T. Teoteoi, 'La conception de Jean VI Cantacuzène sur l'état byzantin vue principalement à la lumière de son *Histoire*', *RESEE*, 13 (1975), 167–86.
[15] Cantac. I, p. 196; II, p. 53.
[16] Cantac. I, pp. 344–5.

the tenacity of the Romans. When addressing his own officers in a moment of crisis, he urged them to model themselves on the invincible Romans of old, 'their own ancestors'. For they were of the same stock as the Romans (Romaioi) of his own time.[17]

Confidence in the unique and exclusive status of the Emperor of the Romans had once been supported by the wealth of the Empire. In the fourteenth century this was no longer the case. The wealth that had once found its way into the imperial treasury in Constantinople had instead been accumulated in the coffers of a number of aristocratic families, such as the Cantacuzenes. It gave them power and influence: and it encouraged their conceit that they had a prescriptive right to rule. John Cantacuzene's riches in land and property were beyond the imagination of ordinary people. The accumulation of such wealth was not generally considered to be reprehensible or anti-social. The rich were blest with unusual opportunities for the exercise of Christian charity; and one of the virtues recommended in an Emperor was philanthropy. To have acquired a fortune, unless by dishonest means, was thought to be a mark of distinction, a sure sign of prudent husbandry, of aristocratic lineage and even of divine approval. The Cantacuzene family were fabulously wealthy, with great landed estates and rich farmland, around Serres in Macedonia, in Thrace along the Marica river, and in Thessaly. They also owned extensive properties in the city of Constantinople. When John's mother Theodora was arrested in 1342 she was found to have hoards of grain, fruit and other provisions stored in her house near the palace and in one of the city monasteries. Her valuables too were confiscated, although she had hidden much of her silver, gold and jewellery in a secret place.[18] Her son also owned real estate in Constantinople and other cities. He found it impossible to estimate his losses when his property was seized by his enemies; and when they expropriated his estates in Macedonia he claims to have lost enormous quantities of livestock. He declares that he uttered no word of complaint about the losses inflicted on him, except to lament that the

[17] Cantac. II, pp. 244, 251.   [18] Cantac. III, pp. 164–5.

proceeds went not into the public domain but only to finance his political enemies.[19] If he and his kind had thought more about the public good in earlier times they might have avoided the unpleasant shock of a form of social revolution which appalled and unnerved them. It is not surprising that Cantacuzenism so easily became a political slogan for the self-appointed champions of the under-privileged.

It is to Cantacuzene's credit that he saw the need, indeed the urgency, to attempt a more equal distribution of the wealth that was left after so ruinous a season of wars. When he became Emperor in 1347 much of it was in the hands of upstarts like Apokaukos, men whom he claimed to despise as *nouveaux riches* with no aristocratic background, no breeding and no God-given right to rule. The rich lands in Thrace and Macedonia had been devastated by years of fighting and plundering. The men with new-found wealth and the influence that went with it were mainly an urban bourgeoisie living in Constantinople. His well-meaning efforts to persuade them to part with some of it for the common good were not well received. It was only when their city was in evident danger from across the water that they were ready to contribute to its defence, and then with a bad grace. That danger came from the Genoese colony of Galata and for a while, since it was a menace visible from the walls of Constantinople, it concentrated the minds of the inhabitants. But Cantacuzene knew that this was only a symptom of the problem. The Empire would never recover until its economy was liberated from the stranglehold of the merchants of Venice as well as Genoa, who had for so long been allowed to dominate its trade and even its food-supply. This, as he often declared, could be achieved partly by the reconstitution of a Byzantine navy and merchant fleet and partly by curbing the privileges and preferential tariffs which his predecessors had granted them. The Italians reacted bitterly and violently to the measures that he tried to enforce. The race between Venice and Genoa to win and keep the prize of the great markets of Constantinople, the Bosporos and the Black Sea brought them to war with each other. Cantacuzene, against his better

---

[19] Cantac. II, pp. 184–5, 192. Nicol, *Last Centuries of Byzantium*, p. 192; A. E. Laiou, 'The Byzantine aristocracy in the Palaeologan period', *Viator*, 4 (1973), especially 143–4.

judgment, was forced to take sides in that war. He saw his new fleet destroyed before it had taken to the open sea.

Yet he gained one small but notable advantage out of his treaty with Genoa in 1352. Byzantine merchant ships were to be allowed to put in at all Genoese ports on the same terms as cargo ships from Galata. There was as a result a perceptible increase in the volume of Byzantine trade. However limited it was, the credit must go to Cantacuzene and the economic and fiscal measures that he introduced. The investment of capital in shipping and trade by sea was something of a novelty for the Byzantines. The monied class had been accustomed to think in terms of landed property. They had expected the sea trade to come to them at Constantinople or Thessalonica. To go out to look for it seemed somehow demeaning. But with the Serbian occupation of northern Greece and the devastation of much of the territory of Macedonia and Thrace during the civil wars landed property was no longer the secure investment that it had once been. Even some of the aristocracy to which Cantacuzene belonged began to turn to commercial activities. It was his policy that helped to encourage them to challenge or even to co-operate with the Italian traders by sea. Their operations were on a small scale. Byzantine merchantmen would not venture far afield; nor could they successfully compete with the well-organised mercantile enterprises of the Italians. The Byzantine war fleet, however, on which Cantacuzene had pinned such hopes, was never restored to its former strength.[20]

The four books of his *Histories* which Cantacuzene composed during the years of his monastic retirement begin with a Prologue and end with an Epilogue. Each is addressed to one Neilos. The author calls himself Christodoulos the monk, a pseudonym which is probably no more than a play on the words 'servant of Christ'. Neilos, however, seems to have been a real person, most probably Neilos Kabasilas, the uncle of Cantacuzene's friend Nicholas Kabasilas. He was Bishop of Thessalonica from 1361 to 1363.[21] In his Epilogue Cantacuzene reveals some of the sources for his information. Lest it be thought strange that he could have had access to the secret

---

[20] Oikonomides, *Hommes d'affaires grecs et latins*, pp. 51–2, 83–7, 120–3.
[21] On Neilos Kabasilas: *PLP*, v, no. 10102.

counsels of his enemies in the civil war, he explains that he learnt them from people who were privy to them, notably the two brothers of the Grand Duke Alexios Apokaukos. There were others too who were so surprised and relieved to be forgiven when he became Emperor that they told him all they knew.[22] This confession tells us something about the character of the man. For one of his redeeming qualities was his tolerance. He was never minded to penalise or persecute his political opponents, still less to try to have them assassinated. This was a side of his character often emphasised and praised by his admirers, such as Demetrios Kydones. It was something which he wanted his readers to know and to applaud. For his *Histories* are really his personal memoirs and often apologetic in tone. To write one's own memoirs is perhaps to court criticism and charges of hypocrisy. John Cantacuzene has had more than his fair share of these. But his detailed and painstaking account of events in the forty-odd years of his active life must be ranked as an outstanding example of Byzantine historiography.

The lucid and simple literary style of his narrative has been rightly praised. What many have seen as being less lucid and simple is the man who wrote it. Autobiographies were rare productions in the world of Byzantine literature. The traditional and conventional form of Byzantine historiography was that written in chronological sequence narrating the course of events year by year, Emperor by Emperor. It was unheard of for an Emperor to write his own history. This alone makes Cantacuzene unique. Constantine Porphyrogenitus wrote the biography of his own grandfather, Basil I, the founder of the Macedonian dynasty. Michael Psellos wrote lives of several of the Emperors of his time in the twelfth century. The princess Anna Comnena wrote the most celebrated of such works in her biography of her father, Alexios Komnenos. Her *Alexiad* is quite shamelessly a panegyric of 'my father the Emperor'. The memoirs of John Cantacuzene do not constitute a panegyric, rather a justification of all his activities through two civil or dynastic wars until he was, with some reluctance, crowned as

---

[22] Cantac. III, pp. 364–5. *Johannes Kantakuzenos, Geschichte*, translated with commentary by G. Fatouros and T. Krischer, I (Stuttgart, 1982), pp. 208–9.

Emperor in Constantinople in 1347. He then describes in detail his part in the events of his seven-year reign, culminating in his despairing acceptance of the fact that the Empire was beyond repair, and his voluntary retirement into the monastic life. The tragic hero and the central figure of the whole composition is not, as with Psellos and Anna Comnena, some third person. He is the author himself. This, as has been well observed, was a new development in Byzantine literature: 'La poésie de la défaite héroïque a été, dans la littérature byzantine, inventée par Cantacuzène.'[23]

The classical simplicity of his Greek style and language, even the paucity of his vocabulary, may be seen as a deliberate ploy to convince his readers of his honesty and sincerity. The antithesis of these admirable qualities is embodied for him in the person and character of Alexios Apokaukos. He devotes a long passage in the second book of his memoirs to a detailed account of the past life and misdeeds of this mischief-maker.[24] One of the charges against him was that he came of a low-class and ignoble family with no money and no breeding. At the same time, however, Cantacuzene claimed the credit for having dragged Apokaukos out of the gutter, promoted his career and even secured his release from prison when he had been convicted of criminal behaviour. The Patriarch John Kalekas, who became Apokaukos's partner in political crime, was also counted as being untrustworthy because of the humble origins of his family. Yet again it was Cantacuzene who befriended him and helped him to become Patriarch in 1334.[25] Another unstable and dishonest adventurer whom he trusted and favoured was Syrgiannes, whom one might call the Alcibiades of late Byzantium. Gregoras compared his defection to the Serbians to that of Themistocles to the Persians. Syrgiannes had at least the merits of being a military man and connected with a noble family. But he danced circles round those who thought they were his friends.[26]

Such misjudgments of character reveal a weakness in Cantacuzene. The fact that he narrates the evidence of this weakness with such candour perhaps speaks for the honesty and

---

[23] Kazhdan, 'L'*Histoire* de Cantacuzène', 287.   [24] Cantac. II, pp. 88–103.
[25] Cantac. I, pp. 532–5.   [26] Greg. I, pp. 490, 498.

integrity of his version of events; or else it was a fault inherent in his nature to which he was blind. He had other such failings. The worst of them was his inability to take resolute decisions. This was a weakness in him often observed and condemned by Gregoras. He should not, for example, have hesitated so long about letting his followers proclaim him Emperor at Didymoteichon in 1341. In 1342, when only a few days' march from Thessalonica, he should not have delayed and procrastinated, 'wasting his time doing nothing', in the hope that the city would surrender without resistance. Thus, in the opinion of one who knew him well, Cantacuzene frequently lost his opportunities, either by delaying his action or by adopting too humble an attitude to his political enemies. He should rather have modelled his actions on those of his great predecessors, like Alexios Komnenos. Gregoras again chastises him for not having taken a firmer line with his opponents after he had entered Constantinople in 1347. It was clear that the treasury was empty and yet many, the Empress Anna among them, had made handsome profits out of the civil war. He should have demanded money from them. He was loth to do so, either from the indecision which was inbred in him or from a natural timidity and fear of causing trouble.[27]

It is arguable that he could indeed have saved himself and his Empire years of trouble, destruction and despair by being more decisive at crucial moments in his career. He might have acted with a greater sense of purpose in 1341 and again in 1347 over the matter of his own proclamation and coronation as Emperor. He could simply have disinherited the young John Palaiologos and openly declared himself to be a usurper of the throne, instead of meekly playing the part of the reluctant Emperor until the decision was thrust upon him. Such hypotheses of history are fascinating but seldom helpful. They are given full rein in the rambling reflections of Val. Parisot on the faults and virtues of Cantacuzene. It is never easy to enter into the mind of *homo byzantinus*. It becomes harder still when the man in question has left such a detailed and prolix account of what he wished posterity to know and to think of his successes and failures. From the beginning of his career he evidently believed

---

[27] Greg. II, pp. 610, 625, 632, 754, 789–90.

that he had a mission to fulfil. It was during his early years as Grand Domestic and most loyal companion and servant of the young Emperor Andronikos III that he began to create his own following of like-minded friends and supporters.[28] After Andronikos's death, however, his mission seemed to become less clear, as if he were afraid of fulfilling it. Yet he never lost his strange conviction that he was under divine protection. He survived numerous attempts made by the agents of the regency in Constantinople to have him captured or assassinated. There was one especially spectacular case of his providential rescue when he was in Berroia in 1343. Apokaukos picked on one of his Cantacuzenist prisoners who was an expert marksman and bribed the man to find Cantacuzene and shoot him down with a poisoned arrow. He located his prey in Berroia and was poised to do the foul deed when the arrow slipped from his bowstring and dropped. The next day he tried again, but again the arrow fell from his grasp at the critical moment. On the third night he took greater care; but when he pulled the string on his bow it snapped, although it was new, as if someone had cut it. He became convinced that Cantacuzene must be under the protection of some divine agency; and, bow and arrow in hand, he fell at his feet and confessed all, begging for mercy. Cantacuzene and all those present were so moved by this clear manifestation of divine intervention that they wept and gave thanks; and Cantacuzene, far from punishing his would-be assassin, rewarded him as one who had revealed the miraculous ways of God.[29]

What then was the mission in life for the fulfilment of which providence so frequently preserved him? It is easy to say that it was to give the time and the scope to satisfy his own ambition. For he was surely ambitious. But his ambitions were not entirely self-centred. They were motivated by a desire to restore his Empire to a measure of its former greatness, to bring back its earlier glory. This is a constant theme of his memoirs. In 1341, when the new Tsar of Bulgaria John Alexander demanded the extradition of his rival Michael Šišman who had been given asylum in Constantinople, Cantacuzene scolded the Bulgarian

---

[28] On Cantacuzene's 'Gefolgschaft', see Weiss, *Johannes Kantakuzenos*, pp. 32f.
[29] Cantac. II, pp. 377–9.

ambassadors who had come to collect the refugee. He reminded
them that since the time of Constantine the Great, the
Emperor of the Romans had given asylum to many lesser
sovereigns who had fallen on bad times and sought comfort and
shelter in Constantinople in the knowledge that the Emperors
were more powerful and more prestigious than any other rulers.
Some of such refugees had been so well treated and received
that they had chosen to stay in Constantinople for life, finding
the service of the Emperor preferable to the government of
their own people. The Bulgars should not get ideas above their
station.[30]

He could call the bluff of the Bulgarians in this fashion. They
were the nearest neighbours of Constantinople. He could and
did frighten them by a show of force. But, as he later came to
learn, the same tactics would not work with the Serbians. For in
Stephen Dušan he found that the imperial myth came face
to face with reality; for the reality was that the Byzantine
Emperor could no longer substantiate his claim to be monarch
of all that he surveyed. Dušan's coronation as Emperor of the
Romans as well as the Serbs was a rude indication that things
had changed; and, although he does not admit it, it was this
event that spurred Cantacuzene on to allowing himself to be
crowned as Emperor at Adrianople only a few weeks later. Both
men knew, however, that it was only the possession of the city
of Constantinople, the New Rome, that could give substance to
the otherwise nebulous claim to be an Emperor of the Romans.

The realities of a changing world were brought home still
more forcibly by events in Asia Minor. By the time that
Cantacuzene became Emperor in Constantinople in 1347 it was
already too late to turn back the clock of history on what had
once been the eastern frontiers of Byzantium. The Turks were
by then firmly established in such ancient urban centres of
Greek and Christian tradition as Nicaea, Nikomedia, Brusa and
Ephesos. As a historian Cantacuzene adhered to the literary
convention of his day by calling the Turks the 'Persians' and
their leaders the 'satraps', the ancient word for Persian rulers.
True to the same convention, he described them as the
'barbarians', though this was no more than accepted usage in

---

[30] Cantac. III, pp. 52–5. See above p. 48.

Byzantine historiography. It did not imply racial hatred or animosity. As a soldier, however, Cantacuzene knew that by the 1340s it was too late to stem the Turkish tide in Asia Minor by military means, unless it were to be by a world war of Christianity against Islam. He knew that the western league of Christian powers sponsored by the Papacy had triumphed over Umur of Aydin and conquered Smyrna in 1345. But in his view they had misdirected their efforts. Constantinople and not Smyrna was the hub of the Christian world in the eastern Mediterranean; and Umur had been his friend, ally and blood brother. It has been suggested that this unusual friendship between Christian and Muslim, first established in 1335, was part of a diplomatic ploy to build up a federation of Turkish leaders, Saruhan, Karasi and others, bound by a common hostility towards the Osmanlis in Bithynia, who were the nearer and more dangerous enemies of Constantinople.[31] The chronology of events seems to be against this interpretation, for the first known treaty of peace which Andronikos III and Cantacuzene struck with Orhan, son of Osman, was in 1333 near Nikomedia. It was their first major military encounter with the Osmanlis at Pelekanon in 1329 which had prompted Cantacuzene, and the idea was surely his, to look for a diplomatic rather than a strategic solution to the problem in Asia Minor. By the terms of his treaty with Andronikos III in 1333 Orhan agreed to respect the remaining territorial rights of the Byzantines in Bithynia. Cantacuzene had not been present at the making of that treaty. His own special relationship with Orhan was to burgeon later and to be broadcast to the world by the extraordinary event of the marriage of his daughter Theodora to Orhan in 1346.

Historians, Byzantine and modern, have expressed pious horror at this callous sacrifice of his daughter as a bride to a ruler whom he himself describes as a 'barbarian'. To him, however, the term barbarian did not imply savagery; and the daughters of Christian princes were often treated as expendable commodities for diplomatic purposes. In principle it might be said that the marriage of Theodora to Orhan was no worse than that of the five-year old Simonis, daughter of

[31] Parisot, *Cantacuzène*, pp. 131–3.

Andronikos II, to the middle-aged Stephen Milutin of Serbia in 1299. It is remarkable, however, that the Patriarch of Constantinople on that occasion had protested vigorously against so scandalous a union, even though both parties were of the Orthodox Christian faith. In 1346, when the union was between an Orthodox princess and an infidel Emir, the church remained silent, for all that the arrangement was indisputably uncanonical. It might have been grist to the propaganda mill of the anti-Cantacuzenists in Constantinople, of the Patriarch John Kalekas and the Empress Anna. But there is no record of their disapproval; and Alexios Apokaukos, who might have made a meal of it, was dead and gone.

Cantacuzene's relationship with Umur of Aydin was of a different character. It was in the nature of a personal friendship and it impressed the Turks as well as the Christians. It had evidently been forged and maintained, perhaps in secret, ever since and probably before Umur's treaty with Andronikos III at Kara Burun. It is also a fact, which Cantacuzene emphasised in a letter to the Empress Anna, that never in the lifetime of her late husband had Umur and his men done any damage to Byzantine possessions. He had come to the aid of Andronikos and Cantacuzene most notably and effectively in their campaign against the rebellious Albanians. But he had never assaulted Greek territory because he regarded it as belonging to his friend Cantacuzene, to whom he was consistently loyal.[32] After the outbreak of civil war in 1341 Umur's loyalty spurred him on to doing as much damage as he could to his friend's opponents and this inevitably caused much devastation of Byzantine territory on European soil. Umur had a simplistic view of the ways in which he could be of assistance. But within the limitations of his Muslim code of chivalry, he was an honest man. He had refused to consider taking one of Cantacuzene's daughters to wife because to do so would have offended against that code. Orhan had felt no such scruples. But Orhan was not morally bound to his ally by the same bonds of blood brotherhood.

In his relationships with his Turkish allies Cantacuzene was undoubtedly naive. In his hours of crisis in the years of the civil

[32] Cantac. II, pp. 396–8; Enveri, *Le Destān*, lines 1309–10.

war he needed and relied upon their military support. His political enemies, who also called upon them, were jealous of his success in cultivating their friendship and even their loyalty. Turkish soldiers had been lured across to Thrace to fight for Christians long before the time of Cantacuzene. The Catalans, who had seized control of Gallipoli in 1305, had invited thousands of Turks to come across and join them. Andronikos II had tried rather unsuccessfully to hire Turkish mercenaries in his war against his grandson.[33] It was his grandson Andronikos III who, on the advice of his commander-in-chief John Cantacuzene, concluded that the Turkish conquest of Asia Minor was a *fait accompli*. The muddled battle and Byzantine defeat at Pelekanon in 1329 seemed to have proved the point. Diplomacy and not warfare should henceforth be the hope of containing the Turks on the continent of Asia. The Byzantines should cut their losses in the east and concentrate on strengthening and preserving the European provinces of their Empire.

Something of this novel conception appears to have been in the mind of Cantacuzene in 1341 when he received a delegation from the Latin lords of the Morea. He was flattered that they came to him on the assumption that he was already Emperor. He was excited by the prospect of an enlarged and reinvigorated Empire in Europe. For, as he said, the addition of the Peloponnese to its territories would restore it to a dominion extending in an unbroken line from Greece to Constantinople.[34] The separatist provinces of Epiros and Thessaly in northern Greece had been brought back to the fold the year before, not least by his own military and diplomatic talents. If the Peloponnese would now accept Byzantine government and if the Catalan rulers of Athens and Thebes in central Greece would do the same, the whole peninsula of Greece from Thessalonica south to Monemvasia would be reunited with its ancient capital of Constantinople as the nucleus of a restored Byzantine Empire in Europe. The Emperors of the Romans might then aspire to reaching a *modus vivendi* with the Turks across the water in Asia. The Byzantines had always known that

---

[33] In 1322: Cantac. I, pp. 151–2.
[34] Cantac. II, pp. 74–6, 80–1. J. Longnon, *L'Empire latin de Constantinople et la principauté de Morée* (Paris, 1949), pp. 325–6; Zakythinos, *Le Despotat grec de Morée*, I, p. 76.

diplomacy was cheaper and often more successful than war. Cantacuzene knew that they could never on their own mount a world war of Christians against Muslims. They had seldom felt attracted by the western idea of a crusade. In times gone by their ancestors had won over the Slavs and the Russians to Orthodox Christianity without killing them all or staging a holy war for their salvation. It was God's will that Christianity would in the end prevail over Islam, though only if its practitioners merited God's protection by mending their ways. This was a constant theme of the sermons of the Byzantine clergy.

The possibility of some kind of peaceful co-existence with the Turks until such time as the Christians earned God's favour seems also to have been in the mind of Cantacuzene's friend Gregory Palamas. He was taken prisoner by the Turks at Gallipoli in 1354 and held captive for about a year. But he was allowed to travel round the new Turkey under escort; and he was impressed by what he saw. He held discussions with Muslim theologians and he wrote two letters to his friends back home.[35] As a saintly Christian bishop Palamas was bound to condemn Islam and to describe the Turks as 'the most barbarous of barbarians'. But he was surprised at the tolerance of the Muslim conquerors towards their Christian subjects. He was housed and comforted in the Christian monastic communities which were still in being. Nowhere does he suggest the possibility of a Byzantine reconquest of the parts of Asia Minor which he was allowed to visit, including Nicaea and Brusa. He was even taken to the summer residence of Orhan not far from Brusa, where he was entertained by the Emir's grandson, whom he found to be a sympathetic and cultured young man. He was naturally welcomed by the Christians wherever he went. He could see for himself that they were not too unhappy under their tolerant barbarian masters.

By 1354, when Palamas was there, the celebrated Christian city of Nicaea had been Turkish for more than twenty years. Many of its Christian inhabitants had already found that it paid to bow to the inevitable and either conceal their faith or embrace Islam. Apostasy was widespread, although repeatedly

---

[35] A. Philippides-Braat, 'La captivité de Palamas chez les Turcs', *Travaux et Mémoires*, 7 (1979), 109–22; Meyendorff, *Introduction*, pp. 154–62.

deplored and condemned by the Patriarchs of Constantinople. They issued encyclicals to boost the morale of members of their flock living perforce *in partibus infidelium*.[36] But no Patriarch could expect all the Christians in Asia Minor to court martyrdom for their faith. Martyrdom was in any case not really on offer. Many of them felt and said that life under the Turks was preferable to the servile existence forced upon the Orthodox Christians of Greece and the Aegean islands by their French and Italian masters. Palamas sensed that the Turkish occupation of Asia Minor had become a normal state of affairs. At the end of one of his discussions with the Muslim theologians in Nicaea, one of them said: 'the time will come when we shall agree with each other. I am glad and I pray that it may come soon.'[37]

Palamas then shared the hope of his friend Cantacuzene that a *modus vivendi* between Byzantines and Turks was possible. Naturally he hoped and prayed that the Muslims might be converted to Christianity by preaching and by example. He never proposed that they should be annihilated or expelled from Asia Minor by force with the help of armies sent from western Europe. For the westerners, the Latins, were less tolerant and more dangerous to the Orthodox faith than the Muslims. This sentiment was to be expressed ninety-nine years later in the memorable phrase: 'Better the Sultan's turban in our midst than the Latin mitre.'[38] Cantacuzene's scheme for cutting his Empire's losses and sharing the world between a Christian Europe and a Muslim Asia was either a visionary's dream or a fool's venture. In either event it was unworkable. It depended too much on his personal friendship and gentleman's agreements with the Turkish leaders, especially Orhan, his son-in-law. When Orhan's son Suleiman showed his disregard for such polite behaviour by occupying the ruins of Gallipoli and establishing a base in Europe, Cantacuzene's policy was also in ruins. He admitted despair if not defeat, gave up the struggle and abdicated. His successor John V promptly turned to the

---

[36] S. Vryonis, *The Decline of Medieval Hellenism in Asia Minor and the Process of Islamization from the Eleventh through the Fifteenth Century* (Berkeley–Los Angeles–London, 1971), pp. 339–42.

[37] Philippides-Braat, 'La captivité', c. 29, pp. 160–1, 205.

[38] Doukas, *Istoria*, ed. Grecu, p. 329.

Latin west for help. Demetrios Kydones saw another new era
dawning with the light of a new understanding, sympathy and
co-operation, not between Greeks and Turks but between
Greeks and Latins. It was again a false dawn.

There can be no doubt that Cantacuzene's dealings with the
Turks and his increasing reliance upon them as friends and
allies contributed more than any other factor to his political
downfall. Many a time he expressed his regret at ever having
called upon their help. He professed to hate them but he could
not manage without them. The earthquake at Gallipoli and
its occupation by Orhan's son Suleiman was the last straw.
Right to the end Cantacuzene hoped to play upon his special
relationship with his son-in-law Orhan to avert the disaster of
yet further warfare in Thrace. He tried to arrange a conference
with him near Nikomedia. He offered Suleiman 40,000 pieces of
gold by way of compensation if he would surrender Gallipoli and
other places.[39] Many in Constantinople regarded this as the
basest form of appeasement. It was said that the bribes which
he offered to Orhan and his son were taken from money which
had been piously subscribed by the Russians for the repair of
the church of St Sophia. It was said among the people that
Cantacuzene had 'delivered them as slaves to the Turks'. The
Patriarch Kallistos, who had refused to recognise Matthew
Cantacuzene as Emperor, bluntly accused his father of having
handed the Empire over to the infidel.[40] One of the chroniclers,
reporting the earthquake of 1354 and its consequences
concludes that after that event there was nothing but woe for
the Christians.[41]

One of the most satisfactory of Cantacuzene's achievements
as Emperor was the appointment of his second son Manuel as
governor of the Peloponnese or Morea. It was a position which
he himself had been offered by Andronikos II in 1321. He had
declined it with the excuse that his own father had died there.[42]
It was a part of the Empire where he had family connections
and memories. It was also a vital link in the chain of provinces
which, twenty years later, he envisaged as stretching from
Greece to Constantinople in his European Empire. He sent

---

[39] Cantac. III, p. 280.   [40] Greg. III, pp. 195–9, 242.
[41] Schreiner, *Chron. brev.*, I, no. 87/3, p. 613.   [42] See above, p. 18.

Manuel to Mistra to take over the province with the title of Despot in 1349. By then the Latin rulers of the northern part of the Peloponnese had forgotten the enthusiasm that they had earlier expressed for binding themselves to the government in Constantinople. But Manuel made it his business to encourage their friendship and alliance. He married a Latin wife, Isabelle of Lusignan from Cyprus; and he joined forces with the Latin lords of Achaia in fending off sporadic attacks on the Morea by Turkish pirate ships. He also imposed order on what had been an unruly province and laid solid foundations on which his successors could build to make the Despotate of the Morea a flourishing microcosm of the Byzantine world. Its capital city of Mistra lived on as a centre of Hellenic and Christian culture for seven years after the fall of Constantinople to the Turks.[43]

It was at Mistra that Manuel was buried in 1380. His father died there three years later and his brother Matthew at about the same time. Their mother Eirene had been laid to rest in her convent some twenty years earlier. Of the three daughters whom she had borne to John Cantacuzene, Maria, who had married Nikephoros of Epiros, died about 1360; Theodora, the wife of Orhan, went back to Constantinople when she became a widow in 1362 and lived at least until 1381; Helena, the long-suffering wife of John V, outlived him by five years and died as a nun in 1396.[44] Her fourth son Theodore Palaiologos carried on the good work begun by Manuel Cantacuzene as Despot of the Peloponnese. But it was her second son who, in 1391, succeeded his father in Constantinople as the Emperor Manuel II; and it was he who most resembled his grandfather John Cantacuzene in character and in appearance. Manuel II too was a scholar, a writer, a theologian and a man of action. As Emperor he had to contend with a political and economic situation still more dire than Cantacuzene had faced. For his own father John V in his long reign had dismally failed to halt the decline and ruin of his Empire. It was from his grandfather that Manuel inherited his sense of duty, of imperial dignity, and of the particular and exclusive quality of being an Emperor of the Romans and protector of Orthodox spirituality. He travelled to Italy, France

[43] On Manuel Cantacuzene: Nicol, *Byzantine Family*, no. 25.
[44] Nicol, *Byzantine Family*, no. 27 (Maria), no. 29 (Theodora), no. 30 (Helena).

and England in search of material and financial help for the defence of Constantinople. But he never imitated his father by striking bargains with the Popes or the Latin rulers of the west by compromising the traditional faith and spiritual identity of his people. In this and in many other respects he was more the grandson of John Cantacuzene than the son of John Palaiologos. There is a striking portrait of Manuel II in a sumptuous manuscript which he presented to the abbey of S. Denys in Paris in 1408. It shows him with his wife Helena and their three eldest sons. Above all, it shows a faithful portrait of a man who even in his appearance was more in the mould of his grandfather than of his father.[45]

The point is proved by comparing the known contemporary portraits of John Cantacuzene. Another sumptuous manuscript in Paris contains four of Cantacuzene's theological and polemical works; and it has two famous representations of him. One shows him in his two guises as Emperor and as monk, as it were beside himself with spirituality.[46] It comes at the beginning of his treatise against Islam. As Emperor, he is depicted standing crowned and in full imperial regalia, clearly labelled as 'John . . . Emperor of the Romans . . . Palaiologos Angelos Kantakouzenos'. His face is stern, his eyes alert, his beard is trimmed but grey. As a monk he stands enveloped in the black angelic habit of his calling, manifestly an older figure, thinner in the face, though still with ruddy cheeks, his eyes more deep set and his beard white and two-pronged. In his left hand he carries a scroll bearing the words 'Great is the God of the Christians', the opening sentence of his anti-Islamic treatise. His right hand points above him to the scene of the three angels being entertained by Abraham, the familiar Orthodox depiction of the Holy Trinity. The portrait of him as a monk is so vivid that it may well have been painted from life when he was in his declining years at Mistra.[47]

The other portrait in the same manuscript shows him as a

[45] J. W. Barker, *Manuel II Palaeologus* (New Brunswick, N.J., 1969), where the portrait in question is reproduced as fig. 5.

[46] Paris BN cod. gr. 1242 fol. 123ᵛ.

[47] J. Spatharakis, *The Portrait in Byzantine Illuminated Manuscripts* (Leiden, 1976), p. 135; Lyn Rodley, *Byzantine Art and Architecture. An Introduction* (Cambridge, 1994), pp. 333–5 and fig. 281.

younger man while he was still active as Emperor.[48] Here he sits enthroned, surrounded by his bishops. He is by far the largest and most commanding figure in the group and again clearly labelled as 'John . . . Emperor of the Romans . . . Palaiologos Angelos Kantakouzenos'. He wears a bejewelled gold crown, a dark brown tunic (*sakkos*), with a gold embroidered belt and sash (*loros*). He holds in his right hand a sceptre and in his left hand the red purse or pouch containing dust. This was called the *akakia* and was supposed to remind the Emperor of the fact of his mortality. The footstool at his feet is adorned with two double-headed eagles, supposedly the device of the Palaiologos family. Attempts have been made to identify the four bishops on either side of the Emperor. One is clearly the Patriarch holding his staff of office and might be Kallistos, who resigned in 1353. Another might be Cantacuzene's friend Philotheos, who succeeded Kallistos. Another is perhaps Gregory Palamas in his role as Bishop of Thessalonica. It is probable that the scene represents the Emperor presiding over the Palamite council of 1351 which took place in a hall of the Blachernai palace in Constantinople. There is no clear indication, however, that this is so; and it may be that the picture is no more than a formal statement of the Emperor's place and authority in the councils of the church.[49] The portraiture of John Cantacuzene, however, is striking and vividly realistic. With his raised eyebrows, alert brown eyes and well-shaped brown beard this is no idealised image of an Emperor. It is a skilful and dignified likeness of the man as he was in middle life. There is a marked facial resemblance between these portraits and those of his grandson the Emperor Manuel II, who came to the throne in 1391.

Another supposed portrait of Cantacuzene in his monastic estate appears in a manuscript in the Historical Museum in Moscow, where he is shown in the middle of a group of six monks.[50] An ivory pyxis or cylindrical box now in the

[48] Paris BN cod. gr. 1242 fol. 5.

[49] Spatharakis, *The Portrait*, pp. 129–36; C. Walter, *L'iconographie des Conciles dans la tradition byzantine* (Archives de l'Orient Chrétien, Paris, 1970), pp. 70–3.

[50] Moscow: State History Museum, Synodal. gr. 429. G. M. Prochorov, 'A codicological analysis of the illuminated Akathistos to the Virgin', *DOP*, 26 (1972), 237–52, fig. 8; Spatharakis, *The Portrait*, pp. 137–8 and fig. 92; Rodley, *Byzantine Art*, p. 337 and fig. 285.

Dumbarton Oaks collection in Washington D.C. is carved in high relief, illustrating ceremonial scenes of a marriage between two imperial families. One of the standing figures labelled as Io(annes) may be John Cantacuzene as Emperor with his wife Eirene and the diminutive figure of their grandson Andronikos between them. The carving of the names of the other persons shown is, however, incomplete and it is hard to be certain of their identity.[51] Such are the known contemporary or near-contemporary portraits of Cantacuzene as Emperor or monk. There are others from later times fabricated or adapted from earlier manuscripts by artists of the fifteenth century or after. The earliest and the best known is in the series of imperial heads decorating the margins of the manuscript of the *History* of John Zonaras in the Biblioteca Estense in Modena. Every Emperor from Augustus to the last Constantine Palaiologos is here depicted. The head of John Cantacuzene is correctly placed between that of Andronikos III son of Michael and that of John V son of Andronikos; but it could hardly be designated as a portrait if it were not so identified by its inscription.[52]

The few coins that have been attributed to the reign of John VI mostly date from the time of his joint reign with John V between the years 1347 and 1352. They therefore display effigies of both Emperors standing side by side. They are stylised representations of figures in imperial robes and crowns. But they are by no means portraits and scarcely works of art. One more elaborate gold coin shows both Emperors kneeling on either side of a figure of Christ; and its reverse bears an unusual sketch of the Virgin standing in prayer within the walls of Constantinople. The only three coin types so far allocated to the few years of John Cantacuzene's rule as sole Emperor show him standing beside a crudely drawn figure of St Demetrios. The reason for this is unclear. Demetrios was the patron saint of Thessalonica, where the mother of John V, Anna of Savoy, then ruled as Empress. It has been suggested that they may have been minted at Adrianople where Matthew Cantacuzene held his imperial appanage in those few years. Of the several gold

---

[51] Spatharakis, *The Portrait*, pp. 138–9; Rodley, *Byzantine Art*, pp. 323–5 and fig. 272. The imperial figures may, however, represent John VII and Manuel II.

[52] Modena: Cod. Mutinensis gr. 122. Spatharakis, *The Portrait*, pp. 172–9 and plate 121.

seals which John VI as Emperor must have appended to his
chrysobulls only one survives. It is in the monastery of Iviron
on Mount Athos and is dated to the year 1351. It portrays
the Emperor standing alone and clearly designated as 'John
Kantakousinos Emperor in Christ'. The obverse of the seal
shows the figure of the enthroned Christ.[53]

The joint coinage of John VI with his son-in-law John V was
surely meant to convey the message that Cantacuzene was no
more than the senior Emperor legally appointed but reigning
only until such time as his son-in-law took over. It is a message
repeatedly advertised in his memoirs. It is typical of his natural
hesitancy that he was for so long reluctant to acknowledge what
many of his friends and advisers considered to be the legitimate
claims to the throne of his own son Matthew. Even when he
conceded that Matthew should be proclaimed as Emperor in
place of John V in 1353, he still insisted that the name of John's
eldest son Andronikos should be commemorated among the
Emperors. It was as if he could not bring himself to admit that
he had finally made the decision that the dynasty of Palaiologos
was being replaced by that of Cantacuzene. It is difficult to
believe that it had all been a pretence, that ever since the death
of his friend and 'brother' Andronikos III in 1341 he had been
merely playing a part, hypocritically acting the role of guardian
of the rights of his friend's son and heir. In the end he left it too
late to replace one dynasty by another. Had he made up his
mind to do so several years earlier, the Empire might have
benefited or at least suffered less. The moment had passed
in 1353, for by then Cantacuzene had lost what little popular
sympathy and loyalty he may have had in 1347. Perhaps the
prophetic Bishop of Didymoteichon had been misinterpreted
when he warned Cantacuzene about eating unripe figs after his
first proclamation as Emperor. For at the end of his reign it
could be seen that he had not plucked the fruits of Empire
too soon. He had done so too modestly and without enough

---

[53] S. Bendall and P. J. Donald, *The Later Palaeologan Coinage* (London, 1979), pp. 138–50.
I am indebted to Professor Philip Grierson for kindly allowing me to see the
relevant section of vol. v of his Catalogue of the Byzantine coins in the Dumbarton
Oaks Collection before its publication. The gold seal of John VI is published
by F. Dölger, *Aus den Schatzkammern des Heiligen Berges*, 1 (Munich, 1948), p. 327,
no. 119. 1.

conviction. Maybe that was why his imperial robes hung so awkwardly on his frame.

The habit of a monk fitted him more comfortably. The firmest and most unshakeable of his convictions was his religious belief. His Orthodox faith would allow no compromise. He could not follow his friend Demetrios Kydones along the road to Rome, much as he admired the writings of Thomas Aquinas. Nor could he share the feeling of his older friend Nikephoros Gregoras that Orthodoxy had lost its way into a fog of mysticism. He believed, and spent many of his monastic years in demonstrating, that the mystical theology of Gregory Palamas had deep roots in the long development of Byzantine Orthodoxy. It was not, as Gregoras insisted, either an innovation or a heresy. It was solidly based on the teachings of the Fathers of the church. It developed and clarified the tradition of Orthodox belief in a matter which defies definition in human terms, namely the nature of the divine light that can illuminate the soul and body of man. This, the potential deification of man, could best be attained after long discipline and vigilance in the stillness of the monastic and solitary life known as *hesychia*. In visible and graphic terms it was symbolised by the scene of the Metamorphosis or Transfiguration of Christ which had dazzled the Apostles on Mount Tabor. There is no evidence that John Cantacuzene was ever schooled in the prayer and practice of the hesychasts. But he understood and approved of what Palamas and his disciples were about. He wrote refutations of their detractors and treatises to defend the truth of their knowledge of God. It is fitting therefore that the beautiful manuscript of his theological works in Paris should be adorned with one of the most striking of the many representations in Byzantine art of the Transfiguration.[54] His devoted and sincere championship of the doctrine of Palamas and the theory and practice of hesychasm was to have a more enduring effect than any of his political and military achievements. For the mystical theology and the veneration of his friend Palamas continue to inspire the Orthodox Christian world to this day.

His influence as a theologian and a monk may therefore appear to have been greater and more memorable than his

---

[54] Paris, BN: Cod. Paris. gr. 1242, fol. 92ᵛ.

career as an Emperor. Byzantine monks of later generations
thought of him as the defender of their faith. The monastery of
Vatopedi on Mount Athos for long claimed him as its own. So
also did the monastery of the Great Meteoron in Thessaly,
whose second founder was another Emperor and monk, the
Serbian John Uroš, who also adopted the monastic name of
Joasaph. The monks of the Meteora in later years either did not
know or did not care that John-Joasaph Cantacuzene had been
dead for five years when John-Joasaph Uroš refounded their
monastery in 1388. There was greater glory to be gained from
associating their foundation with a true Byzantine Emperor
than with an obscure Serbian who called himself Emperor. The
confusion between the two Emperor-monks with the same
names has been aggravated by the fact that the monastery of St
Stephen at the Meteora was reputedly founded in 1400 by one
Antonios Cantacuzene, who could have been a son of John's
daughter Maria.[55] None the less, it is as an Emperor of the
Romans that the name and fame of John Cantacuzene have
been perpetuated through the centuries by those claiming the
distinction of descent from the imperial family. There are many
missing links in the chain of descent for all the devoted labours
of interested genealogists. Certainty about the immediate
descendants of John Cantacuzene in the male line ends with the
two sons of Matthew Cantacuzene. They were John's grandsons
and without doubt scions of the imperial house, for their father
too had been an Emperor.[56] Another and more distinguished of
John's grandsons was the Emperor Manuel II. He never signed
himself with his mother's name of Cantacuzene. But he coined
a version of it as a form of honorific title. In 1415 he honoured
the Italian Count of Cephalonia and his brother by naming
them as 'legitimate Cantacuzenati of the blood'. The signifi-
cance of being dubbed a Cantacuzenatus remains a mystery.
No other such are recorded. But it was evidently a special
distinction implying an honorary relationship with the imperial
family of Constantinople.[57]

[55] D. M. Nicol, *Meteora. The Rock Monasteries of Thessaly*, 2nd edn (London, 1975), pp. 102–3;
Nicol, *Byzantine Family*, no. 28.
[56] Nicol, *Byzantine Family*, nos. 49, 50.
[57] Nicol, *The Despotate of Epiros*, ii, pp. 183–4.

In later and in post-Byzantine times it came to be considered rather more *distingué* to be a Cantacuzene of the blood than to boast ancestral links with the house of Palaiologos. For the reputed descendants of the Emperor John VI played notable parts in the history of the Balkans in the fifteenth and later centuries, in Serbia, Bosnia, Bulgaria and particularly Rumania. Some of them may also have recalled with pride that the very last holder of the Byzantine title of Grand Domestic, which John Cantacuzene had held before he came to the throne, was Andronikos Cantacuzene. For Andronikos died as a martyr in the heroic defence of Constantinople against the Ottoman Turks in 1453.[58] It was a Rumanian scholar who composed the last and the longest eulogy of the Emperor John Cantacuzene in the Greek language. In 1699 the learned Doctor John Comnen of Bucharest completed a biography of the Emperor based on his own memoirs. He wrote it, however, with the special purpose of extolling the virtues of his contemporary, Constantine Cantacuzino, who was at the time Stolnic or High Steward of the reigning prince of Wallachia, Constantine Brincoveanu. John Comnen had no proof, but also no doubt, that the Stolnic Constantine Cantacuzino was a direct descendant of the Byzantine imperial family. The precedent for his role as right-hand man of the reigning prince was neatly provided by his ancestor John Cantacuzene, who had so loyally served the cause of his Emperor Andronikos III, modestly declining to assume the crown for which his birth and talents had so eminently fitted him.[59]

---

58 Nicol, *Byzantine Family*, no. 68.
59 D. M. Nicol, 'The doctor-philosopher John Comnen of Bucharest and his biography of the Emperor John Kantakouzenos', *RESEE*, 9 (1971), 511–26; E. Voordeckers, 'La "Vie de Jean Cantacuzène" par Jean-Hierothée Comnène', *JÖB*, 20 (1971), 163–9.

SELECT BIBLIOGRAPHY

SOURCES

Collections of sources

Archives de l'Athos, ed. G. Millet, P. Lemerle, J. Bompaire *et al.* (Paris, 1937–)
Boissonade, J. F., *Anecdota Graeca*, 5 vols. (Paris, 1829–33)
  Anecdota Nova (Paris, 1844)
Chronica Byzantina Breviora (*see* Schreiner, P.)
Corpus Fontium Historiae Byzantinae (Berlin, Rome, Thessaloniki, Vienna and Washington, 1967–) (*CFHB*)
Corpus Scriptorum Historiae Byzantinae (Bonn, 1828–97) (*CSHB*)
Dölger, F., *Aus den Schatzkammern des Heiligen Berges*, 2 vols. (Munich, 1948)
  Regesten der Kaiserurkunden des oströmischen Reiches, IV: *1282–1341*; V: *1341–1453* (Munich and Berlin, 1960, 1965) (*DR*)
Guillou, A., *Les archives de Saint-Jean-Prodrome sur le Mont Ménécée* (Paris, 1955)
Migne, J. P., *Patrologiae Cursus Completus. Series Graeco-Latina* (Paris, 1857–66) (*MPG*)
Miklosich, F. and Müller, J., *Acta et Diplomata Graeca Medii Aevi*, 6 vols. (Vienna, 1860–90) (*MM*)
Papadopoulos-Kerameus, A., Ἀνάλεκτα Ἱεροσολυμιτικῆς Σταχυολογίας, 5 vols. (St Petersburg, 1891–8)
Schreiner, P., *Die byzantinischen Kleinchroniken* (*Chronica Byzantina Breviora*) (*CFHB*, XII/1–3: Vienna, 1976–8) (Schreiner, *Chron. brev.*)

Individual sources

Athanasios I, Patriarch, *The Correspondence of Athanasius I Patriarch of Constantinople. Letters to the Emperor Andronicus II, Members of the Imperial Family, and Officials*, ed. Alice-Mary Maffry Talbot (*CFHB*, VII: Washington, D.C., 1975)

Cantacuzene (Kantakouzenos, Cantacuzenus), John, *Histories. Ioannis Cantacuzeni eximperatoris Historiarum Libri IV*, ed. L. Schopen and B. Niebuhr, 3 vols. (*CSHB*, 1828, 1831, 1832); German translation with notes and commentary by G. Fatouros and T. Krischer, I–II (Bibliothek der griechischen Literatur, 17, 21: Stuttgart, 1982, 1986). There is an unpublished English translation of Book IV by T. S. Miller (Diss. Catholic University of America, 1975)

Letter to Bishop in Cyprus, ed. J. Darrouzès, 'Lettre inédite de Jean Cantacuzène relative à la controverse palamite', *REB*, 17 (1959), 7–27.

Letter to Pope Clement VI, ed. R.-J. Loenertz, 'Ambassadeurs grecs auprès du Pape Clément VI (1348)', *OCP* 19 (1953), 184–6 (= Loenertz, *BFG*, I, pp. 291–2)

Prologue (Prooimion) to his Treatise against the doctrine of Barlaam and Akindynos, in *MPG*, CLIV, cols. 693–700

Prostagma, Imperial Decree (of March 1347) confirming the synodical condemnation of the Patriarch John Kalekas, in *MPG*, CLI, cols. 769–72

Refutations. Johannis Cantacuzeni Refutationes duae Prochori Cydonii et Disputatio cum Paulo Patriarcha Latino Epistulis Septem Tradita, ed. E. Voordeckers and F. Tinnefeld (Corpus Christianorum, Series Graeca, 16: Turnhout and Louvain, 1987)

Treatise against the Jews, ed. with introduction, text and notes by C. G. Sotiropoulos, Ἰωάννου Στ' Καντακουζηνοῦ κατὰ Ἰουδαίων Λόγοι ἐννέα (Athens, 1983)

Treatises against the Muslims. *Contra Sectam Mahometicam Apologiae IV*; *Contra Mahometem Orationes Quatuor*, in *MPG*, CLIV, cols. 371–584, 583–692

(For the still unpublished works of John Cantacuzene, see: J. Meyendorff, *Introduction à l'étude de Grégoire Palamas*, p. 412; D. M. Nicol, *The Byzantine Family of Kantakouzenos*, pp. 98–100)

Choumnos, Nikephoros, *Letters*, ed. J. F. Boissonade, *Anecdota Graeca*, I–III, V (Paris, 1829–33); *Anecdota Nova* (Paris, 1844)

Doukas (Ducas), *Istoria Turco-Bizantină* (1341–1462), ed. V. Grecu (Bucharest, 1958)

Enveri, *Le Destān d'Umūr Pacha (Düstūrnāme-i Enverī)*, ed. Irène Mélikoff-Sayar (Bibliothèque Byzantine, ed. P. Lemerle, Documents, II: Paris, 1954)

Gabalas, Matthew, ed. D. Reinsch, *Die Briefe des Matthaios von Ephesos im Codex Vindobonensis Theol. Gr. 174* (Berlin, 1974)

Gabras, Michael, ed. G. Fatouros, *Die Briefe des Michael Gabras (ca. 1290–nach 1350)* (Wiener byzantinische Studien, XI/1–2: Vienna, 1973)

Gregoras, Nikephoros, *History. Byzantina Historia*, ed. L. Schopen, 3 vols. (*CSHB*, 1829–55); German translation with commentary by J. L. van Dieten, I–III (Stuttgart, 1973–88)
    Letters, ed. R. Guilland, *La correspondance de Nicéphore Grégoras* (Paris, 1927)
Hyrtakenos, Theodore, *Correspondence*, ed. F. J. G. La Porte-du Theil, *Notices et extraits des manuscrits de la Bibliothèque Nationale*, 5 (1798), pp. 709–44; 6 (1800), pp. 1–48
Kabasilas, Nicholas Chamaetos, *Panegyrics*, ed. M. Jugie, *Izvestija russkago archeologičeskago Instituta v Konstantinopole*, 15 (1911), 112–21; ed. M. Jugie, 'L'éloge de Mathieu Cantacuzène par Nicolas Cabasilas', *Echos d'Orient*, 13 (1910), 338–43
Kalekas, Manuel, *Letters*, ed. R.-J. Loenertz, *Correspondance de Manuel Calécas* (Studi e Testi, 152: Vatican City, 1950)
Kallistos I, Patriarch. *See* D. B. Gonis, Τὸ συγγραφικὸν ἔργον τοῦ οἰκουμενικοῦ πατριάρχου Καλλίστου Α' (Athens, 1980)
Kydones, Demetrios, *Letters*, ed. R.-J. Loenertz, *Démétrius Cydonès Correspondance*, 2 vols. (Studi e Testi, 196, 208: Vatican City, 1956, 1960)
    Speeches, ed. G. Cammelli, 'Demetrii Cydonii orationes tres, adhuc ineditae: Ad Ioannem Cantacuzenum Imperatorem oratio I', *BNJ*, 3 (1922), 67–76; 'oratio altera', *BNJ*, 4 (1923), 77–83; also ed. Loenertz, *Démétrios Cydonès Correspondance*, I, pp. 1–10
Manuel II, Emperor. *Manuel II Palaeologus, Funeral Oration on his brother Theodore*, ed. J. Chrysostomides (*CFHB*, XXVI: Thessaloniki, 1985)
Matthew I, Patriarch, *Testament*, ed. H. Hunger, 'Das Testament des Patriarchen Matthaios I (1397–1410)', *BZ*, 51 (1958), 288–309
Matthew of Ephesos, Bishop, *Letters*, ed. D. Reinsch, *Die Briefe des Matthaios von Ephesos im Codex Vindobonensis Theol. Gr. 174* (Berlin, 1974)
Maximos Kapsokalyvis, monk, *Life*, ed. F. Halkin, 'Deux vies de S. Maxime le Kausokalybe, ermite au Mont Athos (XIVᵉ siècle)', *Analecta Bollandiana*, 54 (1936), 38–112
Metochites, Theodore, *Essays*, ed. C. G. Müller and T. Kiessling, *Theodori Metochitae Miscellanea Philosophica et Historica* (Leipzig, 1821)
Meyendorff, J., 'Projets de concile oecuménique en 1367: un dialogue inédit entre Jean Cantacuzène et le légat Paul', *DOP*, 14 (1960), 147–77
    'Le tome synodal de 1347', *ZRVI*, 8 (1963) (*Mélanges Georges Ostrogorsky*, I), 209–27

Palamas, Gregory, St, *Grégoire Palamas: défense des saints hésychastes*, ed. J. Meyendorff, 2 vols. (Louvain, 1959; 2nd edn 1973)
Saint Gregory Palamas. The One Hundred and Fifty Chapters, ed. and trans. R. E. Sinkiewicz (Pontifical Institute of Mediaeval Studies: Studies and Texts, 83: Toronto, 1988)
Panaretos, Michael, *Chronicle of the Empire of Trebizond*, ed. O. Lampsides, *Archeion Pontou*, 22 (1958), 5–128; also printed separately (Athens, 1958)
Philes, Manuel, *Poems*, ed. E. Miller, *Manuelis Philae Carmina*, 2 vols. (Paris, 1855, 1857)
Philotheos Kokkinos, Patriarch, *Dogmatic Works. Refutations (Antirretika) of Nikephoros Gregoras*, ed. B. Kaimakis, Φιλοθέου . . . Δογματικὰ ἔργα, 1 (Thessaloniki, 1983)
Hagiological Works, ed. D. G. Tsamis, Φιλοθέου . . . τοῦ Κοκκίνου ἁγιολογικὰ ἔργα, 1: Θεσσαλονικεῖς ἅγιοι (Thessaloniki, 1985)
Raoul, Manuel, *Letters*, ed. R.-J. Loenertz, 'Emmanuelis Raoul Epistulae XII', *EEBS*, 26 (1956), 130–63
Thomas Magister, *Speeches*, ed. F. W. Lenz, *Fünf Reden Thomas Magisters* (Leiden, 1963)
Villani, Matteo, in *Croniche di Giovanni, Matteo e Filippo Villani*, ed. A. Racheli, II (Trieste, 1858)

MODERN WORKS

Asdracha, Catherine, *La région des Rhodopes aux XIIIe et XIVe siècles: études de géographie historique* (Athens, 1976)
Balard, M., 'A propos de la bataille du Bosphore. L'expédition génoise de Paganino Doria à Constantinople (1351–1352)', *Travaux et Mémoires*, 4 (1970), 431–69
La Romanie génoise (XIIIe–début du XVe siècle), 2 vols. (Rome, 1978)
Barker, J. W., *Manuel II Palaeologus (1391–1425): A Study in Late Byzantine Statesmanship* (New Brunswick, N.J., 1969)
'The problem of appanages in Byzantium during the Palaiologan period', *Byzantina*, 3 (1971), 103–22
Bartusis, M. C., 'Chrelja and Momčilo: occasional servants of Byzantium in fourteenth century Macedonia', *BS*, 41 (1980), 201–21
The Late Byzantine Army. Arms and Society, 1204–1453 (Philadelphia, 1992)
Beck, H.-G., *Kirche und theologische Literatur im byzantinischen Reich* (Munich, 1959)
Bendall, S. and Donald, P. J., *The Later Palaeologan Coinage* (London, 1979)

Bosch, Ursula V., *Kaiser Andronikos III. Palaiologos. Versuch einer Darstellung der byzantinischen Geschichte in den Jahren 1321–1341* (Amsterdam, 1965)

Bryer, A. A. M., 'Greek historians on the Turks: the case of the first Byzantine-Ottoman marriage', *The Writing of History in the Middle Ages: Essays presented to R. W. Southern*, ed. R. H. C. Davis and J. M. Wallace-Hadrill (Oxford, 1981), pp. 471–93

Cammelli, G., 'Demetrii Cydonii orationes tres, adhuc ineditae: ad Ioannem Cantacuzenum oratio I', *BNJ*, 3 (1922), 67–76
'Oratio altera', *BNJ*, 4 (1923), 77–83

Charanis, P., 'Imperial coronation in Byzantium: some new evidence', *Byzantina*, 8 (1979), 39–46

Clucas, L., 'The triumph of mysticism in Byzantium in the fourteenth century', *Byzantina kai Metabyzantina*, IV (*Byzantine Studies in Honor of Milton V. Anastos*), ed. S. Vryonis (Malibu, 1985), pp. 163–224

Constantinides, C., *Higher Education in Byzantium in the Thirteenth and Early Fourteenth Centuries* (Nicosia, 1982)

Ćurčić, S. and Mouriki, Doula, *The Twilight of Byzantium: Aspects of Cultural and Religious History in the Late Byzantine Empire* (Princeton, N.J., 1991)

Darrouzès, J., 'Conférences sur la primauté du Pape à Constantinople en 1357', *REB*, 19 (1961), 76–109

Dennis, G. T., 'The deposition of the Patriarch John Calecas', *JÖBG*, 11 (1960), 51–5
The Reign of Manuel II Palaeologus in Thessalonica, 1382–1387 (Orientalia Christiana Analecta, 159: Rome, 1960)

Dölger, F., 'Die dynastiche Familienpolitik des Kaisers Michael Palaiologos', in Dölger, *ΠΑΡΑΣΠΟΡΑ: 30 Aufsätze zur Geschichte, Kultur und Sprache des byzantinischen Reiches* (Ettal, 1961), pp. 178–88
'Johannes VI. Kantakuzenos als dynastischer Legitimist', in Dölger, *ΠΑΡΑΣΠΟΡΑ*, pp. 194–207

Dräseke, J., 'Kaiser Kantakuzenos' Geschichtswerk', *Neue Jahrbücher für das klassische Altertum*, 30 (1914), 489–506
'Kantakuzenos' Urteil über Gregoras', *BZ*, 10 (1901), 106–27
'Zu Johannes Kantakuzenos', *BZ*, 9 (1900), 72–84

Failler, A., 'La déposition du patriarche Calliste I (1353)', *REB*, 31 (1973), 5–163
'Note sur la chronologie du règne de Jean Cantacuzène', *REB*, 29 (1971), 293–302
'Nouvelle note sur la chronologie du règne de Jean Cantacuzène', *REB*, 34 (1976), 118–24

Fatouros, G., 'Textkritische Beobachtungen zu Johannes Kantakuzenos', *BS*, 37 (1976), 191–3

Ferjančić, B., *Despoti u Vizantiji i južnoslovenskim zemljama* (Despots in Byzantium and on South Slav territory) (Posebna Izdana Vizantološkog Instituta, 8: Belgrade, 1960)
Tesalija u XIII i XIV veka (Thessaly in the thirteenth and fourteenth centuries) (Belgrade, 1974)
Filitti, I. C., *Notice sur les Cantacuzène du XIe au XVIIe siècles* (Bucharest, 1936)
Fine, J. G. A., *The Late Medieval Balkans: A Critical Survey from the Late Twelfth Century to the Ottoman Conquest* (Ann Arbor, 1987)
Finlay, G., *A History of Greece from its Conquest by the Romans to the Present Time, B.C. 146 to A.D. 1864*, ed. H. F. Tozer, III (Oxford, 1877)
Florinskij, T., 'Andronik Mladšij i Ioann Kantakuzin', *Žurnal ministerstva narodnago prosveščenija*, 204 (July–August, 1879), 87–143, 219–51; 205 (September–October, 1879), 1–48; 208 (March–April, 1880), 327–34
Frances, E., 'Narodnie dviženija osenju 1354 g. v Konstantinopole i otrečenie Joanna Kantakuzina' (The popular movement in Constantinople in the autumn of 1354 and the abdication of John Cantacuzene), *Vizantijskij Vremennik*, 25 (1964), 142–7
'Quelques aspects de la politique de Jean Cantacuzène', *Rivista di studi bizantini e neoellenici*, n.s. 5 (1968), 116–76
Gay, J., *Le Pape Clément VI et les affaires d'Orient (1342–1352)* (Paris, 1904)
Geanakoplos, D. J., *Emperor Michael Palaeologus and the West, 1258–1282. A Study in Late Byzantine Latin Relations* (Cambridge, Mass., 1972)
Gibbon, E., *The History of the Decline and Fall of the Roman Empire*, ed. J. B. Bury, VI (London, 1898)
Gibbons, H. A., *The Foundation of the Ottoman Empire. A History of the Osmanlis up to the death of Bayezid I, 1300–1403* (Oxford, 1916)
Gill, J., *Byzantium and the Papacy 1198–1400* (New Brunswick, N.J., 1979)
'John VI Cantacuzenus and the Turks', *Byzantina*, 13 (1985), 57–76
Guilland, R., *Essai sur Nicéphore Grégoras: l'homme et l'oeuvre* (Paris, 1926)
Etudes byzantines (Paris, 1959)
'Etudes de civilisation et de littérature byzantines, I: Alexis Apocaucus', *Revue du Lyonnais* (1921), 523–54
'Les empereurs de Byzance et l'attrait du monastère', in Guilland, *Etudes byzantines*, pp. 33–51
Halecki, O., *Un Empereur de Byzance à Rome. Vingt ans de travail pour l'union des églises et pour la défense de l'empire d'Orient, 1355–1375* (Warsaw, 1930)
Halkin, F., 'Deux vies de S. Maxime le Kausokalybe, ermite au Mont Athos (XIVe siècle)', *Analecta Bollandiana*, 54 (1936), 38–112
Hendy, M., *Studies in the Byzantine Monetary Economy c. 1300–1450* (Cambridge, 1985)

Hunger, H., *Die Hochsprachliche Profane Literatur der Byzantiner*, 2 vols. (Munich, 1987)
'Das Testament des Patriarchen Matthaios I (1397–1410)', *BZ*, 51 (1958), 288–309
'Thukydides bei Johannes Kantakuzenos. Beobachtungen zur Mimesis', *JÖB*, 25 (1976), 181–93
'Urkunden und Memoirentext: der Chrysoboullos Logos des Johannes Kantakuzenos für Johannes Angelos', *JÖB*, 26 (1978), 107–25
Hussey, Joan M., *The Orthodox Church in the Byzantine Empire* (Oxford, 1986)
Imber, C., *The Ottoman Empire, 1300–1481* (Istanbul, 1990)
Janin, R., *Constantinople byzantine: développement urbain et répertoire topographique*, 2nd edn (Paris, 1964)
  La géographie ecclésiastique de l'Empire byzantin, I: *Le siège de Constantinople et le patriarcat oecuménique*, III: *Les églises et les monastères*, 2nd edn (Paris, 1969)
Jireček, C. J., *Geschichte der Serben*, 2 vols. (Gotha, 1911–18); revised edn by J. Radonić, *Istorija Srba*, 2 vols. (Belgrade, 1952)
Jorga (Iorga), N., 'Latins et grecs d'Orient et l'établissement des Turcs en Europe, 1342–62', *BZ*, 15 (1906), 179–222
Jugie, M., 'L'éloge de Mathieu Cantacuzène par Nicolas Cabasilas', *Echos d'Orient*, 13 (1910), 338–43
Kalligas, Haris A., *Byzantine Monemvasia. The Sources* (Monemvasia–Athens, 1990)
Kazhdan, A. P., 'L'*Histoire* de Cantacuzène en tant qu'oeuvre littéraire', *B*, 50 (1980), 279–335
Kyrris, K. P., *Τὸ Βυζάντιον κατὰ τὸν ΙΔ' αἰῶνα: Ἡ πρώτη φάσις τοῦ ἐμφυλίου πολέμου καὶ ἡ πρώτη συνδιαλλαγὴ τῶν δύο Ἀνδρονίκων (1321)* (Leukosia, 1982)
'John Cantacuzenus and the Genoese 1321–1348', *Miscellanea Storica Ligure*, 3 (Milan, 1963), 8–48
'John Cantacuzenus, the Genoese, the Venetians and the Catalans (1348–1354)', *Byzantina*, 4 (1972), 331–56
Laiou, Angeliki E., 'The Byzantine aristocracy in the Palaeologan period: a story of arrested development', *Viator*, 4 (1973), 131–51
  Constantinople and the Latins: The Foreign Policy of Andronicus II, 1282–1328 (Cambridge, Mass., 1972)
Lemerle, P., *L'Emirat d'Aydin. Byzance et l'Occident. Recherches sur 'La geste d'Umur Pacha'* (Paris, 1957)
  Philippes et la Macédoine orientale à l'époque chrétienne et byzantine (Paris, 1945)

Loenertz, R.-J., *Byzantina et Franco-Graeca*, 2 vols. (Storia e Letteratura, Raccolta di Studi e Testi, 118, 145: Rome, 1970, 1978) (*BFG*, I, II)

'Ambassadeurs grecs auprès du Pape Clément VI (1348)', *OCP*, 19 (1953), 178–96 (= *BFG*, I, pp. 285–302)

'Démétrius Cydonès, I: De la naissance à l'année 1373', *OCP*, 36 (1970), 47–72

'Ordre et désordre dans les mémoires de Jean Cantacuzène', *REB*, 22 (1964), 222–37 (= *BFG*, I, pp. 113–50)

Longnon, J., *L'Empire latin de Constantinople et la principauté de Morée* (Paris, 1949)

Maksimović, Lj., *The Byzantine Provincial Administration under the Palaiologoi* (Amsterdam, 1988)

'Politička uloga Jovana Kantakuzina posle abdikacije (1354–1383)' (The political role of John Cantacuzene after his abdication, 1354–1383), *ZRVI*, 9 (1966), 116–93

'Regentsvo Alexija Apokavka i društvena kretana u Carigradu' (The regency of Alexios Apokaukos and social movements in Constantinople), *ZRVI*, 18 (1978), 165–88

Matschke, K.-F., *Fortschritt und Reaktion in Byzanz im 14. Jh.: Konstantinopel in der Bürgerkriegsperiode von 1341 bis 1354* (Berlin, 1971)

'Johannes Kantakuzenos, Alexios Apokaukos und die byzantinische Flotte in der Bürgerkriegsperiode 1341–1355', *Actes du XIVe Congrès International des Etudes Byzantines*, II (Bucharest, 1975), 193–205

Medvedev, I. P., 'Pozdnie kopii Vizantijskich dokumentov v sobranii Biblioteki Akademii Nauk SSSR', *Vizantijskij Vremennik*, 33 (1971), 223–31

Meyendorff, J., *Byzantium and the Rise of Russia* (Cambridge, 1981)

Introduction à l'étude de Grégoire Palamas (Patristica Sorbonensia, 3: Paris, 1959)

'Projets de concile oecuménique en 1367: un dialogue inédit entre Jean Cantacuzène et le légat Paul', *DOP*, 14 (1960), 147–77 (reprinted in Meyendorff, *Byzantine Hesychasm: Historical, Theological and Social Problems. Collected Studies* (London, 1974), no. XI).

'Le Tome synodal de 1347', *ZRVI*, 8 (*Mélanges G. Ostrogorsky*, I: Belgrade, 1963), 209–27

Miller, T. S., 'The plague in John VI Cantacuzenus and Thucydides', *Greek, Roman and Byzantine Studies*, 18 (1976), 385–95

Millet, G., 'Les inscriptions byzantines de Mistra', *Bulletin de Correspondance hellénique*, 23 (1899), 97–156

Moravcsik, Gy., *Byzantinoturcica*, 2 vols., 3rd edn (Berliner byzantinische Arbeiten, 10: Berlin, 1983)

Nicol, D. M., *Collected Studies*, 2 vols. (London, 1972, 1986)
'The abdication of John VI Cantacuzene', *Byzantinische Forschungen*, II (*Polychordia: Festschrift F. Dölger zum 75. Geburtstag*: Amsterdam, 1967), 269–83 (= *Collected Studies*, II, no. VI)
The Byzantine Family of Kantakouzenos (Cantacuzenus) ca. 1100–1460. A Genealogical and Prosopographical Study (Dumbarton Oaks Studies, XI: Washington, D.C., 1968)
The Byzantine Lady. Ten Portraits, 1250–1500 (Cambridge, 1994)
'Byzantine requests for an oecumenical council in the fourteenth century', *Annuarium Historiae Conciliorum*, I (1969), 69–95 (= *Collected Studies*, I, no. VIII)
Byzantium and Venice: A Study in Diplomatic and Cultural Relations (Cambridge, 1988)
Church and Society in the Last Centuries of Byzantium (Cambridge, 1979)
The Despotate of Epiros, II, *1267–1479: A Contribution to the History of Greece in the Middle Ages* (Cambridge, 1984)
'The doctor-philosopher John Comnen of Bucharest and his biography of the Emperor John Kantakouzenos', *RESEE*, 9 (1971), 511–26 (= *Collected Studies*, II, no. VIII)
'Hilarion of Didymoteichon and the gift of prophecy', *Byzantine Studies/Etudes Byzantines*, 5 (1978), 185–200 (= *Collected Studies*, II, no. IX)
The Last Centuries of Byzantium, 1261–1453, 2nd edn (Cambridge, 1993)
Meteora. The Rock Monasteries of Thessaly, 2nd edn (London, 1975)
'A paraphrase of the Nicomachean Ethics attributed to the Emperor John VI Cantacuzene', *BS*, 29 (1968), 1–16 (= *Collected Studies*, II, no. VII)
Nicol, D. M. and Bendall, S., 'Anna of Savoy in Thessalonica: the numismatic evidence', *Revue numismatique*, 19 (1977), 90–102
Obolensky, D., *The Byzantine Commonwealth: Eastern Europe 500–1453* (London, 1971)
Oikonomides, N., *Hommes d'affaires grecs et latins à Constantinople (XIIIe–XVe siècles)* (Conférence Albert-le-Grand: Montreal, 1979)
Ostrogorsky, G., 'The Byzantine Empire and the hierarchical world order', *Slavonic and East European Review*, 35 (1956), 1–14
History of the Byzantine State, translated by Joan Hussey (Oxford, 1968)
Ousterhout, R., 'Constantinople, Bithynia, and Regional Developments in Later Palaeologan Architecture', in S. Ćurčić and Doula Mouriki, eds., *The Twilight of Byzantium* (Princeton, N.J., 1991), pp. 75–110
Parisot, Val., *Cantacuzène homme d'état et historien, ou examen critique des Mémoires de l'Empereur Jean Cantacuzène et des sources contemporaines et*

notamment des 30 livres dont 14 inédits de l'Histoire Byzantine de Nicéph.
Gregoras qui controlent les Mémoires de Cantacuzène (Paris, 1845)
Philippides-Braat, Anna, 'La captivité de Palamas chez les Turcs.
Dossier et Commentaire', *Travaux et Mémoires*, 7 (1979), 109–22
Podskalsky, G., *Theologie und Philosophie in Byzanz: Die Streit um die theologische Methodik in der Spätbyzantinische Geistesgeschichte* (14./15. Jh.) (Munich, 1977)
Politis, L., 'Jean-Joasaph Cantacuzène fut-il copiste?', *REB*, 14 (1956), 195–9
'Eine Schreiberschule im Kloster τῶν 'Οδηγῶν', *BZ*, 51 (1958), 17–36, 261–87
Prochorov, G. M., 'A codicological analysis of the illuminated Akathistos to the Virgin', *DOP*, 26 (1972), 237–52
'Publicistika Ioanna Kantakuzina 1367–1371 godov' (Publications of John Cantacuzene in the years 1367–1371), *Vizantijskij Vremennik*, 29 (1968), 318–41
Prosopographisches Lexikon der Palaiologenzeit, ed. E. Trapp, H.-V. Beyer, R. Walther, *et al.* (Österreichische Akademie der Wissenschaften, Kommission für Byzantinistik: Vienna, 1976–) (*PLP*)
Radić, R., *Vreme Jovanna V Paleologa (1332–1391)* (The Time of John V Palaiologos) (Vizantološki Institut, Serbian Academy of Sciences and Arts: Belgrade, 1993)
Rodley, Lynn, *Byzantine Art and Architecture: An Introduction* (Cambridge, 1994)
Runciman, S., *The Byzantine Theocracy* (Cambridge, 1977)
The Emperor Romanus Lecapenus and his Reign: A Study of Tenth-Century Byzantium (Cambridge, 1929; reprinted 1963)
The Fall of Constantinople 1453 (Cambridge, 1965)
The Great Church in Captivity: A Study of the Patriarchate of Constantinople from the Eve of the Turkish Conquest to the Greek War of Independence (Cambridge, 1968)
The Last Byzantine Renaissance (Cambridge, 1970)
Mistra: Byzantine Capital of the Peloponnese (London, 1980)
Setton, K. M., *The Papacy and the Levant (1204–1571)*, I: *The Thirteenth and Fourteenth Centuries* (Philadelphia, 1976)
Ševčenko, I., *Collected Studies: Society and Intellectual Life in Late Byzantium* (London, 1981)
Soulis, G. C., *The Serbs and Byzantium during the Reign of Tsar Stephen Dušan (1331–1355) and his Successors* (Washington, D.C., 1984)
Spatharakis, J., *The Portrait in Byzantine Illuminated Manuscripts* (Leiden, 1976)
Tafrali, O., *Thessalonique au quatorzième siècle* (Paris, 1913)

Teoteoi, T., 'La conception de Jean VI Cantacuzène sur l'état byzantin vue principalement à la lumière de son *Histoire*', *RESEE*, 13 (1975), 167–86

Tinnefeld, F., 'Byzantinisch-Russische Kirchenpolitik im 14. Jahrhundert', *BZ*, 67 (1974), 356–84

Todt, K.-P., *Kaiser Johannes VI. Kantakuzenos und der Islam: Politische Realität und theologische Polemik im palaiologenzeitlichen Byzanz* (Religions-wissenschaftlichen Studien, XVI: Würzburg, 1991)

Voordeckers, E., 'Un empereur palamite à Mistra en 1370', *RESEE*, 9 (1971), 607–15

'La "Vie de Jean Cantacuzène" par Jean-Hierothée Comnène', *JÖB*, 20 (1971), 163–9

'Quelques remarques sur les prétendus "Chapitres théologiques" de Jean Cantacuzène', *B*, 34 (1964), 610–21

Vries-Van der Velden, Eva de, 'A propos d'une lettre inexistante de Jean VI Cantacuzène', *B*, 46 (1976), 330–53

L'Elite byzantine devant l'avance turque à l'époque de la guerre civile de 1341 à 1354 (Amsterdam, 1989)

Vryonis, S., *The Decline of Medieval Hellenism in Asia Minor and the Process of Islamization from the Eleventh through the Fifteenth Century* (Berkeley–Los Angeles–London, 1971)

Walter, C., *L'iconographie des Conciles dans la tradition byzantine* (Archives de l'Orient Chrétien, 13: Paris, 1970)

Ware, K., 'St. Maximos of Kapsokalyvia and fourteenth-century Athonite hesychasm', *ΚΑΘΗΓΗΤΡΙΑ. Essays presented to Joan Hussey for her 80th birthday* (Camberley, 1988), pp. 409–30

Weiss, G., *Joannes Kantakuzenos – Aristokrat, Staatsmann, Kaiser und Mönch – in der Gesellschaftsentwicklung von Byzanz im 14. Jahrhundert* (Wiesbaden, 1969)

Werner, E., 'Johannes Kantakuzenos, Umur Paša und Orhan', *BS*, 26 (1965), 266–76

Zachariadou, Elizabeth A., *Trade and Crusade: Venetian Crete and the Emirates of Menteshe and Aydin (1300–1415)* (Venice, 1983)

Zakythinos, D. A., *Crise monétaire et crise économique à Byzance du XIIIᵉ au XVᵉ siècle* (Athens, 1948) (= Zakythinos, *Collected Studies* [London, 1973], no. XI)

Le Despotat grec de Morée, I: *Histoire politique*; II: *Vie et Institutions*, rev. edn by Chryssa Maltezou, 2 vols. (London, 1975)

Živojnović, M., 'Jovan Paleolog i Jovan Kantakuzin od 1351 do 1354 godine' (John V Palaiologos and John VI Cantacuzene from 1351 to 1354), *ZRVI*, 21 (1982), 127–41

INDEX